D09955903

MISTRUST

ALSO BY ETHAN ZUCKERMAN

Digital Cosmopolitans:
Why We Think the Internet Connects Us,
Why It Doesn't, and How to Rewire It

MISTRUST

Why Losing Faith in
Institutions Provides the
Tools to Transform Them

ETHAN ZUCKERMAN

W. W. NORTON & COMPANY

Independent Publishers Since 1923

For information about permission to reproduce selections from this book,
write to Permissions, W. W. Norton & Company, Inc.,
500 Fifth Avenue, New York, NY 10110

For information about special discounts for bulk purchases, please contact
W. W. Norton Special Sales at specialsales@wwnorton.com or 800-233-4830

Manufacturing by LSC Communications, Harrisonburg
Production manager: Anna Oler

Library of Congress Cataloging-in-Publication Data

Names: Zuckerman, Ethan, author.
Title: Mistrust : why losing faith in institutions provides the tools to
transform them / Ethan Zuckerman.
Description: First Edition. | New York : W. W. Norton & Company, 2021. |
Includes bibliographical references and index.
Identifiers: LCCN 2020038408 | ISBN 9781324002604 (Hardcover) |
ISBN 9781324002611 (ePub)
Subjects: LCSH: Trust—Political aspects—United States. | Political alienation. |
Political participation. | Social change.
Classification: LCC JA74.5 .Z83 2021 | DDC 306.20973—dc23
LC record available at https://lccn.loc.gov/2020038408

W. W. Norton & Company, Inc., 500 Fifth Avenue, New York, N.Y. 10110
www.wwnorton.com

W. W. Norton & Company Ltd., 15 Carlisle Street, London W1D 3BS

1 2 3 4 5 6 7 8 9 0

For Amy Price,
my favorite insurrectionist.

CONTENTS

Introduction   xi

Chapter 1   IS THIS THING WORKING?   1

Chapter 2   WHY WE LOST TRUST   21

Chapter 3   WHAT WE LOSE WHEN WE LOSE TRUST   47

Chapter 4   THE LEVERS OF CHANGE   79

Chapter 5   INSTITUTIONALISTS TO THE RESCUE   107

Chapter 6   COUNTER-DEMOCRACY AND
             CITIZEN MONITORING   124

Chapter 7   PRODUCTIVE DISRUPTION   141

Chapter 8   DECENTRALIZATION   159

Chapter 9   DO SOMETHING: EFFICACY AND
             SOCIAL CHANGE   180

Afterword: Katrina and COVID-19   207

Acknowledgments   217

Notes   221

Index   251

INTRODUCTION

IN SHEFFIELD, MASSACHUSETTS, THIRTY MILES SOUTH OF where I live, a stone marker stands at the edge of a corn field. It's about three feet high, neatly maintained, but visited mostly by through-hikers who pass by on the nearby Appalachian Trail.

The marker commemorates the final battle of Shays's Rebellion, the first major instance of domestic insurrection in the postrevolutionary United States. When farmers from western Massachusetts returned home after fighting for independence from Britain, they often found themselves in dire financial straits. Despite promises of pay for their military service, most veterans went unrewarded, and taxes levied by the state government led farmers to lose their only asset, their farmland. Daniel Shays, a former captain of the Fifth Massachusetts regiment in the Continental Army, led protests for debt relief, helping shut down courthouses throughout the western part of the state.

Militarily, Shays's Rebellion was a brief, sloppy, and ultimately unsuccessful affair. Shays and two other commanders attempted to converge their forces on the federal armory in Springfield, hoping to seize a cache of weapons there. But their communications were intercepted, and when the rebels arrived, a private militia paid for by wealthy supporters of the governor in Boston quickly routed them and drove them out of the state. The monument in Sheffield, assembled in 1904 from a piece of marble that had been rejected by a nearby quarry, reads, "Shays Rebellion was here, Feb 27 1787," but fails to mention that the battle was a last gasp before Shays's remaining followers fled, through upstate New York to the lawless, unincorporated territory of Vermont.[1]

Despite the almost total lack of military glory for its participants, Shays's Rebellion had an enormous effect on early America. Alexander Hamilton and other Federalists considered the inability of the young nation to defend itself against domestic insurrection to be proof that the United States needed a strong central government, capable of raising an army and maintaining domestic order. Predictably, Thomas Jefferson disagreed. In a letter to James Madison, dated January 30, 1787, he opined, "I hold it that a little rebellion now and then is a good thing, and as necessary in the political world as storms in the physical."[2]

This was easy for Jefferson to say—he was in France, as ambassador to America's most important ally. Furthermore, his prosperous farm in Monticello was almost five hundred miles away from Shays and his angry men. Other leaders of the American Revolution were deeply panicked about the rebellion, and only three months after Shays retreated through Sheffield, the Constitutional Convention began its work in Philadelphia. The recent conflict was so much on the minds of the framers that the Federalists and other Constitution supporters were commonly referred to as Washingtonites and those in opposition as Shayesites.[3] Historians have argued that the strong single executive that the United States enshrined in the Constitution was a direct response to the difficulty of suppressing insurrection.[4]

But while Hamilton's arguments won the day, Jefferson's words still resonate. A nation formed through a revolution must recognize that rebellion is an essential aspect of its character and its destiny. Jefferson's letter to Madison continued: "Unsuccessful rebellions indeed generally establish the encroachments on the rights of the people which have produced them. An observation of this truth should render honest republican governors so mild in their punishment of rebellions, as not to discourage them too much. It is a medicine necessary for the sound health of government."[5]

Perhaps reflecting Jefferson's idea, punishment of the Shaysites was surprisingly moderate. More than four thousand participants in the rebellion were given amnesty, and while eighteen ringleaders were convicted and sentenced to death, most were later pardoned or had their sentences commuted. The only two who were hanged for rebellion had also been convicted of looting. Shays himself was pardoned in 1788 and returned from the Vermont woods to Massachusetts. In his old age, he received a pension from the federal government for his military service.

From its inception, then, America has experienced a tension between institutions and insurrection, between the need for a carefully crafted structure designed to separate and counterbalance governmental powers and the need to respond to "encroachments on the rights of the people" in forms that may involve protest, dissent, and ultimately rebellion. The United States has survived as the first modern democracy because its institutions have been resilient to insurrection, a flexibility exemplified by the fact that only three years after our founding document was ratified, it was significantly amended by a bill of rights.

Institutions maintain their resilience by being flexible and capable of change. With age, though, they calcify and become brittle. The danger is that institutions that once bent to accommodate insurrectionism in their youth may snap under similar pressure in their old age.

I write this book at a moment when it feels like America might snap. A global pandemic has revealed the fragility of our institutions and shown the nation to be woefully underprepared for a significant crisis. President Donald Trump has vacillated between disclaiming responsibility and claiming absolute power. But even before the United States began struggling with COVID-19, institutions like Congress and the Supreme Court often seemed paralyzed. Political partisanship had morphed into tribalism, and debates over the issues of the day had come to feel less like differences of opinion than like disagreements about the nature of reality. Beyond concerns about the strengths and weaknesses of our government, civility, trust, and a collective sense of purpose seem absent. A broad swath of institutions—the press, the corporations, and the digital platforms—both connect and divide us, but none of them seems up to the task of holding us together.

It's useful—and scary—to remember that the United States is not alone in this moment of existential crisis. Many people in Britain reacted to Brexit with a mix of disbelief and denial, a refusal to accept that their neighbors would vote to leave a community that has kept Europe at peace for seventy years. Some Britons initially understood Brexit as the result of political machinations and deceptive advertising that could be reversed with a do-over in the polls, but that view has slowly given way to the disconcerting realization that many Britons genuinely do support a rebellion against the European Union—and against "politics as usual"—even if the implications of that path forward are murky in the extreme.

The ascent of strongmen in India, Brazil, Hungary, and Poland reminds us that democracy is fragile, easily crushed. The "illiberal democracies" that have taken over in these countries no longer pretend to seek dialogue or compromise with their political opponents. They've embraced tribalism on a national scale and see their opponents not as fellow citizens but as enemies of the state. Ominously, their examples warn free people elsewhere that the fall from a liberal democracy to an illiberal one can be swift and unexpected.

Despite its connections to the current political moment, this book was years in the making. When I began my research, Donald Trump was a reality television star, a weird relic of the 1980s who'd managed to gain marginal relevance by promoting an out-

landish conspiracy theory about Barack Obama's birth certifi-
cate. But by the time I submitted the manuscript to my publisher,
Trump was the forty-fifth president of the United States, three
years into a surreally turbulent presidential term. Despite being
under investigation for almost his entire presidency and surviving impeachment, his popularity has been surprisingly persistent,
with roughly 40 percent of Americans approving of his leadership.

But this is not a book about Donald Trump. Nor is it a book
about Vladimir Putin, Recep Tayyip Erdoğan, Viktor Orbán,
Rodrigo Duterte, or any number of other ethnonationalist leaders emerging around the world. I share the concerns raised by
former US secretary of state Madeleine Albright that the recent
turn toward authoritarianism and ethnonationalism uncomfort-
ably evokes the rise of fascism in the middle of the past century.[6]
But that's not the warning I want to offer.

Instead, I want to warn people about the conditions that led to
the election of Donald Trump.

The conservative columnist David Brooks, who self-identified
early and often as a "never Trump" Republican, likes to say that
Trump was the wrong answer to the right question.[7] I agree.
Many of the people who supported Trump for election in 2016,
particularly during the Republican primaries, were expressing
frustration with a system of democratic representation that they
felt was not furthering their interests. Candidates like Jeb Bush
and Marco Rubio promised more of the same. Trump promised
to tear those existing systems down.

While we tend to associate the impulse to tear down government institutions with the political right, many on the left are
frustrated with the limits of our government and corporate systems as well. Trump's rise followed the Occupy movement and
leftist anti-austerity movements in Spain and Greece—all of
them based on critiques of a capitalist system of representative
democracy in which markets seem to overpower popular will.

How seriously do we take this impulse to challenge systems

that seem broken? Leaving aside existing political rivalries, we are all grappling with questions about whether to fix the powerful institutions in our lives or to abandon them and replace them with something better, perhaps something entirely different. Do we march with Daniel Shays? Do we convene a new constitutional convention?

Trump's presidency makes this question harder to answer. Centrists and even some progressives have a strong impulse to protect democratic institutions that they hope will serve as bulwarks against the excesses of the Trump administration. At a moment when the United States is in the throes of an antigovernment crusade captained by the elected head of the government, it's only reasonable to advocate preserving the institutional guardrails designed to keep representative democracy from devolving into raw populism or naked cronyism. But we still need to know how we got here.

Mistrust is the single, critical factor that led to the election of Donald Trump in the United States and that may be empowering ethnonationalist, populist autocrats around the world. On the left and the right, people are losing trust in their institutions. It's this loss of trust, both in our institutions and in our ability to change our societies, that should worry us more than the rise of any specific leader or movement.

Whether Trump leaves office in 2020 or persists, reflecting a deep nativist shift in the United States, we need to focus on this uncomfortable truth: our current democratic, free market institutions aren't working for most Americans. Outside our borders, young democracies are discovering that free and fair elections don't automatically address economic imbalances and weaknesses. From China to Rwanda, authoritarian states that emphasize economic growth over political freedom are challenging the open models of North America and western Europe. Not only are these autocracies and illiberal democracies growing faster than democracies, they enjoy higher trust among their citizens.

This book takes seriously the voices of those who are loudly announcing that they no longer support a system that fails to support them. Instead of looking to restore an American consensus that is now long gone, I want to explore the ways the system is cracking and crumbling and learn from those who are working to install new, more just, and more robust systems in its place.

Despite my best intentions, this book's focus is not global. While it finds inspiration in places ranging from Ghana to Taiwan, much of its story unfolds within the United States and, to a lesser extent, Britain and western Europe. That's necessary, because the rising tide of mistrust is strongest there. This may reflect a backlash against the ways the United States has celebrated and sought to export its system globally, or it may have to do with a shift from its lofty status of sole superpower to that of another player in a multipolar world. But a loss of faith in institutions is a problem that can infect any society, not just the so-called "mature democracies" of North America and Europe. The struggles that the United States presently faces point to the danger of assuming that any system is destined to work forever and to the need to ensure that governments change and adapt as their citizens and the world they live in change.

Many of the ideas in this book, particularly about social change, are not new. Social movements that mistrust existing systems of power have been endlessly creative in their tactics for seeking change. When I asked Rashad Robinson, the head of the American racial justice NGO Color of Change, whether his organization had had to change tactics under the Trump administration, he laughed off my question, telling me, "People of color in the United States almost never have a political majority. We've always had to seek change in ways that take for granted that the system is not working for our benefit."[8] Many of the strategies I explore here have their roots in the American civil rights movement and in other racial and economic justice movements around the world—I've tried to honor those sources. I don't pretend that my contribution to this discussion is a novel way to think about social change; rather, I hope to increase the visibility of strategies and approaches that have been used for ages by people—especially women and people of color—who've been excluded from decision making and formal institutions of power.

Finally, despite its title, *Mistrust,* this book is optimistic. It celebrates the approaches individuals and groups are using to make change in the world as much as it describes the challenges many democracies currently face. Many people, overwhelmed by sudden shifts that reveal the weakness of institutions and the lasting, corrosive power of racism and ethnocentrism, feel this time to be overwhelming. I find solace in two phenomena.

First, many people—and especially young people—around the world are reacting to this moment of political and social disruption by developing effective and creative approaches to changing the world for the better. Black Lives Matter, Never Again, #MeToo, and other movements offer hope that social transformation is possible, even if it comes about differently than it did in the past. In the face of the pandemic, mutual aid networks have sprung up around the world as people look for opportunities to help each other out. Our desire for a better world—and our willingness to work for it—seems bent but unbowed by the shortcomings of our institutions.

Second, in the process of finding strategies to change the world, a new generation of activist citizens are expanding the range of possible options so we can organize and govern ourselves. This development has good and bad implications. The joy of seeing progressive leaders like Elizabeth Warren and Alexandria Ocasio-Cortez emerge as high-profile figures in American politics is counterbalanced by the terror of seeing ideas that should have been buried alongside eugenics reemerge into popular discourse. I draw hope from the idea that few, if any, people are satisfied with the choices they are currently presented with, and that whatever directions emerge from this period, we are likely embarking on a different path.

I offer this book as a stone in the ground, a rough-hewn marker of a moment when it seems like everything might change, for the worse or for the better. Here's hoping that some years in the future, someone might step off the trail and pause to read its inscription.

MISTRUST

Chapter 1

IS THIS THING WORKING?

THE IMPACT HUB IN ACCRA, GHANA, HAS ITS HOME IN A sleek, glass-walled modern office filled with contemporary West African art and the cluttered offices of technology start-ups. I arrived there at the tail end of a business trip in the spring of 2014, on a day when a dozen bloggers, social media experts, and programmers were at work. I'd agreed to give a talk about social media to some of Ghana's entrepreneurs, but I focused on one young man in the crowd. Efo Dela, a poet, provocateur, and comedian, had previously urged his fourteen thousand Twitter followers to participate in Ghana's Dumsor protests. Now Efo, wearing a jaunty red fez, was discussing the future of social media in Ghana. I wanted to know how he and fellow activists were using the Internet to organize protests.

Dumsor is a word in the Twi language that means "on/off," and *on/off* is the best way to characterize Ghana's creaky electrical grid. In the past two decades, the country has become a middle-income nation, and the millions of Ghanaians have bought televisions, air conditioners, computers, and mobile phones, placing a heavy load on an inadequate electrical system. Ghana's grid goes down in rolling blackouts, leaving neighborhoods without power for hours or days at a time. Young Ghanaians have taken to the streets wearing T-shirts emblazoned with the Twitter hashtag #*dumsormuststop,* carrying kerosene lanterns, a symbol of their life without electrical power.

Since Efo had been active in calling young Ghanaians to join a five-thousand-person march to Independence Square, the city's most prominent public space, I asked him, "What's the best digital tool for organizing political movements in Ghana? Twitter? Facebook? WhatsApp?"

Efo shook his head and said, "Whoa, man, I'm not political."

In many countries *I'm not political* means "Shut up before we both get arrested." But Ghana is one of the world's most politically open societies, with a free press and democratic elections that have continued for two decades. Efo wasn't warning me off a dangerous topic. Rather, he was making it clear to the rest of the people in the room that he had nothing to do with Ghana's two-party political system.

"I won't even let someone take a photo of me with someone who's political," he explained. If he were seen with his arm around a supporter of either of Ghana's main political parties, he'd lose credibility with his readers, who—like him—see politics as a rigged game played by professionals, not something ordinary Ghanaians engage in.

I didn't know it at the time, but Efo had just explained how Donald Trump, two years later, would win the American presidency.

Antipolitics

For the past two decades, I've worked with, advised, and learned from activists around the world who are using technology and media to take on hard problems. In Russia, where wildfires have destroyed villages outside Moscow and turned the air in the capital into choking smog, young Russians self-organized aid for their neighbors, filling cars with blankets, clothes, and food, delivering them to communities in need. Not only did they disprove the stereotype that Russians don't volunteer, they created a safety net for the elderly and the poor where the state had failed to provide one. Years after the fires, the network remains, helping community members find new apartments and jobs, providing mutual support and stability in a country that's often chaotic and dysfunctional.

In India, the Pink Chaddi Campaign began in Mangalore in 2009 after an attack on women in a pub by members of an orthodox Hindu group, Shri Rama Sene. The leader of Shri Rama Sene, religious extremist Pramod Muthalik, justified the attack, blaming the women for behaving immorally. Muthalik threatened further attacks on Valentine's Day, promising that he and his supporters would confront men and women found consorting romantically and drag them into Hindu temples to be forcibly married. In response, Nisha Susan, a political writer, organized the Consortium of Pub-Going, Loose, and Forward Women, who launched a campaign to send pairs of pink underpants—*chaddi,* in Hindi—to Muthalik's office. The protest received widespread media attention and led to Muthalik and his supporters being held in protective custody on Valentine's Day to prevent them from attacking couples.[1]

In Alexandria, Egypt, in June 2010, plainclothes police officers pulled Khaled Said, a twenty-eight-year-old Egyptian businessman, from an Internet café and proceeded to beat him to death in the lobby of a residential building. A few days after his murder, an Egyptian Google employee based in the United Arab Emirates, Wael Ghonim, set up a Facebook page called *We Are All Khaled Said*. The page, which exposed and protested police violence, attracted almost half a million followers, then became the key source of information about protests in Tunisia, which ultimately drove Egyptian youth into Cairo's Tahrir Square.[2] The goal of Ghonim's page was not regime change in Egypt, and Ghonim himself had not been engaged in Egyptian politics before the government arrested him for his role in administering the Khaled Said Facebook page.

None of these movements was overtly political—in fact, many participants identified themselves as antipolitical. The issues they address are ones of sexism, social justice, consumer rights, and the failure of government safety nets. The solutions they prescribe rarely involve the passage of new laws or the election of new officials. They see problems that can be best addressed not through politics as usual, but through organizing, direct action, and even humor.

In American politics, antipolitics has been a strong force for years, as generations of politicians have run for office by asserting their distaste for Washington, DC, and their opposition to politics as usual. In 1980 Ross Perot, a Texan software billionaire with no government experience, mounted a modestly successful third-party bid for the US presidency that channeled contempt for both political parties and a belief that the government needed to shrink both its spending and its ambitions to maintain fiscal viability. The Tea Party, active in the late 2000s, reframed many of Perot's themes into an explicitly conservative, anti-Washington movement that succeeded in electing dozens of members of Congress.[3] This antipolitical tendency runs deep in the American mythos, serving as a the key plot point in films and television shows from *Mr. Smith Goes to Washington* (1939) to *Dave* (1993) to the TV drama *Designated Survivor* (2016–19). In each story, principled outsiders prove to be better at running the nation than corrupt professionals.[4]

But while antipolitics—an approach to social change that rejects involvement with traditional political processes—has been a constant in American history, young Americans are routinely blamed for their lack of interest in politics. Former Supreme Court justice Sandra Day O'Connor has dedicated her life, after leaving the bench in 2006, to countering a "crisis on our hands when it comes to civics education."[5] For O'Connor, the failure of high school students to understand the American system of checks and balances clearly indicates that we are failing to prepare young people to participate in civic life. The wide gap in voter turnout between people under thirty and those above— generally around 20 percent of people under thirty vote in presidential elections,[6] while more than 50 percent of people over forty-five turn out[7]—is sometimes seen as further evidence that youth have disengaged from politics, though the statistical gap has been pretty much constant since 1986.

The United States certainly could do a better job educating its young people to be effective citizens. The political philosopher Danielle Allen makes a powerful argument that the fundamental purpose of the American public education system is to ensure an informed citizenry. Educating citizens requires teaching critical thinking, the humanities, and STEM, as well as ensuring that students can name all three branches of government.[8] But there's a danger that we have misdiagnosed the problem. Are we facing a crisis because young people are bad at civics? Or are people rightly mistrustful of the institutions that dominate their lives and skeptical about their ability to influence or change them?

Mistrust

In 1958 the American National Election Study began asking Americans whether they trusted the federal government to do the right thing all or most of the time.[9] By this measure, American trust in government peaked at 77 percent in 1964, shortly after the assassination of John F. Kennedy and the election of Lyndon Johnson. By the end of Jimmy Carter's presidency in 1980, trust had fallen below 30 percent, and while the exact percentage has fluctuated, briefly rising above 50 percent shortly after the terror attacks of September 11, 2001, it has never returned to the lofty heights of the early 1960s. Fewer than 20 percent of Americans now express strong trust in the government to do the right thing all or most of the time—an inversion of thirty years ago, when only a small minority consistently mistrusted the government.

We might blame a decline in trust in the federal government on the uniquely dysfunctional presidency of Richard Nixon—indeed, trust in government fell 20 percentage points during his time in office. But Americans didn't lose trust only in the federal government. We lost trust in institutions of all sorts. Between the 1970s and now, Americans report having less trust in the police, organized religion, the medical system, the Supreme Court, public schools, banks, organized labor, newspapers, television news, the criminal justice system, and big business. The only major institution that has earned greater American trust in these past four decades is the military. In part, that's because surveys began measuring trust in the military during the Vietnam War, when it was at a historic low. (Pew's surveys show an increase in trust in small business, but small businesses are less an institution than a collection of individuals.)

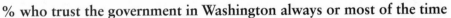

% who trust the government in Washington always or most of the time

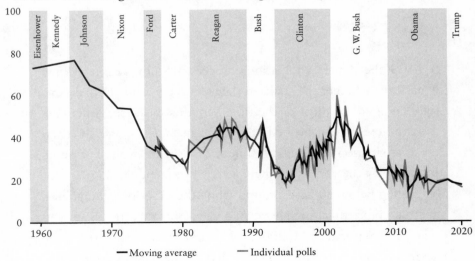

The erosion of trust in the United States has been extreme and dramatic, but Americans are not alone. The PR and polling firm Edelman, which tracks trust in institutions around the world, finds that Germany, Italy, Spain, Britain, Sweden, Japan, and others have even lower institutional trust than the United States. Notably, some of the nations with the highest trust in institutions—Singapore, the United Arab Emirates, China, India—are autocracies or are taking steps to becoming closed societies.[10]

As institutions mature—and we might think of an institution as anything without a face, an organization in which our interactions are with a bureaucracy or a policy rather than with autonomous individuals—we seem to become both reliant on them and mistrustful of them. In the United States, trust in the medical system plummeted from 74 percent in 1977 to 34 percent in 1993,[11] suggesting that the rise of the HMO and other forms of managed health care[12]—and the increase in bureaucracy they represent—helped collapse public trust in a key institution. It's one thing to trust the medical system when the main person you interact with is your doctor, and another entirely when it's the anonymous processor of your insurance claims.

When mistrust is on the rise in a society, it becomes increasingly difficult to know how to fix problems. If you trust the president or the legislature, you can elect representatives who will advocate for your preferred solutions. But once you've concluded that government can't be trusted to do the right thing, you're less likely to rely on voting as a useful form of civic expression.

Mistrust presents a problem for protesters as well. The most iconic protest in twentieth-century America, the 1963 March on Washington, which culminated in Martin Luther King, Jr.'s, "I Have a Dream" speech, demonstrates the value of protest when electoral influence doesn't succeed. The march was designed to force President Kennedy to support the Civil Rights Act, which had been stalled in Congress. The massive march and accompanying media coverage persuaded Kennedy to act on civil rights—

or gave him plausible cover to act—and gave his successor, Lyndon B. Johnson, a mandate to push for its passage.

This march, which set the template for so many subsequent protests, was a march *on Washington*. If we believe that partisan paralysis prevents Washington from making compromises and changes, it is no longer rational for us to try to influence Congress, or even a president, through protest. The international women's march, announced the day after Donald Trump's election and held the day after his 2017 inauguration, was not an attempt to persuade the new president to change his policies. Instead, it offered a howl of anger at his election and what it symbolized. That it was likely the largest protest in American history made little difference in influencing the Trump administration.

Insurrectionists and Institutionalists

In his book *Twilight of the Elites*, the MSNBC host Chris Hayes suggests that left versus right is no longer the most important dichotomy in American politics.[13] More important is the tension between *institutionalists* and *insurrectionists*. Institutionalists believe that the key to solving a nation's problems is to revitalize and strengthen existing organs of power: congresses and parliaments, political parties and unions, businesses and civic organizations. By contrast, insurrectionists believe existing systems are rigged, ineffective, or wholly broken, and that change will come only from overthrowing existing systems and replacing them with new systems . . . or perhaps with no system at all.

If you've lost trust in institutions, perhaps because they've systemically failed to make your life better, insurrectionism may be both a reasonable and an honorable stance. But we've been trained not to take it seriously. Serious People, we are taught in schools and reminded in the news, know that decisions about our collective future are made by people debating within the government—in the halls of Congress, in the White House—and within corporate boardrooms. A web of Sunday-morning talk shows, designed for consumption by Serious People, reminds us that our role is to closely follow these discussions, to have opinions on these matters, to discuss them with our friends, and to vote based on what we believe. The subtle implication remains: there's little else we can do.

We don't take insurrectionism seriously because it feels like a dream or a utopian fantasy. We are so accustomed to our relative powerlessness within contemporary representative democracy that the idea that we could imagine something better, could make changes that go beyond voting one party in and another out, feels silly or frivolous.

We also tend to equate insurrectionism with revolution, the violent overthrow of an existing system. While many of us cheered revolutions in Tunisia, Egypt, and throughout the Arab world, we remember that most ended with the violent suppression of dissent or decayed into civil war. Revolutions seem both dangerous to hope for and unlikely to end well, even when they are the best we can imagine for societies that neglect or actively transgress citizens' rights or humanity.

Finally, we don't take insurrectionism seriously because we do a poor job of teaching and learning our own history. Replacing a colonial government that ineptly ruled from across an ocean with one that allowed citizens direct influence over their government feels like the work of civic superheroes, people with no equals today. We can sometimes forget that American democracy initially excluded women, people of color, and even white men who didn't own land. Expanding that democracy required a series of insurrectionist movements, some peaceful, some bloody, but all hard fought. American institutions began changing almost the moment they were created. We continue to change our government even now, with six amendments to the Constitution since World War II.

This book is an exercise in taking insurrectionism seriously.

While revolutions are a violent rejection of a government, insurrectionism identifies individual institutions that aren't functioning well—in the government, business, or elsewhere—and works to overhaul them, transform them, or replace them with something better. Those transformations are usually far slower and less romantic than occupying a public square until the government falls. Unfortunately, it's easier to promise insurrection than to successfully implement it.

The election of a man with no governmental experience and no apparent interest in the functioning of a federal government to the nation's highest office suggests the deep alienation of a large percentage of the American electorate. Trump was elected by people who had lost faith in the government's ability to meet their needs and to make meaningful change. That the change he promised was primarily the return of white men to positions of authority and power, rolling back progress achieved by antiracist, feminist, and LGBT movements, can disguise the fact that many people of all political stripes were unhappy with the status quo.

In this sense of frustration, Brexit offers a direct parallel to the rise of Trump. For Britons who understand themselves as disempowered, it's easy to understand how rejecting a powerful institution like the European Union seems like an important step, even without a clear sense of what a post-Brexit Britain might look like. If you believe you are unable to change the world you live in, electing Trump or exiting the European Union feels like recovering your efficacy.

Both Trump and Boris Johnson have used their position as insurrectionist leaders to launch a broad attack on any institutions that might hold them in check. Johnson's maneuverings to take Brexit discussions out of the hands of a deeply divided Parliament and move forward with his preferred plans for exit, citing his desire to implement the people's will, threatened to cripple the possibility of parliamentary oversight. Trump's endless attacks on the media as "fake news" continue even as he turns his sights to intelligence officers, diplomats, and career public servants, who he sees as agents of a "deep state," conspiring to check his authority. In a world where no institution can be trusted, there are only superempowered individuals like Trump and Johnson.

But considering Trump as the avatar for insurrectionism limits our understanding of the phenomenon. First, it suggests that insurrectionist movements come primarily from the right. That's not true. In recent years, strong insurrectionist tendencies have come from the left as well. At its peak, the left-insurrectionist Occupy movement had a presence in almost a thousand cities in more than eighty countries, demanding the rejection of current economic and political systems. While the movement dissipated in the United States, in Spain the closely related 15M movement morphed into a new political party, Podemos, which revitalized the Spanish left.

It's helpful to think of the 2016 US presidential election in terms of four quadrants, with a left-right axis and an insurrectionist-institutionalist axis. Hillary Clinton is identified as a left insti-

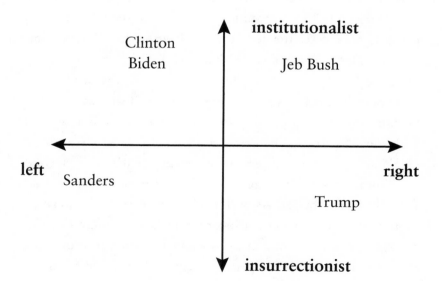

tutionalist: her selling point was her deep knowledge of the institutions of government from her time as a senator, as secretary of state, and as first lady. She expected to face off against Jeb Bush, Ted Cruz, and a pack of right institutionalists. Instead, she fended off a challenge from Vermont senator Bernie Sanders, who despite his decades-long tenure in Washington could believably position himself as a left insurrectionist. He identified as a socialist and pushed radical overhauls of broken systems, like replacing America's dysfunctional health care system with government health care. Ultimately, Clinton was done in by Trump, a right insurrectionist, who ran roughshod over his Republican challengers by presenting himself as genuinely coming from outside the existing political system. Two thousand sixteen was a good year for insurrectionists and a lousy one for institutionalists. Two thousand twenty repeated these dynamics for the Democrats: the showdown between Sanders and Biden, an insurrectionist and an institutionalist, once again resulted in a left institutionalist facing a right insurrectionist.

But Trump is no model insurrectionist; he's far more interested in tearing institutions down than in building something new in their place. His initial cabinet has been referred to as the "wrecking crew,"[14] a recognition that many of the secretaries he chose wanted to see the departments they ran defanged or eliminated. (The best example, perhaps, is Trump's first secretary of energy, Rick Perry, who thought so little of the department that controls America's nuclear power and nuclear weapons that he campaigned on a promise to eliminate it and was rewarded with the keys to it.) The desire to dismantle these institutions, combined with the reckless incompetence that's characterized the Trump presidency, suggests a vision of insurrectionism that burns but never builds. As we'll explore, insurrectionism can be more than a roar of rage. It incorporates a continuum of strategies, from transforming institutions from within to pressuring them from the outside, replacing them with novel institutions, or most radically, working to eliminate institutions altogether. What it doesn't do is smash things and move on.

Finally, Trump isn't remotely serious about addressing the forces that have led so many people to lose confidence in institutions. The tax cuts and deregulation that represent his core successes as president are designed to increase, not decrease, the inequality that fuels the frustration and alienation behind American insurrectionism. Trump talks like an insurrectionist, but his vision is about smashing the social progress of the past decades and returning the nation to an earlier, even less just order. Should 2020 return the United States to a more conventional presidency, there's no reason to believe that everyday Americans' widespread dissatisfaction will dissipate.

Frustration with institutions and the ways we interact with them—electing representatives and influencing how they pass laws—is concerning, but it's deeply encouraging that we're also seeing a wave of people using an expanded set of techniques to seek change. While in the past several decades, activists on the left and the right have seen law as the most powerful lever for change, a new wave of engaged citizens is leveraging markets, writing code, and working to reshape and influence social norms. As we look beyond the paralysis that grips many governments and consider a broader vision of engagement, it becomes apparent that this is both a dark moment for civics and one of the brightest we've seen in generations.

Good Citizens

For Christmas 2012, my friend Quinn Norton sent me a brick.

Specifically, she sent me a handmade print depicting a brick, emblazoned with an "I voted" sticker, a symbol of civic virtue immediately recognizable to any American voter.

The picture was an inside joke for regular readers of Norton's provocative and sometimes controversial blog. A celebrated tech journalist, she had expanded her beat to cover the Occupy movement, spending a year living in different encampments in the United States and Canada. After Occupy ended, she published a piece on why she would no longer vote in US elections. Explaining that her great-grandmother had marched for women's right to vote in Boise, Idaho, Quinn reflected that her vote now feels contradictory and meaningless: "We are told both that we must perform our kabuki democracy, and that our vote doesn't really matter." Instead of lining up at the polls, she urged readers to "vote with every dollar, in every relationship. Vote in how you work and how you speak. Vote in how you treat others and what you will accept from them. Vote your dignity and the dignity of others."[15]

Quinn's essay is so provocative because most democracies treat voting as a near-sacred duty. In some countries, like Australia, it's mandatory, and nonparticipation is fined. In the United States, outing yourself as a nonvoter is likely to prompt a lesson about the women, African-Americans, and others who marched, protested, and risked their lives for the right to vote. Nonparticipants are told that if you don't vote, you shouldn't complain about the state of the nation. In short, voting defines what it means to be a good citizen in the United States. But what it means to be a good citizen can, and does, change.

In his groundbreaking 1998 book *The Good Citizen,* the journalism scholar Michael Schudson explains that expectations for "good citizens" in the United States have changed at least four times in the past two hundred years.[16] At the inception of our democracy, elections were less about politics than about a community affirming its worthiest and most prominent member. Whoever that august person was would logically be chosen to represent the community in government.

The notion of a professional politician, or of modern political parties, didn't gain currency until the early 1800s, when politics moved into barrooms, with loud, drunken parties pre-paring men to vote, a process that often involved fighting one's way to the ballot box through supporters of the other party. A candidate's party affiliation had less to do with his stances on specific issues than with his alignment with certain professions and social classes.

Representative democracy as we know it didn't really emerge in the United States until the 1920s, when a set of progressive reforms ushered in the secret ballot, the possibility of split tickets, and the presence of questions and ballot initiatives at the polls. These election reforms were paired with a rise in investigative, muckraking journalism and were closely linked to the temper-ance movement, which sought to take politics out of the barroom and turn it into a sober, serious process. Schudson refers to this conception of democracy as the Informed Citizen model and notes that it came with undesirable consequences. For one thing, it places heavy demands on citizens to inform themselves about candidates and issues. After the progressive reforms, American democracy saw a massive fall in electoral participation, from about 70 percent in the boozy years of party politics to 35 percent in nonpresidential years.

While we teach the Informed Citizen model as the ideal for citizenship, Schudson notes, many of us find it hard to keep up with its demands. Working at a California polling station, he found that for every voter who'd examined and notated their four-hundred-page California voters' guide, dozens more quickly voted a straight party ticket, or voted in the few races where they'd done the research, then moved on. Citizens today, Schud-son speculates, understand that they can't master every issue that we ask them to opine on. Instead, they monitor a set of issues they know and care about and take action when they think they can make a difference.

In other words, citizens care less about civic duty—the obliga-tion to engage in political life in a particular, prescribed way—

than about efficacy, their ability to make meaningful changes on issues they care about. I choose to read Quinn Norton's provocation as a call for efficacy. Norton wants us to spend time on the causes where we can and will be able to make a change, not to waste our time and energy on ones that demand our participation but lead to no lasting changes.

Scholars of civic participation study efficacy as a way to understand who does and doesn't participate in elections and other parts of civic life. The reasoning is logical enough: if you didn't believe you could make a change through your actions, why would you bother participating? Questions about efficacy often start with political knowledge: Do you know when and where to vote? Do you know how to reach your local representative with a question or a concern? Answering yes to these questions suggests that you are knowledgeable enough to be politically effective. But as scholars have examined the idea, they've been forced to refine it, distinguishing between internal and external efficacy.

If you've got the knowledge you need to participate in civic life, you've got internal high efficacy. But you may be thwarted by a political system that doesn't value or respond to your participation. The organizers of the US civil rights movement in the 1960s had tremendous internal efficacy. Activists taught classes on how and where to vote and on strategies for nonviolent protest and economic activism. Actions like the Montgomery Bus Boycott required complex organization and coordination. Protest leaders essentially had to create a parallel public transportation system to ensure that participants in the year-long boycott could get to work and didn't lose their jobs. As a number of historians have pointed out, the March on Washington was organized to the level of providing sandwiches dressed with mustard, not mayonnaise, because the organizers worried the mayo might spoil in the heat. Activists who are organized to the level of condiment choice don't need civics classes to increase their internal efficacy.[17]

The civil rights movement struggled to make progress against the entrenched system it was trying to oust. Segregation was not only the law in much of America, but it was also a powerful set of norms and behaviors, held in place by all those who benefited from it and even by many who were harmed by it. For years, Martin Luther King, Jr., and others had high internal efficacy and low external efficacy—their knowledge of American civics came up against a system that wasn't ready to adjust. And when King and others tried to make change through means other than winning elections, those in power condemned them as dangerous and potentially violent.

Clergy leaders in Alabama wrote a letter opposing demonstrations against desgregation, demanding that King and his followers work within existing systems: "When rights are consistently denied, a cause should be pressed in the courts and in negotiations among local leaders, and not in the streets. We appeal to both our white and Negro citizenry to observe the principles of law and order and common sense."[18]

When insurrectionists work within dysfunctional systems, they often find those systems resist their attempts at change: they experience the low external efficacy that civil rights leaders felt. When they change tactics and try to work outside those systems, they're told they don't know how to participate effectively: as King was criticized for working outside the system, they are accused of having low internal efficacy, of lacking an understanding of how systems work.

At a certain point, activists can't win: they are thwarted by broken systems, or they are told they are ignorant of how those systems work. But their problem is not ignorance but a lack of efficacy. When systems won't respond to attempts at change, that's the time to look for new tactics. When we are organized, competent, creative, and deliberate, and when systems are rigid and brittle, it is time for broken systems to be replaced with new ones.

At this moment of deep frustration with political institutions—

from the left and from the right—we are seeing real and meaningful change through mechanisms that combine conventional protest with social media to mobilize mass movements online. After footage emerged of then-candidate Trump bragging about sexually abusing women, a movement demanding accountability for violence against women has grown stronger in the United States. From the women's march in Washington that dwarfed the size of the presidential inauguration and brought out crowds in over six hundred cities around the world,[19] to the protests against appointing Brett Kavanaugh, accused by Dr. Christine Blasey Ford of sexual assault as a youth, sexual violence has proved to be an issue capable of mobilizing protests.

A large share of the impact of the #MeToo movement has come through social media, from the phenomenon of hundreds of thousands of women identifying as survivors of sexual violence, echoing the hashtag #MeToo. Within a year of the movement's rise to prominence with the exposing of Harvey Weinstein's systemic abuse of actresses and staffers, dozens of high-profile men accused of sexual abuse have been ousted from positions of power, and Weinstein has gone to jail. While feminists had hoped for years that the inclusion of more women in professional spheres would make those institutions more open and less abusive, it took a brick through the window rather than a seat at the table to force institutions to confront abuse and inequity that had persisted for decades.

Insurrectionists make change in the world by harnessing their mistrust of existing institutions. For the best of these movements, their skepticism is not an obstacle to their effectiveness but their key strength. Unpacking how these movements work requires us to understand a much broader range of actions as civic participation. As Norton urges, civics becomes how we speak, how we spend, how we work, and how we treat each other.

Our understanding of what it means to be a good citizen is in flux. At some point soon, we may understand a good citizen to be one who chooses not to vote because she is finding other, better ways to change society. To navigate this transition, we need to guard against civic piety, the sense that we know how civics should be done and that anyone not following established rules should stop what they are doing and apologize.

We're used to understanding civic actions as ones where citizens engage with their government. But insurrectionist civics sees law as only one of four levers that citizens can manipulate. The #MeToo movement isn't primarily seeking new laws: sexual assault in the workplace has been illegal for years. But norms about reporting and facing consequences for sexual assault need to change, and #MeToo is using a combination of media attention and legal actions to alter those norms. Other engaged citizens see markets and code as key levers to move, taking successful action on climate change, privacy, and other critical issues that have been difficult to advance through law alone.

Not every engaged insurrectionist is plotting an end run around existing institutions. Some are becoming experts on how those institutions work, using their rules and practices in order to reimagine them. These radical institutionalists accept that institutions need to evolve, but they see the seeds of rebirth in their particular institutional history and capacities to adapt. Another camp of insurrectionists, the counter-democrats, see institutions as broken but place primacy on scrutinizing them, publicizing their weaknesses, and forcing them to adapt and improve. They confront institutions in ways that are often uncomfortable but ultimately seek to preserve these (better, more accountable) institutions. As mistrust grows, we encounter those working to disrupt existing institutions and replace them with new, fairer systems or with no institutions at all. Here many of the most ambitious projects look less like activism as we know it and more like ambitious Silicon Valley start-ups.

As much as exploring insurrectionism can lead us to futuristic directions, it's critical to remember that mistrust in social institutions is not a new phenomenon. For those who've experienced exclusion from civic life—African-Americans and other people of color, LGBTQIA people—mistrust in institutions is often a default stance. For marginalized groups, engaged citizenship has always required working outside institutions while simultaneously demanding inclusion within them. The tensions in the civil rights movement between those who wanted recognition within existing systems—as exemplified by Reverend King—and those who wanted to build fairer, parallel systems—the Black Panthers—still play out today. Institutionalists and insurrectionists can too easily see each other as the enemy. Institutionalists see insurrectionists as unreasonable and unrealistic. Insurrectionists see institutionalists as compromised and self-deluding.

Institutionalists and insurrectionists have a common enemy: disengagement. As mistrust in institutions rises, most people don't abandon institutions and become insurrectionists—they exit civic life. The Efo Delas of the world, who abandon the political and embrace the civic, are the exception and not the rule. What institutionalists and insurrectionists have in common is a belief that change is still possible and that the work is worth their time.

Understanding how disengagement became a default stance requires us to understand the origins of mistrust. Like everything else in a society that's far from achieving equity, mistrust is unevenly distributed. Understanding the transformation of the United States from a nation that trusted institutions to one that systemically mistrusts them is a first step in understanding how we can mobilize mistrust, turning what could be a corrosive chemical into rocket fuel that propels engaged citizenship.

Chapter 2

WHY WE LOST TRUST

IN 1995, RALPH KINSEY BENNETT LOST HIS WALLET IN Greensboro, North Carolina. And in Boston. And again in Seattle. The *Reader's Digest* staff editor was not uncommonly forgetful. Rather, he was conducting a simple and compelling experiment in trust and trustworthiness.[1]

Bennett and other *Reader's Digest* editors left wallets containing fifty dollars, family pictures, identification, and a local address and phone number—120 separate times—in locations in big cities and small towns around the United States. Each time a reporter dropped a wallet and left, another reporter waited secretly nearby, then followed whoever picked it up to see where they went and what they did with it.

Eighty of the 120 wallets that *Reader's Digest* editors dropped were returned. Women slightly outperformed men in terms of trustworthiness, and small-town residents were on average more honest than city dwellers, though nine of ten wallets dropped in Seattle were returned. Strikingly, many of the people who returned wallets told interviewers that while they personally felt compelled to return the wallet, they didn't think most people would be. Most estimated that fewer than 50 percent of wallets would be returned.

Pollsters at Gallup realized that the "wallet test" was a concrete gauge of how much trust people had in different sectors of society. In their 2006 Gallup World poll, they asked people in eighty-six countries whether they would expect a neighbor, a stranger, or the police to return their wallet if they found it.[2] In most countries, people trust their neighbors more than the police, and they trust strangers very little. In high-trust New Zealand, 94 percent anticipated that their neighbors would return a wallet, and 44 percent predicted that strangers would. In Cambodia, only 24 percent believed their neighbors would return the wallet, and only 1 percent thought strangers would.

Canadian economist John Helliwell saw an opportunity to check the Gallup study against an experiment run by a Toronto newspaper, which had replicated the *Reader's Digest* experiment. While only 25 percent of Torontonians believed that a stranger would return a lost wallet, in practice, 80 percent of the wallets were turned in with cash intact. Helliwell, a scholar of "subjective well-being"—or as nonacademics put it, happiness—worried that his countrymen were selling themselves short and suffering emotional damage in the process.[3]

High-trust societies, those in which many people believe their lost wallet would be returned, are generally happier than low-trust societies. Controlling for myriad other factors that correlate to happiness, Helliwell found that moving from a low-trust society like Cambodia to a high-trust society like New Zealand would realize an increase in happiness equivalent to having household income increase by 40 percent. If Torontonians only knew how trustworthy their neighbors actually were, the whole city might be a happier place!

The wallet experiment illustrates several key dimensions of trust. We trust particular individuals, groups, and institutions: we might trust our neighbors but not strangers or the police. Trust is situational: I might trust you to return my wallet, but I might not trust you to care for my child. Trust inherently involves risk: if I'm guaranteed to get my wallet back, there's no trust involved in the situation. Trust is voluntary: no one can force me to believe that my neighbors, the police, or complete strangers can be trusted.

Scholarly analyses of the wallet experiment reveal some less obvious aspects of trust. Trust is extremely variable, both within and between societies. It's difficult to predict whether a particular individual will be trusting or mistrustful, though people with more education and greater wealth are generally more trusting than those who struggle economically. Still, people in China show more interpersonal trust and trust in government than do richer and better educated Germans, and both Germans and Chinese are far more trusting than Spaniards, though Spain and Germany have similar levels of education and prosperity.

These differences in trust levels have led to speculation that certain cultures are more trusting than others. Francis Fukuyama looked at differences in economic prosperity between high-trust northern Italy and low-trust southern Italy and argued that the ability to trust beyond a narrow circle of family and friends left northern Italians better positioned to compete in national and global markets. For Fukuyama, trust helps explain not only the economic but also the political success of nations.[4]

Fukuyama offers one argument for why trust matters: the absence of trust adds immense costs to transactions. When we do business with people we know and trust, we are willing to extend credit, send orders before we receive payment, and otherwise take steps to speed a transaction. When we lack that trust, we invoke intricate mechanisms to prevent bad behavior.

The Internet auction site eBay took on this problem when it built a business around strangers selling and buying goods online. To make trade possible in the absence of trust, eBay had to build a reputation system where participants reported on whether the person they purchased from was reliable. It launched an escrow system, in which it acted as a trusted third party, verifying that expensive items were delivered before releasing payments. A large percentage of eBay's capitalization comes from its ability to make trust-free transactions possible—we might think of those tens of billions as the price we have collectively agreed to pay for eBay to create trust where there was none. Virtually all other online retailers have adopted eBay's core discoveries—that people need signals that someone is trustworthy and financial protections to do business with untrusted parties—and they now are standard operating practice in digital commerce.

The economists Paul Zak and Stephen Knack have a mathematical explanation for eBay's success. In a 2001 paper, they conducted a thought experiment in which people made investments through brokers who operated at various levels of trustworthiness. While these brokers could cheat their clients, the clients could investigate the brokers. Zak and Knack used this model to investigate the economic impact of trust in societies and found that "because trust reduces the cost of transactions (ie less time is spent investigating one's broker), high trust societies produce more output than low trust societies." They also found that societies could fall into a "trust trap," wherein people are unwilling to invest because trust is so low. In these societies, informal mechanisms to punish cheaters don't work. EBay faced precisely this trust trap before it invested in the formal mechanisms that made it possible for customers to trust each other.[5]

People in low-trust societies pay social prices as well as economic prices. High-trust societies are filled with "weak ties," or casual relationships with neighbors and co-workers. In his 2000 book *Bowling Alone*, sociologist Robert Putnam feared that by spending less of our time interacting with our neighbors, and more time alone in front of the TV set, we would lose these weak ties and become less trusting in and more hostile toward those around us.[6] Subsequently, Putnam has explored what can happen if we live in communities where we feel little trust: we hunker down and hide in our houses rather than connecting with our neighbors. Without a network of weak ties to the people we're surrounded by, we are likely to be less happy and potentially to be as unsatisfied with our lives as if we were fiscally much poorer.

Trust affects our health, wealth, and happiness. It also affects our ability to govern ourselves. Representative democracy isn't possible without trust. If we cannot trust our representative in Parliament or Congress to advocate on behalf of our interests or those of our community, instead of advancing her own interests, we—gradually or rapidly—lose faith. Trust in government doesn't require that we trust each individual person in a position of power. We may despise the man or woman serving as our current representative, but that distaste need not equal distrust in the larger system, as long as we believe that our positions will be heard and influence decision making.

Oddly, democracy demands far less trust than do the systems of government it has replaced. Monarchies require either no trust at all or absolute trust in a ruler. The innovation of American democracy was to introduce points of transparency into governance. You can review what's been said in Congress, an idea that was unthinkable in England, where a 1620 declaration by King James I made divulging parliamentary proceedings a crime.[7] The strong protections given to the press under the First Amendment make it possible for journalists to interrogate government decisions, a relationship that requires a certain amount of mistrust to animate the process.

Democracy thrives in a sweet spot between too much trust and too little. Trust Barometer, a survey developed by public relations firm Edelman, tracks people's trust in four key institutions—government, press, corporations, and NGOs—in twenty-five nations. The countries with the highest trust in government are not necessarily the healthiest democracies. They include China (79 percent), India (72 percent), the United Arab Emirates (71 percent), and Singapore (62 percent). In closed societies, trust can be extremely high because citizens are satisfied . . . or because they're unable to review what the government is actually doing . . . or because they're scared to report that they don't trust the government![8]

With too little trust, democracies may not be able to function at all. On January 1, 2012, the government of Nigeria removed a subsidy that had made gasoline extremely inexpensive. Nigeria's minister of finance, the internationally respected economic reformer Ngozi Okonjo-Iweala, explained that the subsidy disproportionately rewarded wealthy Nigerians who could afford cars, and that by removing the subsidy, the government would be able to allocate more money toward programs that would benefit all Nigerians. Bus and truck drivers responded to the loss of the subsidy by doubling their prices, which led to price increases on basic goods like bread and cooking oil. Millions of Nigerians took to the streets to protest the removal of the subsidy in a movement called Occupy Nigeria.

Minister Okonjo-Iweala was correct, at least on paper: the fuel subsidy did benefit wealthy Nigerians, who were far more likely to own cars than poor ones, and shifting subsidy money to government spending on health care or education would benefit many more Nigerians. But after decades of government corruption, most Nigerians had very low trust that the government would spend money to benefit ordinary citizens. Even if poor Nigerians didn't benefit from the fuel subsidy as much as rich ones, taking the subsidy away was an economic loss, as very few Nigerians believed they'd ever see the broader gains promised by the government. At a very low level of trust, governments may literally be unable to do anything right—citizens will simply assume that any changes made will benefit those in power and harm the citizenry.

The Occupy Nigeria protests are an extreme case, but it's worth noting that in Nigeria, confidence in government is slightly higher than in the United States and much higher than in Spain, according to the 2011–14 World Values Survey, a massive, global social science survey conducted twice a decade in dozens of countries.[9] Since at least 1999, political scientists in the United States and Europe have warned that confidence in government is reaching low enough levels that democracy itself might be threatened.

While some in the United States and Britain see mistrust emerging from Trump's systemic attacks on institutions and from Brexit sentiment, citizen confidence in government has been falling for decades in the United States and in several parts of western Europe. While the decline of trust in the United States neither directly parallels nor prefigures declines in other parts of the world, it's informative as a possible illustration of how a society's trust can decay.

The trust shift in the United States, from a society where four in five trusted the government to one where one in five does, snowballed toward the end of the Nixon presidency. Mistrust rose during Nixon's impeachment and alongside increasing resistance to the Vietnam War. Democrats and Republicans alike lost faith in Nixon, Ford, and Carter, and in 1980, near the end of Carter's recession-plagued presidency, trust in government bottomed out at 25 percent. While trust rebounded under Ronald Reagan, a partisan shift also emerged, with confidence in the presidency rebounding more for Republicans than Democrats. The gap in trust between the two parties expanded to 24 points under the George W. Bush presidency, the highest gap Gallup's polling has shown.[10]

Since Barack Obama's election to the presidency in 2008, American trust in government has been in a trough, simultaneously low and highly partisan. Democrats trusted Obama, and Republicans trust Trump more than Democrats do. But average trust in government hovers below 20 percent, significantly lower than when President Carter warned of a "crisis in the growing doubt about the meaning of our own lives and in the loss of a unity of purpose for our nation."[11] President Trump did not cause mistrust in the United States. Rather, he is a result of a decade of bipartisan low trust, following a long, partisan sequence where trust has been both low and tightly tied to perceptions of the party in power.

The situation is vastly more complicated in Europe, if only because levels of trust vary so sharply between different nations. While in 2005 only one-third of Swedes trusted their government, by 2017, 58 percent expressed a high level of trust. In contrast, only 17 percent of Italians trust their government, the result of a long slide from a high of 35 percent trust in 2001. At the risk of offering vast generalizations, central and eastern European nations are less trusting than western European nations. Southern Europe is less trusting than northern Europe.[12] And while Europe may be experiencing a trough of trust similar to the United States, trust in Europe appeared to hit bottom after the economic crisis of 2007–8 and has recovered only somewhat since.

While the decrease in trust in the United States is especially dramatic, there's evidence that this country is not alone in its crisis of confidence in democratic institutions. In early 2017 the Harvard lecturer Yascha Mounk and the Australian political scientist Roberto Foa released a paper that was so shocking, it made headlines in national newspapers before it was officially published. Mounk and Foa had gathered evidence that a trend toward liberal democracy as a dominant model of political organizing might be "deconsolidating," with fewer people reporting a conviction that democracy was the best possible model of governance, more people showing openness to rule by the military or by experts, and an accompanying rise in "antisystem" political parties. Strikingly, Mounk and Foa found less support for democratic institutions from younger people than from older ones. While nearly 60 percent of Europeans born in the 1950s told pollsters that it was essential to live in a democracy, less than 45 percent of those born in the 1980s felt the same way. And while 5 percent or fewer Europeans over thirty-five told pollsters that democracy was a "bad" or "very bad" way to run a country, almost three times as many sixteen-to-twenty-four-year-olds reported that they felt democracy was a bad system of government.[13]

Unfortunately for Americans, Foa and Mounk's findings about the United States are even starker. Twenty-four percent of Americans aged sixteen to twenty-four consider democracy a bad form of government, and while Americans born in the 1950s are as enthusiastic as Europeans, only 32 percent of Americans born in the 1980s see it as essential to live in a democracy. One critic of Foa and Mounk's work, Ron Inglehart (the founder of the World Values Survey, who's been studying political and social opinions for fifty years), suggests that Europe shows only modest signs of democratic deconsolidation, whereas the effects are more serious in the United States, noting, "One reason may be that in recent years US democracy has become appallingly dysfunctional."[14]

Ingelhart blames American dysfunction in part on hyperpartisanship leading to regular face-offs between the governing parties, which leads to shutdowns of the government. Indeed, Congress emerges as the least trusted major institution in Gallup's surveys, with only 8 percent of Americans expressing a great deal or quite a lot of confidence in America's highest legislative body. Congress is also the institution that's suffered the greatest loss in American public confidence, falling from 42 percent in 1973 to its current dismal levels. What's most striking about America's crisis in trust is that faith in almost all American institutions has dropped sharply over the past forty years.

In the mid-1970s, the majority of Americans expressed high trust in organized religion, the medical system, public schools, banks, and newspapers. Trust in all had dropped sharply by 2010. Sometimes a clear, single event leads to a collapse. Trust in organized religion in the United States plunged fifteen points in 2002, the year *The Boston Globe* began reporting on a pattern of child abuse by Roman Catholic priests that the Church hierarchy had covered up.[15] Confidence in big banks dropped from 49 percent in 2006 to 22 percent in 2009 as the 2007–8 financial crisis unfolded. But other falls were slow, gradual, and less easily explained by a single catastrophic event.

The overall trend is unmistakable. In the most recent Gallup polls, the only three institutions that a majority of Americans expressed trust in were the military, the police, and small business. That a majority of Americans trust the police and the military over all other institutions is an uncomfortable statistic, one we might expect to see in a fragile state, not in the birthplace of liberal democracy.

Trust in these institutions has continued to slide under Donald Trump's leadership. Some of these declines are partisan—a large number of Democrats have recently decided that they have no faith in the presidency—but the fact that confidence in all but one American institution has fallen between late 2016 and early 2018 suggests a zeitgeist of institutional mistrust.[16] The only institution to gain trust in the most recent survey? Newspapers, one of Donald Trump's favorite targets.

The United States is not alone in suffering a widespread crisis of institutional trust. Edelman's Trust Barometer examines trust in a range of institutions, not just in government. Britain, Germany, France, South Korea, Japan, and Australia all report levels of trust 10 points lower than what's reported in the United States. In France and Italy, more than 70 percent of the population believes that "the system is failing."[17]

What we've seen between the 1960s and the present is a thorough transformation of the relationship between citizens and the institutions they encounter in their lives. In the United States in the 1960s, it was as difficult to find someone skeptical of government as it is to find someone now with high confidence in Washington. This raises the obvious question: what happened to trust?

Again, looking at factors that have eroded trust in the United States won't explain the erosion of trust elsewhere in the world. But many of the underlying factors that affected trust here are likely to explain drops in other countries. Others, including conflicts over racism and civil rights, are likely peculiar to the American experience.

It's Nixon's Fault

Karl Marlantes, who served as a Marine lieutenant in Vietnam, tells the story of how he lost his political innocence during the war. Talking to friends in his unit before deploying, "One said that Lyndon B. Johnson was lying to us about the war. I blurted out, 'But . . . but an American president wouldn't lie to Americans!' They all burst out laughing." Before Vietnam, Marlantes argues, most Americans were like him. After the war, we were like his comrades; the idea of an honest politician was laughable.[18]

The Vietnam War damaged trust in American institutions in successive waves. Lyndon Johnson presided over the partially fabricated Gulf of Tonkin incident in 1964. Nixon's credibility took a serious hit when the Senate Armed Services Committee discovered in 1973 that the president had ordered a fourteen-month campaign of carpet bombing in Laos and Cambodia, using complex deceptions to avoid reporting those actions. In 1985, ten years after the end of the war, two-thirds of Americans polled believed Johnson and Nixon had deliberately misled the country about the war.[19] In the same survey, 73 percent of veterans said they were mistrustful of the government because of its handling of the war. Those soldiers who saw heavy combat were the most disillusioned.

The revelation of the secret bombings in Cambodia was concurrent with congressional debate over impeaching Nixon for his role in ordering the Watergate burglaries. While the Senate Armed Services Committee ultimately voted against including the secret bombing in the list of impeachment charges against Nixon, the simultaneous unraveling of his presidency and the war transformed the attitudes of many Americans, replacing deference to the authority of the office with suspicion at the concentration of executive power. Between 1972 and 1974, American trust in government fell from 53 to 36 percent, the steepest decline on record.[20]

The historian Julian Zelizer argues, "We still live in the era of Watergate," because the lasting impacts of the loss of trust in government still shape politics today.[21] Ironically, though Watergate drove a Republican president from office, it likely has harmed Democrats more in the long run, as left political agendas lean more heavily on government programs than those offered by the right.

But Watergate can't fully explain the current challenges to American institutions. Less than 40 percent of Americans today were alive during Watergate,[22] and while its cultural influence is lasting and profound, 9/11—an event that greatly increased confidence in government—was a seminal event for more living Americans than was Watergate or Vietnam. And while Watergate and Vietnam eroded trust in government, they increased trust in other institutions, notably in the media, which was lionized for the successes of investigative journalism in revealing Nixon's deceptions.

Racism and Mistrust

America's fraught history with race offers an uglier explanation for the loss of trust in government institutions. The civil rights movement of the 1950s and '60s expanded rights and opportunities for African-Americans, who had been systemically oppressed through segregation, suppression of voting rights, employment and housing discrimination, and financial exploitation by the few institutions that would serve them. The ongoing and profound effects of this discrimination are visible in the racial wealth gap between white and Black Americans: in 2013 the median wealth of white families in America was $134,230, while for Black families, it was $11,030.[23]

While many of the best-known events of the civil rights movement—the Montgomery Bus Boycott, the Freedom Rides, the integration of southern universities, the March on Washington—occurred during the high-trust years of the 1950s and early '60s, the signature legislation that prohibited discrimination by race at the federal level, the Civil Rights Act and the Voting Rights Act, were passed in 1964 and 1965, just as trust in government peaked in the United States.

Civil rights leaders persuaded the federal government to legislate changes that many Americans were not personally ready to make. While more recent civil rights struggles, like the acceptance of equal marriage for gays and lesbians, found congressional support after they'd found widespread public support, African-Americans won rights that many Americans would not have voted to give them. In 1956, when *Brown v. Board of Education* mandated the integration of schools, national polling on the question of whether Black and white children should attend school together was evenly divided, and opinions were far more negative in southern states.[24] The violence associated with school integration was a predictable result of the Supreme Court mandating a change that many Americans resisted—and a sign of the Supreme Court's willingness to promote social justice counter to prevailing popular opinion.

For some white Americans, the changes brought about by the civil rights movement signaled that the government didn't care about them or their desire for a segregated nation. Republicans harnessed this resentment by adopting the "Southern Strategy," which began associating the Republican Party with support for white supremacy.

But racism in the United States is not confined to white southerners, and resentment of the government's equal treatment of African-Americans may have been a contributing factor to government mistrust since 1964. When American politicians have made coded attacks on African-Americans, they've seen rises in trust. Ronald Reagan demonized "welfare queens," in language that evoked African-American women profiting from government largesse. Bill Clinton, himself a white southerner, greatly expanded Reagan's war on drugs, a policy that disproportionately imprisoned Black men and changed the dominant complexion of American inmates from light to dark. Both leaders enjoyed high levels of trust during their time in office, while the first Black president, Barack Obama, faced the lowest trust ratings of any American leader up to that point.

Simply put, Americans may trust their government less when it actively seeks equality between its Black and white citizens, and they may support it more when it signals a willingness to marginalize and demonize people of color. We might expect the partial transformation of the Republican Party into an ethnonationalist party under Donald Trump to increase trust in government. However, Trump's campaign and time in office have explicitly aimed at reducing trust in government institutions, which his most ardent supporters sinisterly refer to as the "deep state," suggesting that a decrease in trust in government is an increase in trust in Trump. In fact, trust in government has remained relatively stable and low under Trump, at rates similar to those Obama suffered from.

Many white Americans will protest the idea that endemic racism may be responsible for a broad decay in institutional trust. But many Americans of color see this dynamic as a critical and obvious component in understanding our country. As Michelle Alexander demonstrated in her groundbreaking book *The New Jim Crow,* major social transformations like the rise of mass incarceration have a strong racial component.[25] And as Ta-Nehisi Coates has argued in his case for reparations for the economic harms done to Black citizens, the ongoing effects of endemic racism are often as invisible to majority populations as they are visible to minority populations.[26]

We must not minimize the impact of racism in American politics, especially as Trump's election has normalized some racial supremacists and revealed the persistence of white nationalism. But it's difficult to explain the fall in trust in all institutions solely based on race. Americans losing trust in Congress and the presidency after seeing the government provide rights and benefits to a visible "other" is easier to attribute to race than is declining trust in the health care system, for example. And America's uniquely screwed-up racial dynamics don't map neatly to declines in trust in Britain and France, though rising mistrust in those countries has exposed and stoked strong anti-immigrant sentiments. When it comes to the fall in trust, there are other factors to consider.

Trust Didn't Fall. It Was Pushed.

Ronald Reagan and Margaret Thatcher, leaders of two of the world's most powerful governments, were the greatest proponents of mistrust in government. Understanding the rise of what George Monbiot memorably terms the "self-hating state" requires that we consider the economics of Reagan and Thatcher's formative years.[27]

To escape the Great Depression, President Franklin D. Roosevelt turned to the ideas of the British economist John Maynard Keynes, who argued that when mature economies were in a depression, they would need governments to intervene and increase spending. Keynes was prescribing government spending as a cure for Britain's woes, but his fingerprints were all over the massive US public works programs of the mid-1930s, including the Tennessee Valley Authority, the Works Progress Administration, and the Civilian Conservation Corps. These programs sent the government deep into debt, but they also put Americans back to work at a moment when unemployment hovered near 25 percent.[28] When government spending slowed in 1937, the recovery sputtered, and FDR became a full-throated Keynesian. Deficit spending would continue through World War II.[29]

The postwar emergence of the United States as the world's dominant industrial power led to a period sometimes called the "golden age of capitalism." It was also a golden age of public goods and government spending, including support for education through the GI Bill and the development of infrastructure, including the interstate highway system. This period of intense government spending coincided with peaks of trust in the federal government. The economic ideas that FDR championed in the 1930s—government intervention to correct market failures and provide services that corporations would or could not—were accepted as orthodoxy.

That orthodoxy came under assault in the 1960s, first in Britain and later in the United States. "Stagflation," a combination of economic stagnation and high inflation, threatened Britain starting in 1965.[30] To tackle stagflation—which should be impossible in certain "Keynesian" models of the economy, which held that high unemployment would lead to low inflation—British prime minister Margaret Thatcher turned to a set of ideas championed by University of Chicago economist Milton Friedman, which cautioned against government interventions in markets through spending. Friedman and other neoliberals advocated an extremely limited role for government, believing that any functions that could be devolved to the private sector should be.

Britain under Thatcher privatized more than fifty government-held businesses, including gas, electric, and water utilities, the national telecommunications system, and the national airline.[31] Reagan focused on deregulation rather than privatization—in part because there was far less to privatize in the United States—

removing constraints and oversights that had been designed to ensure that businesses operated with public interests and benefits in mind. Both Thatcher and Reagan combined their enthusiasm for free markets with a fear of collectivism that targeted not just the Communist states of China and the Soviet Union but also labor unions at home.

The historian Tony Judt argued that Reagan and Thatcher did something far more profound than simply turning public assets into private ones: they attacked the very concept of public goods. The governments of the postwar expansion, in addition to providing employment, had sought to build infrastructures, like highways, that would benefit all citizens. These public goods are economically useful in that they lower the costs for everyone to do business, but Judt argued they had another, equally important function: they legitimated government, reminding us what we were paying for with our taxes. When we ask private companies to provide services instead, we run the risk of "eviscerating" our relationship with government. Today, said Judt, "the thick mesh of social interactions and public goods has been reduced to a minimum, with nothing except authority and obedience binding the citizens to the state."[32]

Late in his life, Judt worried that something had gone terribly wrong in the United States and Britain, the countries most associated with neoliberalism: they had lost the ability to imagine solving problems by investing in public goods. By contrast, China is undertaking a massive infrastructure project, the Belt and Road Initiative, a set of rail, highway, port, and electrical grid projects designed to increase trade throughout Asia.[33] It's almost impossible to imagine the United States or Britain undertaking an infrastructure project of this scale.

Reagan and Thatcher made public goods unthinkable in part by denigrating the capabilities of governments. In his inaugural address in 1981, Reagan explained his theory for why the

United States was struggling economically: "In this present crisis, government is not the solution to our problem; government is
the problem."

In articulating this view of government as incompetent and
unwanted, Reagan and Thatcher set up a self-fulfilling prophecy.
If you believe government can do nothing, you will underfund
it, as both leaders did. Once government agencies were stripped
of funding, demoralized leaders vacated positions in government,
leaving their departments weaker and less capable of undertaking
ambitious projects. Over time, competent and functional government become incompetent, through the simple process of a leader
asserting their incompetence and behaving as if it were true.

The Brexit campaign rejects the idea that the bloated, bureaucratic European Union could possibly benefit British citizens as
much as it costs them. (In a fascinating twist, the main aspect
of British independence around which Brexit mobilized was Britain's state-run health care system, a clear example of a valued
public good.) Similarly, Trump took office appointing a wrecking
crew of cabinet secretaries, some of whom had previously advocated the abolishment of the bureaus they ended up running.[34]

The British attacks on the European Union are an extension
of Reagan's argument that the bigger the government, the less
competent it can possibly be. The Trump administration attacks
go beyond questions of competency and suitability into darker
waters, suggesting that institutions that have tried to check the
president's power—notably the FBI, the Justice Department, and
the media—are corrupt and engaged in a conspiracy to undermine his authority. Trump's argument may also be self-fulfilling,
though in a different way. If these institutions continue to act as
checks on power, they lose credibility with Trump's supporters.
If they stop acting as a check on power, they lose credibility with
Trump's opponents. Once leaders begin attacking the legitimacy
and motivations of core government institutions, it's difficult to

avoid destroying trust in those institutions, on one partisan side or the other.

While neoliberalism helps explain an overall shift away from trust in government, it doesn't track historical polling very well. During Reagan's presidency, trust in government rose steadily from 30 percent to the mid-40s, suggesting that it may more closely parallel a sense that the economy is expanding and individuals' lives are getting better. Arguably, the deeper consequences of Reagan and Thatcher—the disappearance of public goods and the demonization of bureaucracies—might take years or decades to impact public trust.

Inequality

The adoption of neoliberal policies in the 1980s did more than undermine confidence in government institutions—it also dismantled policies that redistributed income. The welfare state that Thatcher railed against was funded through a series of taxes that claimed large shares of firms' profits and individual investment income, as well as heavy taxes on luxury goods, shifting wealth from the well-off to those less advantaged. When Thatcher took office in 1979, she cut the top tax rates on personal income from 83 to 60 percent, starting a trend in tax reductions that continued through the 2010s. Reagan followed a similar path, slashing a 70 percent tax rate on the highest earners down to 28 percent by the end of his term.

The gap between wealthy and poor citizens began to widen, after decades of closing. In 1928 the top 1 percent of Americans earned 24 percent of the nation's total income. That concentration of wealth collapsed from the 1929 market crash, then through FDR's New Deal and World War II. By the late 1940s, the top 1 percent of Americans earned only 12 percent of the national income. That figure bottomed out below 10 percent before Reagan's tax cuts started an inexorable rise in inequality. This same U-shaped pattern (high inequality before 1940, low inequality in the postwar years, increasing inequality since 1980) holds in other Anglo-Saxon countries (Britain, Canada, Australia), though with a less dramatic rise in inequality post-1980.

The French economist Thomas Piketty became a household name with his 2013 book *Capital in the Twenty-First Century,* based on research suggesting that for much of the twentieth century, falling inequality was an exception to a general rule.[35] Using financial records that go back centuries, Piketty offers a formula to understand when inequality will rise: when the rate of return on capital is higher than economic growth, the rich will get richer. That's because few people in an economy have substantial capital to invest; most of us make our money from wages, which tend to grow as the whole economy grows. During the postwar golden age, economic growth outpaced returns on capital, both because government spending rebuilt war-damaged economies and because tax policies redistributed many of the profits from investment. Piketty speculates that current attitudes toward taxation and government spending are likely to continue, leading returns on capital to be higher than wage growth, concluding that the "consequences for the long-term dynamics of the wealth distribution are potentially terrifying."[36]

In highly unequal countries, consumer spending and economic growth tend to be low because poor people don't have much discretionary income. Highly unequal countries also have low social mobility, as those who are poor and talented have a hard time advancing while rich mediocrities remain in power. And it's possible that unequal societies are less stable than more equal ones. Behavioral economists have found evidence that humans may simply be hardwired to resent inequalities and favor fairness.[37] As citizens become more aware that a small elite controls the majority of a nation's wealth, the realization fuels populist movements that seek to disrupt the existing order.

Walter Scheidel, a professor of history and classics at Stanford, has developed a disturbing thesis that builds on Piketty's research on inequality. Intrigued by Piketty's observation that the twentieth century may have been the exception to a generalized pattern of high inequality, Scheidel constructed a portrait of economic inequality that stretches back ten thousand years, to the era when hunter-gatherer societies transitioned to agricultural societies. Scheidel sees inequality as the state of nature, the default for human societies, and suggests that economic equality increases only after massive social and political shocks: plagues, catastrophic wars, or the collapse of existing states.[38]

The implications of Scheidel's idea for mistrust are straightforward. Perhaps the period of high trust in government in the postwar years aligned with the "great compression," the period between World War I and neoliberalism where inequality shrank rather than expanded. As people saw their personal economic positions improving, they recognized the value of government and other institutions and rewarded them with their trust. As we've returned to our default state of inequality, we may be returning to a default state of mistrust. Scheidel would predict that any rise in equality would follow an event on the scale of the bubonic plague, the collapse of the Roman Empire, or a world war—the events that have reversed inequality in the past. It's unclear whether COVID-19 and its economic effects are anywhere near the scale of a disruptive event that would reverse trends toward inequality, though the US government's steps to patch social safety nets is a surprising and encouraging move.[39]

But it's too early to conclude that inequality is the state of nature. Both Piketty and Scheidel rely on historical records that are incomplete and spotty and, in Scheidel's case, nonexistent for large swaths of time. Research connecting recent high inequality with political instability is brittle—results found using one method to analyze data often can't be replicated using another method of analysis.[40] The political scientist Jay Ulfelder notes that major social upheavals, like revolutions, are relatively uncommon, offering fewer chances to find a pattern to their distribution.[41]

What is clear is that high inequality as an explanation for social ills, including mistrust, is an idea that's gaining acceptance, at least within the United States. In 2015 the Princeton economists Anne Case and Angus Deaton documented rising death rates in middle-aged non-Hispanic white Americans who do not have college degrees, opening a debate about "deaths of despair"—suicide, drug use, and alcoholism—that appear to disproportionately affect this demographic group.[42] Case and Deaton connected these deaths to the disappearance of well-paying occupations, mostly union jobs in manufacturing, that could support high school graduates and offer a relatively high level of economic security.[43] While Case and Deaton's papers have generated a wealth of academic debates about the statistical techniques they're using,[44] they've captured the attention of political commentators and pundits who link Trump's presidential victory to working-class white voters. Authors like J. D. Vance have risen to prominence on their promise to explain the anger and alienation of these voters.[45]

Rising inequality doesn't affect only working-class whites. In 1967, President Lyndon Johnson charged the Kerner Commission with investigating riots that broke out in majority-Black neighborhoods in several large American cities. A year later the commission reported that America was in danger of becoming two nations, "one black, one white—separate and unequal." Johnson was furious with the report and not only rejected its conclusions but refused to meet with the commissioners. Fifty years later a study released by the Economic Policy Institute showed that no progress has been made in closing gaps between white and Black populations in American homeownership, unemployment, and incarceration. Worse, the "wealth gap" between Black and white Americans tripled in the ensuing five decades.[46] If we blame rising mistrust in the United States on the increasing alienation of working-class whites, we have to acknowledge that for a large number of citizens, America has never been equal.

Explaining rising mistrust in terms of increasing inequality is appealing: why would anyone trust institutions that appear to be stacking the deck against them? Furthermore, variations in inequality between the United States and different parts of Europe track differences in mistrust. Both inequality and mistrust have risen fastest in the United States, next in southern Europe, and slowest in strongly redistributive economies like those of the Nordic countries.

A purely economic explanation for a broad cultural change isn't entirely satisfying. Are people really considering their economic circumstances before making judgments about whether they trust churches? Alongside the economic reality and the neoliberal attacks on government, we also must consider a set of cultural explanations.

Awareness

Alexis de Tocqueville, the great scholar of revolution in the United States and France, believed that revolutions began in part with a "break in consciousness" brought about by thought leaders: artists, writers, and journalists. These men and women of letters "help[ed] to create that general awareness of dissatisfaction, that solidified public opinion, which . . . creates effective demand for revolutionary change."[47]

Tocqueville's observation seems to hold true in the twenty-first century, with massive protests unfolding with little warning, sending the citizens of Tunisia into the streets to oust their long-serving dictator, and in turn inspiring the Arab Spring. While the technologies used to spread the "general awareness of dissatisfaction" have changed since Tocqueville's day, the basic mechanism is the same. The Turkish-American political scientist Timur Kuran explains that in many societies, people "falsify their preferences," pretending to support a regime they dislike in order to minimize conflict with their neighbors.[48] When they become aware that their friends and neighbors don't like the regime either, they are more likely to stand up and rebel. Or as Kuran has put it, "Public opinion starts to transform when, for elites, the cost of speaking the truth falls."[49]

It's possible that Americans are experiencing the phenomenon that Kuran describes: when our neighbors tell us they don't trust institutions, we realize we don't trust those institutions either. And between the 1960s and today, we have experienced social transformations that have caused the cost of speaking the truth to drop.

In the early 1960s, prior to the twin shocks of Vietnam and Watergate, the US press was remarkably deferential to power, especially presidential power. Michael Schudson argues that during that decade, "news coverage became at once more probing, more analytical, and more transgressive of conventional lines between public and private."[50] The press was aware of President Kennedy's marital infidelities but buried stories about them, including one in which the president sexually assaulted a female reporter.[51] By the time President Clinton was impeached for lying about his relationship with Monica Lewinsky, such deference to power, and willingness to turn a blind eye to personal failings, had shrunk significantly.*

---

* The media's treatment of Paula Jones's accusation that Bill Clinton exposed himself to her suggests that this willingness to explore these stories was far from totally transformed.

Schudson argues that this change in behavior by the press was accompanied by a shift in "presence," an awareness by leaders of institutions that the press was watching and willing to call out misbehavior. A rise in investigative journalism and analysis, where reporters focused less on newly discovered facts and more on explaining "the story behind the story," led to the sense that the press was no longer one of the controlling institutions of society but a counterinstitution, watching the powerful and waiting to hold them to account.[52]

A critical press relies on an educated readership, and that's what the United States and Britain created between 1950 and 1980. In 1950, 33 percent of the US population over 25 had completed some high school and only 3.3 percent had completed college.[53] Now 90 percent of US students graduate from high school and 36 percent from college.[54] The rise is even larger in Britain, with 3.4 percent attending university in 1950 to 49 percent in 2012.[55]

Shifts in trust from the 1960s to the present may reflect the transformation of an undereducated and compliant citizenry into one that's better positioned, via education and access to information, to question institutions. Add another element—the rise of participatory media, the ability for people to share their opinion through social media and other online expression—and we have a recipe for overcoming Kuran's preference falsification.

Feeling free to speak the truth as you see it has downsides. Previously, if you realized you no longer trusted the medical system, for instance, you would likely reach only a small audience with your thoughts. Now you're able to find a community of antivaccination activists online, who are only too happy to reinforce your doubts and lead you to a selection of literature designed to confirm your hypotheses.

But the same mechanisms that allow medical misinformation to spread, bringing measles back to some US states, have also allowed survivors of a school shooting in Florida to lead a national movement of students demanding gun control. For better and for worse, shifts in journalism, education, and communications have helped create a population that is more skeptical, more engaged, less credulous, and less trusting.

While the Internet has amplified the spread of counternarratives, including false narratives, we can't blame the Internet for the entire rise in mistrust. The time scales don't line up. During the first major shift in trust during the 1970s, the Internet was an experimental academic technology used by fewer than several thousand individuals. Trust may be harder to recover in an Internet age than in the broadcast era, making institutions less resilient to losses of trust rooted in their public failings.

Years ago, when Francis Fukuyama theorized that trust was a base characteristic of a society's values and Robert Putnam posited a relationship between trust and the breakdown of community ties, the British social scientist Pippa Norris offered a simpler solution: trust is easy to lose, and hard to regain, and institutional mistrust is usually the result of institutions underperforming. In a society increasingly aware of institutional failure and increasingly willing and able to call it out, Norris's notion has strong appeal. Confidence in business and banks shrank dramatically after the global financial crisis of 2008. Confidence in the US government dropped when the George W. Bush administration proved unable to cope with the aftermath of Hurricane Katrina,[56] and it may well decrease again once the costs of COVID-19 become clear. When you lose a wallet and no one returns it, you might lose trust for some time to come.

Norris's theory carries with it the uncomfortable implication that there's no easy way to reverse mistrust. We need to reform our institutions into ones that deserve our trust, and simultaneously to understand the civic dynamics of our post-trust world so we can work within it.

Chapter 3

WHAT WE LOSE WHEN WE LOSE TRUST

WHEN SHE WAS A COLLEGE STUDENT, THE ESSAYIST SARAH Vowell became obsessed with the classic 1972 Francis Ford Coppola film *The Godfather*. While ostensibly studying art history in Holland, she took a thousand-mile detour to Sicily to visit Michael Corleone's hometown, to eat cannoli and find a sense of direction and certainty she'd lost by leaving her small town and church for college and the secular world.

Instead, she found deep hostility. "Hunched, old men glared as if the sight of me was a vicious insult. I felt like a living, breathing faux pas." Sheepishly, she realized her error: the central lesson of the film was to trust no one outside the family. La Cosa Nostra—"our thing"—implies that it's for us and not for anyone else. That a girl from Oklahoma would find acceptance in rural Sicily was about as likely as Vowell being asked to head a New York crime family. She quickly returned to Amsterdam, perhaps before Fabrizio could betray her and place a bomb in her car.[1]

Sicily's cultural differences from the rest of Italy, and stereotypes of the island as poor, violent, and backward, are rooted in its history. Palermo, its main city, was settled by the Phoenicians, a Levantine people who also settled regions of North Africa. Parts of the island were then conquered by Romans, Byzantines,

Arabs, Normans, French Angevins, Spanish Bourbons, Napo-
leon, and—only since 1860—Italians. The nineteenth-century
scholar Leopoldo Franchetti placed the blame for Sicily's peculiar
development on Spanish Hapsburgs and Bourbons, whose loose
grip on the distant island led to centuries of Sicilian inability to
trust the law for fairness or protection. Rather than do the hard
work of building a functioning state in a far-off island with challenging terrain and bad roads, Spanish administrators embraced
a divide and conquer policy, actively working to keep Sicilians
from trusting each other.[2]

The inability to trust anyone—your government, your neighbors, anyone outside your family—leads to everyday problems.
What if you want to sell a cow? Diego Gambetta, Italy's foremost
scholar of mafias and criminal organizations, begins his book
The Sicilian Mafia with a story about a *vaccaro* (cattle breeder)
in Palermo.[3] The breeder wants to cheat the butcher, and the
butcher wants to cheat the breeder, but each needs to work with
the other to sell the cow and turn it into meat. The solution: a
third party who makes butcher and *vaccaro* agree and who takes
a cut from each. That third party—a private source of trust and
protection to make commerce possible—is the true origin of the
Sicilian mafia, Gambetta argues.

It's easy to misunderstand the mafia, he explains, in part
because it's so violent, so colorful, and such an apparently per-
verse way of organizing a society—in other words, such good
cinema. But the mafia survives because it serves a real need:
creating trust in economies that can't trust official institutions.
Gambetta discovered that, rather than "running" the drug trade
or smuggling operations, the Sicilian mafia's real function is to
regulate markets and settle conflicts between people who can't
go to the police because their business itself is illegal. Historically, the mafia has functioned in Sicily as its own legal system—
ordinamento giuridico—in a way that's often complementary,
not explicitly at odds, with the state. (It sometimes does remark-

ably well. A commission in Palermo explained that the low rate of drug overdose in the city was likely due to quality control of street drugs, enforced by the mafia.)

While it's remarkable that Sicilians created the mafia as a solution to weaknesses in the state and interpersonal trust, it's a lousy solution. Gambetta, a northern Italian, was fascinated by economic development in his home country, wondering why the South remained consistently underdeveloped while multinational companies sprouted up in the North. The disparity led Gambetta to study trust, hypothesizing that "the weakness of this social lubricant in the South could be at the source of its tenacious development difficulties."[4] While the mafia may provide trust as a private good, the endemic underdevelopment of southern Italy suggests that the cost is a high one. One economist estimates that the average business in Sicily pays 600 euros a month in *pizzo*— protection—and that the protection industry consumes 1.4 percent of the gross regional product.[5]

Francis Fukuyama's ambitious 1995 book *Trust: The Social Virtues and the Creation of Prosperity* offers an expanded theory of the economic implications of trust. Germany, Japan, and the United States have prospered because a strong culture of trust, nurtured through powerful civic institutions, allows economic actors to work together with little suspicion and high cooperation. Countries like France, South Korea, and Italy, Fukuyama argues, are built on strong family ties and often have difficulty extending bonds of trust beyond those rigid, often dysfunctional loyalties. Southern Italy in particular is a cautionary tale for Fukuyama. He sees the region as crippled by "amoral familism," the zero-sum mentality that helping a stranger harms one's own family. That attitude is antithetical to the cross-social bonds of trust that Fukuyama sees as essential for economic growth.[6]

Mistrust is expensive. And providing trust through other means, like private trust brokers, has unintended negative consequences, not limited to waking up with a severed horse head in your bed. However we interpret the rise of institutional mistrust in the United States—as the fault of Nixon's criminality, Reagan and Thatcher's attack on the state, inequality, or a transformed news industry—the consequences of mistrustful societies are not well known. But we need to understand them.

What happens to a society that defaults toward mistrust, rather than trust, in institutions? What happens to our power as citizens when we lose confidence that the prescribed methods of civic participation have real impact? Can we reverse this tide of mistrust? If we don't, who benefits in a world of high mistrust?

Cases like the Sicilian mafia give us glimpses of social arrangements in high-mistrust societies. But these possibilities are more intriguing than predictive. Mafia-like organizations developed quite differently in China and Northern Ireland, societies with low trust but with different government, religious, and family structures at work. Indeed, the mafia isn't even a phenomenon across Sicily, with some communities apparently immune to its influence. We can't predict specific outcomes as we watch mistrust rise in US and European communities, but history and experimental research offer general rules we can use to anticipate what may come.

One rule the Sicily example illustrates: when we lose faith in institutions, the market often intervenes to provide services that those institutions are responsible for. *Mistrust means we cede public functions to private actors*. In a functioning state, police and courts protect people who are conducting (legal) business. In a dysfunctional state, providing protection becomes a commercial opportunity.

When the State Is No Longer in Charge

As the COVID-19 pandemic began to spread in Brazil, the world's sixth most populous nation, its far-right president, Jair

Bolsonaro, took a combative approach. He didn't combat the virus, just anyone who suggested Brazilians should take it seriously. Describing the disease as "a little flu" and urging supporters to ignore social distancing guidelines,[7] Bolsonaro may have outpaced Donald Trump in the sheer ignorance and dangerousness of his approach to the pandemic. In May 2020, as the virus spread more quickly in Brazil than in any other nation, an editorial in *The Lancet* described Bolsonaro as "perhaps the biggest threat" to successfully fighting the virus.[8]

While the Brazilian president was downplaying the risk of the virus, another group was taking COVID-19 precautions seriously: street gangs. In the Cidade de Deus favela of Rio, the community made famous in the 2002 film *City of God,* the Red Command street gang began enforcing an eight p.m. curfew designed to slow the spread of the disease. Loudspeakers mounted on vehicles snaked through the community, broadcasting instructions to stay home and warning, "We will do a curfew because no one is taking the disease seriously. Anyone found messing around or walking outside will be punished and made an example of. It is better to stay home and chill."[9]

In another favela of Rio, traffickers ordered people not to walk on the streets in groups any larger than two; another gang handed out soap and placed signs asking residents to wash their hands before entering the favela. In Complexo de Maré, a favela near Río's airport, gang leaders ordered shops and churches to shorten their operating hours, making an exception only for the local bakery.[10]

Favela dwellers are used to being ignored by Brazilian authorities, and gang members are a much more visible presence in many *cariocas'* lives than the government is, but Bolsonaro's unwillingness to take the disease seriously has created a unique situation. The gangs feel a real need to protect their members and their communities from a disease they take seriously, and the absence of the government provides them an opportunity to rebrand themselves not just as ruthless drug lords but as concerned members of the community.

When an institution fails, citizens will look toward whatever might take its place.

But it's not always the idiosyncrasies of a populist leader that causes a state to abandon its responsibilities. Sometimes it can be an ideological choice.

The shift of services provided by state institutions to the private sector is a conscious strategy for many conservatives, a key part of the neoliberal project. Those who believe that big governments are inherently undesirable, and that providing services through markets is more virtuous, regard the loss of trust in government institutions as desirable. There's no doubt that there are circumstances where the private sector offers better outcomes than do broken bureaucracies. Many African nations went from having less than one phone per one hundred people to sixty per hundred when private mobile phone operators displaced government-owned telephone companies.[11]

But running government like a business doesn't always go so smoothly, especially when existing services are cut as a result. In 2008 the global financial crisis led the city of Colorado Springs to experience sharp declines in tax revenue. A bastion of fiscal conservatism, the city government decided not to raise taxes but to cut services. The parks department removed trash cans and put up signs telling citizens to remove their own litter. It also encouraged volunteers to bring their mowers to the parks, as city employees would cut the grass only twice a month.[12] The city cut bus service on weekends and evenings, disproportionately impacting people who didn't have their own cars to get to and from work. And in perhaps the most symbolic gesture, it turned off almost ten thousand streetlights, inviting residents to "adopt" a streetlight at the cost of $75 to $180 a year.[13]

The decision to run Colorado Springs like a business was initially popular with voters, who elected Steve Bach, a real estate broker who ran on his business sensibilities, as mayor. But the experiment proved unwieldy very quickly. Colorado Springs had trouble convincing businesses to relocate to the city, given concerns over public services. The streetlight experiment ended in a blaze of irony: disabled streetlights proved popular targets for copper "bugs," thieves who stripped the poles of their wiring, assured that they wouldn't be electrocuted in the process. Once the economy recovered and the city decided to turn the lights on again, they discovered that their effort to save a few hundred thousand dollars had led to $5 million in damage. At the end of Bach's term, he was replaced by a new mayor who, while conservative, promised to raise taxes and restore services.[14]

The move of key civic functions—maintaining public spaces like parks and streets—from the government to the citizens shifts questions of accountability. Who's responsible when your bus route shifts and leaves you with a long walk to the train you need to catch? In 2007 mySociety, a British organization dedicated to improving civic systems, launched a site, FixMyStreet, allowing citizens to report potholes and other issues so their local city council members could follow up and address them. The site became successful and beloved.

In 2011 mySociety launched FixMyTransport, and quickly discovered it had taken on a much harder problem. London transportation is the responsibility of dozens of bus companies, independent railway operators, boat services, and other entities, all under the management of Transport for London, a local government body. FixMyTransport had to maintain a massive database of email addresses for people at dozens of entities who might be responsible for fixing problems. If you reported a problem, rather than routing it to your local council, FixMyTransport had to warn you that posting your problem and waiting for it to be fixed was unlikely to work. The developers then turned the site into a community-building tool, hoping to recruit groups of people affected by the same problem to advocate for solutions. While

FixMyStreet survives, mySociety gave up on FixMyTransport in early 2015. The thankless work of maintaining all the moving parts required to get London's complex transportation challenges fixed remains.[15]

But while a complex web of private operators make reporting transit problems challenging in London, on certain issues citizens are finding it more effective to lobby corporations than governments. In the United States, after a mass gunman killed seventeen students and teachers in Parkland, Florida, a group of the surviving students took to social media to campaign for change in America's peculiar attitudes toward guns. While protests at the Florida state house gained little initial traction—legislators chose to address mass shootings by passing a resolution that identified pornography as a public health threat—protests aimed at corporations very quickly returned results.[16] Delta and United Airlines, rental car companies, banks, and insurers all ended discount programs for National Rifle Association members, under pressure of social-media-driven boycott campaigns.[17] Dick's Sporting Goods decided to stop selling assault-style rifles and raised the gun purchasing age in its stores from eighteen to twenty-one, responding to public pressure. Walmart, the nation's largest gun seller, immediately followed suit. Within a week of the Parkland shooting, it was significantly harder to buy an assault rifle in the United States—and legislators had nothing to do with it.[18]

Mistrust encourages us to influence those we see as movable, not necessarily those most responsible for a problem. Rashad Robinson, executive director of the antiracism organization Color of Change, explains the logic of targeting campaigns on influencing corporations: "It's about finding the strategic avenue and giving people the ability to feel useful, to feel like they make a difference. That is important in a democracy."[19]

While Color of Change's focus on efficacy is smart activism, it suggests serious and deep problems for participatory democracy. If Robinson is right that people are more likely to feel useful influencing brands rather than their elected representatives, our confidence in democratic institutions will fall further. Left unsaid is another uncomfortable question: what happens when neither democratic nor commercial institutions are well trusted?

Between 2015 and 2017, the St. Petersburg, Russia–based Internet Research Agency ran over three thousand different ads on Facebook, aimed at influencing the 2016 US presidential election and its immediate aftermath. Rather than advocating for Donald Trump or against Hillary Clinton, the ads focused on existing tensions in American society, around immigration, race, and religion.[20] Despite their crude nature, the ads were often very effective in bringing people into the streets and into conflict. On May 21, 2016, the Facebook group Heart of Texas organized a rally at the Islamic Da'wah Center of Houston to "Stop Islamification of Texas." Another Facebook group, United Muslims of America, held a "Save Islamic Knowledge" rally at the same place and time. Both groups had been created by Russian provocateurs working for the Internet Research Agency. Predictably, the rallies ended in verbal confrontations between supporters of each fictional group. The cost for all this chaos? Two hundred dollars in Facebook ads.[21]

US intelligence agencies have confirmed Russian interference in US elections and anticipate increasingly sophisticated efforts targeting elections in 2020.[22] More important, the Trump administration has been slow to take significant proactive action against future Russian interference, possibly fearing that any acknowledgment of meddling in the 2016 election would call into question the legitimacy of the Trump presidency.

Not wanting to be blamed for the manipulation of subsequent US elections, social media companies like Google and Facebook are beginning to understand that they will be expected to protect their infrastructure from foreign interference. This leads to odd situations like a confidential meeting at Facebook headquarters between Christopher Krebs, undersecretary for the Department of Homeland Security, and officials from seven technology companies. Tech companies shared information on some of the strategies they were using to combat misinformation but were surprised when the government didn't offer any insights of its own: "One attendee of the meeting said the encounter led the tech companies to believe they would be on their own to counter election interference."[23]

Unfortunately, technology companies are experiencing their own moment of intense mistrust, sometimes referred to as the "techlash." In the wake of the Cambridge Analytica scandal, where an academic researcher released data from his experiments to a political consultancy so that the pro-Brexit and Trump campaigns could segment Facebook users for targeted advertising, Facebook in particular came under intense scrutiny over their handling of users' personal information. A Reuters/Ipsos poll in March 2018 found that only 41 percent of American adults trust Facebook to "obey laws that protect your personal information," a much lower number than the majority who trusted platforms like Google, Amazon, and Apple.[24]

Trust in Facebook will likely slip even further as the company has refused to remove false political advertising from its system, arguing that political claims are a form of protected speech. It's likely, as the media scholar Siva Vaidhyanathan explains, that Facebook is reluctant to position itself as the arbiter of truth in political debates around the world.[25] But a defense of disinformation suggests Facebook might not solve the problem of online manipulation even as it stands to profit directly from it.

In other words, the responsibility for preventing future interference in US elections rests with a government whose leader refuses to acknowledge the problem and with technology companies that the left mistrusts for spreading fake news and the right, for constraining online speech. Shifting the burden of responsibility from one institution to another works only when the new institution is more trustworthy than the old one.

The Trouble with Transparency

Facebook's primary response to this climate of mistrust has been to take steps toward *transparency*, beginning with a policy that requires political advertising to be labeled, giving users the ability to see who paid for a particular ad.[26] Demanding increased transparency is a predictable and reasonable response to the problem of low trust in institutions.

Facebook had at least three reasons to release this information, two good and one bad. The simple act of revealing hidden data is designed to increase trust: *See, we've got nothing to hide*. Second, close scrutiny of the data will likely show that Facebook's internal systems are usually working as they should—if we click on hundreds of disclosures on the platform, only to discover that the overwhelming majority of them are legitimate political ads and not Russian malfeasance, we may regain some of our trust that the system is working as it should. Third, efforts at transparency create reams of data that very rarely get interrogated or analyzed. From Facebook's point of view, that may be an advantage—it gets credit for taking steps toward transparency, but any scandals will emerge only if a journalist or committed citizen has the time and resources to analyze the data released in detail.

A global movement toward transparency in government took its first steps in the 1950s, when American newspapers fought to open the secrecy of the wartime US government. Pressure from the American Society of Newspaper Editors led Congress to pass the Freedom of Information Act in 1966. The legislation helped spark a global movement to demand transparency and accountability from governments by requiring them to respond to requests for documents. A second wave of transparency enthusiasm developed in the mid-2000s, as advocacy organizations around the world adopted the Internet. The Obama administration embraced this wave but also muddied the language of "open government," which had previously referred to governments releasing previously secret data. The Obama administration made available reams of government data that were open, usable, and utterly innocuous. Meanwhile a global movement toward open government data, complete with a multilateral task force (the Open Government Partnership) and widely funded both by governments and charitable foundations, made transparency one of the pillars of international development.

But opening government data has little to do with whether a government is, in fact, open. As the transparency activists Harlan Yu and David Robinson pointed out in a 2012 analysis of the Open Government movement, Hungary was able to open data about public transit in Budapest and Szeged at the same time that Viktor Orbán's government lurched toward autocracy.[27]

Ukraine, after the 2014 pro-EU Euromaidan revolution ousted the pro-Russian president Viktor Yanukovych, experienced a whirlwind romance with transparency. When Yanukovych fled the country for Russia, he dropped boxes of his personal files into the reservoir near his palatial home, Mezhyhirya. Ukrainian journalists worked with divers to retrieve the boxes and used Yanukovych's sauna to dry them, then photographed them and posted them online as "Yanukovychleaks."[28] The twenty-three thousand pages rescued were eventually handed off to the state prosecutor's office, which opened twenty cases against Yanukovych and his family based on the evidence discovered.[29] International funders like the Open Society Foundation* supported journalism and transparency organizations, hoping that Ukraine under the Euromaidan generation could be a beacon proclaiming the power of transparency.

But transparency works differently in low-trust societies than

---

* In the interests of full disclosure, I am a consultant to and former board member of the Open Society Foundation.

in ones with established high trust: it reveals the brokenness of existing institutions. The transparency revolution in Ukraine is an unfortunately classic case. In October 2016 new transparency legislation required Ukrainian politicians to disclose their assets in a searchable online database. Legislators disclosed that they owned millions of dollars in cash, collections of art and watches, fleets of expensive cars, and other luxuries that should be difficult to afford on parliamentary salaries that, until 2014, were about $280 a month.

The disclosures stoked disillusionment in the average Ukrainian. A soldier who'd volunteered to fight on Ukraine's front lines in Crimea posted on Facebook, "I personally feel unwell. Or rather, like someone who has been beaten and is therefore unwell. I had no illusions about our political and official elite. But all the same, what's come out is beyond the pale."[30] To elect less corrupt parliamentarians, Ukraine will need to pay officials better, but attempts to raise official pay have been rolled back due to the fact that corrupt officials are better paid than the average Ukrainian.[31] Trust in government in Ukraine was lower in 2015, the year after Euromaidan, than it had been in 2005 and 2010, an abysmal 7 percent.[32]

Transparency as a strategy has further traps. Hillary Clinton's legendary emails—hosted on a private server rather than in State Department email accounts—became an issue due to (vague, unclear) federal rules that required her to transfer her work emails to the National Archives and Records Administration.[33] The scrutiny of those emails, and the proliferation of news stories about them in the run-up to the 2016 US presidential election, have persuaded many in government to minimize their use of email and rely on the phone or face to face conversations to transact business. Because US transparency laws are a hodgepodge, written mostly for the age of letters and memos, not informal text communications, there are dozens of ways to stay within the letter of transparency law while violating its spirit. The journalist Matt Yglesias observes that the easiest way for a White

House official to avoid entering a meeting in the Secret Service logbook (which is a public document) is to simply meet someone across the street at a coffee shop: "In a world of imperfect transparency, the main effect of mandatory transparency is to push people into workarounds."[34]

The most worrisome unintended consequence of transparency is apophenia, defined by Swiss psychologist Peter Brugger as the "pervasive tendency . . . to see order in random configurations," to be "overwhelmed by meaningful coincidences" that falsely appear to betray a deeper pattern.[35] Conspiracy theorists suffer from apophenia, and well-meaning efforts at transparency have added to the availability of raw material in which they find those "meaningful coincidences."

When Clinton emails were found on the laptop of disgraced Democratic congressman Anthony Weiner, a Twitter user claimed that Weiner was being investigated for child exploitation, and that Clinton and her team were involved with a vast child trafficking ring. When WikiLeaks, an organization that has portrayed itself as focused on technologies for transparency, released emails that had been illegally obtained from Clinton aide John Podesta, Internet users concocted a theory Podesta wasn't only a Democratic Party insider but also a secret pedophile child trafficker. The evidence: references to "pizza" in Podesta's emails, which online sleuths read as "cheese pizza," which they argued was code for "child pornography." The pizza references led conspiracists to research Comet Ping Pong Pizza, a popular restaurant and music venue in Washington, whose owner had contributed to Democratic causes. After weeks of speculation about what might be hidden within Comet Ping Pong and neighboring businesses—kill rooms, underground tunnels, satanism, cannibalism—Edgar Welch, a twenty-eight-year-old from North Carolina, arrived at the pizza parlor with a handgun and assault rifle, planning to "self-investigate" the dungeons below. Welch fired three shots, discovered that there was no basement to the pizzeria, and was arrested.[36]

Despite the apparent absurdity of the Pizzagate conspiracy, the core idea—that senior Democratic Party officials profit from child trafficking—resurfaced in the QAnon conspiracy, which seems custom-designed to exploit apophenia and mistrust. "Q," who claims to be a member of Donald Trump's inner circle, communicates with his followers by posting cryptic questions ("crumbs") on the 8chan and 8kun anonymous message boards. Q's followers ("bakers") investigate Q's questions, picking through media stories for details that fit a narrative in which Trump is about to arrest Barack Obama and Hillary Clinton for running a child sex ring.

Believing that opposition politicians are criminals requires a deep distrust in the legitimacy of institutions, but both Pizzagate and QAnon additionally draw on the availability of data and news that can be interpreted to support these complex clandestine narratives. In the mind of a determined conspiracy theorist, data released by governments as well as data leaked from other sources becomes raw material for connections, a sky full of unordered stars ready to be sorted into constellations.

Mistrust and Disengagement

Thankfully, not everyone responds to conditions of high mistrust by adopting complex conspiracies and investigating them with guns in hand. *The most common reaction to high mistrust in institutions is disengagement.* Roberto Stefan Foa and Yascha Mounk, whose research on the World Values Survey suggests a "deconsolidation of democracy" and a rising tolerance for authoritarianism, also see evidence that young people are less interested in politics. There's always been a gap between Americans older than thirty five and those younger in terms of their interest in politics. In 1990 the gap was 10 percentage points between older and younger Americans who reported themselves as "fairly" or "very" interested in politics (63 versus 53 percent). Twenty years later that gap has expanded to 26 percentage points (67 versus 41 percent), mostly due to a sharp drop in interest among young people. The pattern is similar in Europe, where the difference in interest in politics between young and old expanded from a 4-point gap to a 14-point gap in the last two decades (from 52 versus 28 percent in 1990 to 52 versus 38 percent in 2010.)

One way this decreasing interest in politics emerges is the decrease in voter turnout. While Americans are used to being scolded for our poor turnout rates, those rates have been roughly stable (and poor, some of the worst in the OECD) since the 1950s. Europe is another, uglier story. The Voter Turnout Database, an international effort to study voting trends globally, reports a significant fall in voter turnout from the 1980s to 2015, dropping from 76 to 66 percent. (Rates had been much more stable over the previous four decades, falling only from 78 to 76 percent between 1940 and 1980.) Much of this decline can be attributed to Europe, where the fall in voting rates is especially sharp in post-Communist countries. There enthusiasm for elections waned quickly, dropping an average of 20 percentage points since the fall of the Soviet Union. But the mature democracies of western Europe have not gone unscathed: turnout has fallen 10 percentage points in the same interval.[37] This trend reversed somewhat in 2019, where attacks on the concept of the European Union by the UK Brexit campaign likely led more voters to the EU polls.

Despite the mobilization due to Brexit, there is evidence of rising disinterest in politics via disengagement from political parties. More Americans (37 percent) now identify as independents than with either major political party (30 percent each for Democrats and Republicans.) In Britain's 1951 election, 97 percent of voters chose from their two major parties; by 2009, only 60 percent did. Britain in particular has seen a steep slide in party membership, from nearly 4 million combined across the big parties in the 1950s, down to less than half a million in 2010 despite a steady population size.[38] France and Italy have seen less dramatic but also significant, declines, losing between one- and two-thirds of their party members in the past three decades, and the average European party has seen its membership cut in half since 1980.[39]

The exception to the trend in declining party membership has been on the far right, among parties whose views have historically been outside the mainstream of political discourse. Founded in 2013, the populist and nationalist Alternative for Germany (AfD) became Germany's largest opposition party in the Bundestag in 2017. Italy's anti-immigrant Northern League became the nation's third most popular party in the 2018 elections, and leader Matteo Salvini became the nation's deputy prime minister. One way to understand the rise of these parties is that an expansion of the ideological spectrum to voters is encouraging increased participation. Another way is to see these parties as the result of protest votes. Their leaders invariably identify themselves as fighting "politics as usual," and their positions usually include withdrawing from the European Union. Voter support for AfD, the Northern League, or Marine Le Pen's National Front may reflect mistrust in government more than faith in the existing party system.

If mistrust in government is leading people—and especially young people—away from political parties, political news, and polling places, protests provide evidence that many young people remain engaged with civics if not with political processes. The wave of protests that swept the globe after 2010, when Tunisian citizens threw out dictator Zine al-Abidine Ben Ali and sparked the Arab Spring, has been a wave of antipolitics and antipower, focused more on ousting those who control broken institutions than on proposing specific fixes. Inspired by the overthrow of governments in Tunisia, Egypt, and Libya, anti-austerity pro-

tests brought as many as one in seven Spaniards into the streets
as part of the Indignados movement in May 2011. Occupy Wall
Street began in that fall, expanding into a global movement with
protests in nearly a thousand cities.[40] A protest over the redevel-
opment of Gezi Park in Istanbul turned into months of protests
across Turkey. Lebanon's protests in 2019 brought hundreds of
thousands of protesters into the streets across sectarian lines
and succeeded in ousting the prime minister, while Hong Kong's
resistance to Chinese authority through the figure of Carrie Lam
is bringing a generation of youth into the streets. The women's
march in the US vastly overshadowed Trump's inauguration in
terms of turnout. Protest seems to be emerging as an alternative
to engagement through conventional politics.

The outcome of these protests, however, has generally been
disappointing. The hopes of the Arab Spring have faded in most
of the affected countries: Libya and Syria slid into war and Egypt
into military dictatorship. Turkey's summer of protest was overshadowed by a coup attempt in 2016 and a descent into authoritarian rule, cemented by President Erdoğan's decisive victory
in 2018 polls.[41] Occupy's signature achievement of getting citizens to discuss inequality was undercut by the 2016 election of
a US president whose chief ambition appears to be increasing
inequality and whose chief qualification is his (disputed) status as
a billionaire. Even Lebanon's victory rings hollow, as the movement's slogan, "Everyone means everyone," demands a whole-
sale transformation of the country's political culture, which
remains unlikely. While Prime Minister Saad Hariri has resigned,
his successor is another member of the administration, the former education minister, and Lebanon's political elite remains
firmly entrenched.

A scholar of—and participant in—the Gezi Park protests,
Zeynep Tufekci, offers one possible explanation for the apparent
weakness of protests in achieving lasting change: it's much easier
to organize a protest than it used to be. Calling people into the

streets is trivially easy, she argues, using tools like Facebook and Twitter, platforms that recruit and document protests simultaneously. But because it's easier to bring people into the streets, a movement that mobilizes one hundred thousand people today is likely to be much more fragile and inexperienced than one that achieved that turnout in the 1970s. Authoritarians like Erdoğan understand this and are less threatened and influenced by protests than they would have been in decades past.[42]

The Bulgarian political scientist Ivan Krastev offers an even darker interpretation of the rising trend toward protest: "Citizens are losing trust in democratic institutions not because these institutions are less efficient or more corrupt, but because we have lost our power to influence them." The people in the streets are powerless because the institutions themselves are often powerless to make the changes protesters demand. If the governments of Greece or Spain had taken steps to end economic austerity measures, global financial markets would have quickly punished them by (further) downgrading their bonds. The uncomfortable truth for these protesters is that they are wise in their lack of trust: their governments have far less policy-making power over economic issues than do faceless, voterless global markets. As a result, "many of the participants aren't protesting specific governmental policies so much as they are expressing a general belief that powerful interests have captured democratic institutions in many Western democracies and that citizens are powerless to bring change. Not surprisingly, a growing number of people tend to vote for protest or extreme parties."[43]

If Krastev and Tufekci are right, it may explain why a decade-long wave of global protests crashed and dissipated into foam. Despite the comparative ease of organizing protests and the compelling logic of protesting mistrusted institutions, for protests to achieve change, they require that institutions can be influenced and have the power to meet protesters' demands. Leaders have learned, Tufekci suggests, that that activist presence in the streets means less than we hope it does. And those leaders, Krastev suggests, often can't do what we want them to, even if they listen. Those who invoke the March on Washington during America's civil rights struggle as a high point for protest and social change would do well to remember that it was *a march on Washington,* specifically a very receptive Washington. Without a receptive audience in Presidents Kennedy and later Johnson, who were willing to pressure Congress to make meaningful changes, protesters would have found themselves pushing on an immovable object.

Without trust in the presidency, parliament, or other government institutions, it's not clear how long protesters will continue to push. In the United States, more baby boomers (1 in 11) reported participating in protests than millennials (1 in 15). (In Europe, more protesters are young, but fewer of today's youth participate in protests than previous cohorts did at the same age.)[44]

Mistrust May Mobilize the Right and Disengage the Left

For all the concerns raised about declining participation in both conventional and unconventional civics, it's fair to observe that the left is having a harder time mobilizing mistrust than the right is. The Tea Party movement, whose protests in 2009 led to a wave of conservative congressional candidates in 2010 and to a federal shutdown over the national debt in 2011, was an explicitly anti-tax, antigovernment spending movement that rallied members with language about institutional mistrust. While the Tea Party's emphasis on the deficit and shrinking government power seems a long time ago and a galaxy far away from the Trumpist Republican Party, its populist power still gives mainstream Republican politicians nightmares. The Brexit campaign in Britain heavily leveraged mistrust in the institutions of the European Union to persuade Britons that they would be better going it alone. Viktor Orbán and Andrzej Duda have cemented power in Hungary and Poland respectively through campaigns that have relied heavily on skepticism about the European Union and on conspiracy theories that see their nations threatened by international institutions. Along with disengagement from these institutions, many citizens seem to react to high levels of mistrust by supporting right-wing policies, especially nationalist stances on issues like migration.

Returning to the insurrectionist-institutionalist distinction discussed in Chapter 1, it's worth noting that the movements that have gained power are right insurrectionist movements, not right institutionalist movements. In Britain, David Cameron lost control of his party and the prime ministership when a large percentage of Conservative voters sided with the insurrectionist United Kingdom Independence Party (UKIP) to demand Brexit. American institutionalist Republicans like Jeb Bush were crushed in the 2016 Republican primaries, and the split between pro-Trump insurrectionists and Never-Trumper institutionalists threatened to tear the party apart. To the dismay of institutionalist conservatives, their parties in the United States and Britain have moved further to the insurrectionist right. British prime minister Theresa May's cabinet suffered defections from two senior leaders who believed her approach to Brexit was too accommodating, after which she was forced to yield to the more extreme Boris Johnson. President Trump has been unswayed by Republicans who wanted compromise with Democrats on immigration, instead deferring to those who support the stricter policies favored by his base.

Historically, insurrection has been more closely associated with liberal than with conservative movements. From the American and French revolutions to the Russian Revolution, the conservatives are usually the ones trying to stay in power rather than campaigning to overturn the established order. But there are at least two reasons why a current spirit of rising insurrectionism should favor the right.

In 1960 Arizona senator Barry Goldwater published *The Conscience of a Conservative,* a stunningly popular book—it sold half a million copies in its first five months—that established a core ideological tenet for American conservatives.[45] For Goldwater, "Politics is the art of achieving the maximum amount of freedom for individuals that is consistent with the maintenance of social order."[46] With this formulation, Goldwater united two ideological camps—libertarians concerned with freedom from government interference and cultural conservatives resistant to social change—and tied their concerns to a fierce opposition to Communism. While Goldwater was crushed in the 1964 presidential election, the rise of conservatism combined with the explicitly racist "Southern Strategy" led Richard Nixon to power in 1968 and to two decades of Republican near-dominance of American politics.

Prior to Goldwater, Republican leaders had been exemplified by Dwight D. Eisenhower, a committed institutionalist, building the interstate highway system and expanding Social Security. After Goldwater, Republicans seeking office made explicit promises to limit the role of government and dismantle institutions.[47] By the time the Tea Party arrived to yoke the language and imagery of the American Revolution to small government and lowered taxes, the Republican Party had been staggering toward the anti-institution pole for decades, in part inspired by the neoliberal project in Britain.

There's no clear parallel to Goldwater in the American left. To the extent that Bernie Sanders advanced an insurrectionist agenda in his 2016 and 2020 presidential campaigns, his signature policy proposal—government-provided health care—is an idea that centers on massive, trusted institutions. Elizabeth Warren's endless policy prescriptions see government as a powerful regulatory force, and Alexandria Ocasio-Cortez, emergent bête noire of the American right, advocates legislation that would be comfortable within most centrist European parties. Right-wing media and activists routinely paint all three politicians as socialists.

After decades of antigovernment rhetoric, American conservatives may be more receptive to insurrectionism than the left. But declining trust in institutions may be tilting them toward a particular flavor of insurrectionism: nationalist authoritarianism. A world in which institutions are failing to protect us from attack, is a scary world. Research suggests that fear plays a strong role in a person's political viewpoint and orientation. A 2011 study by the neuroscientist Ryota Kanai at University College London found that young adults who identify as conservative have structurally different brains from those who identify as liberals: they have a larger right amygdala, a part of the brain associated with emotion processing, especially anxiety and fear responses.[48] Brain differences, which may underpin fear and ideology, begin at very young ages. R. Chris Fraley and colleagues at the University of Illinois found some correlation between children who showed fearful behavior when they were four years old and their political identification as adults, with the more fearful children identifying as conservative in adulthood. (The authors also found a stronger correlation between less permissive "authoritarian parenting" and conservative identification.)[49]

The social psychologist John Bargh has an elegant demonstration of the ways fear can affect political ideology. He invited a set of liberals and conservatives into a lab and led them through an exercise in which they imagined themselves with superpowers. Some had the ability to fly; others imagined themselves as invulnerable to harm. Those who imagined flying tested predictably on a questionnaire about political indicators—those who identified as Republicans were more conservative and resistant to social change. But among those who'd been primed to think about invulnerability—a prompt to encourage the unconscious to suppress fear responses—Republicans responded more like Democrats. Bargh argues that this is a possible technique for converting conservatives into liberals: "The boiling water of our social and political attitudes, it seems, can be turned up or down by changing how physically safe we feel."[50]

Our contemporary political and media environment is designed to activate fear. Commercial news media need attention to survive, and stories about crime, terrorism, and violence feature disproportionately, as these problems generate fear, and fear generates views.[51] Those views keep advertising dollars flowing. The elected authoritarians that rule Russia, Hungary, and the Philippines generated and rode waves of fear to power. And stoking fear that our existing institutions are not protecting us against threats from immigrants is core to the political strategies that have put Viktor Orbán in power in Hungary and Donald Trump in the United States. The right insurrectionist strategy of replacing slow, careful bureaucratic institutions with a strong leader is one that presents itself explicitly as an answer to fears.

Everything Is PR

The predictable responses to mistrust—engagement only where we feel we are making a difference, the transfer of public functions to private entities, transparency, disengagement, and fear—all present significant challenges to a culture of healthy civic engagement. Unfortunately, a more daunting challenge has emerged as a consequence of mistrust: the loss of a single collective reality.

Well before the election of President Trump, Americans' trust in the institution of journalism had fallen precipitously from the heights it enjoyed after ousting President Nixon after Watergate. But Trump's election brought the unprecedented spectacle of a US president attacking the press as the "enemy of the people,"[52] while at the same time social-media-based campaigns to manipulate public opinion during the UK's Brexit campaign and the US presidential election came to light. *Fake news,* a term originally coined to describe fabricated media that appealed to political prejudices, was adopted by Trump to describe any media critical of himself.[53] These sustained attacks on the media are having an effect. A 2018 Gallup/Knight study found that while 54 percent of Democrats had a favorable view of the media, only 15 percent of Republicans did. Ninety-one percent of Republicans saw "a fair amount" or "a great deal" of political bias in news, while 42 percent of Republicans believe that accurate stories that cast a politician in an unfavorable light constitute "fake news."[54] In this media environment, Republicans and Democrats are having a hard time agreeing on what they can believe about their nation.

President Trump's behavior has not improved the situation. He shocked many Americans, including some in his own administration, by affirming his belief that Putin had told the truth in asserting that Russia did not interfere with the 2016 US presidential election. At that point many prominent Republicans broke with the president. The late Republican senator John McCain termed Trump's press conference "one of the most disgraceful performances by an American president in memory."[55] The conservative columnist George Will declared Trump "America's child president" and a "sad, embarrassing wreck of a man."[56]

Other Republicans touted Trump's performance as a work of genius. Senator Mike Rounds of South Dakota offered the theory that Trump was playing chess, while other leaders were playing checkers: "The president just looked right back at [Putin] and with the same straight face . . . basically sent a message: 'If you can sit here and tell me that with a straight face and that's what it takes it to move forward in other negotiations, I most certainly can match you on this, and in fact I can stand here and say, 'Of course you didn't do it,' even though we all know that [you did].'" The senator explained further, "So to me, Mr. Putin tried to tell the whopper with a straight face and President Trump basically laid out, 'You wanna play that game? Fine. I can do the same thing because we all know you did.'"[57]

It's possible to point to Senator Rounds as an example of the Republican Party's craven support for a leader who's an extremely effective tool for forwarding its partisan ambitions. But the peculiar phenomenon of praising an apparent misstep as a strategy is reminiscent of Hannah Arendt's observations of how totalitarian leaders use propaganda, as expressed in her masterwork, *The Origins of Totalitarianism*:

> The totalitarian mass leaders based their propaganda on the correct psychological assumption that, under such conditions, one could make people believe the most fantastic statements one day, and trust that if the next day they were given irrefutable proof of their falsehood, they would take refuge in cynicism; instead of deserting the leaders who had lied to them, they would protest that they had known all along that the statement was a lie and would admire the leaders for their superior tactical cleverness.[58]

In other words, by constructing a reality in which he lies all the time—and forces his supporters to accept, defend, and explain those lies—Trump guarantees that his strongest defenders will see his most shocking statements as an example of "tactical cleverness" rather than either lack of conviction or incompetence.

We might be tempted to see Trump's deployment of "fake news" as a form of "working the ref," making it less likely that criticism will stick and that his supporters will see controversies not as presidential missteps but as the work of a biased press. Trump has confirmed as much, telling the veteran CBS journalist Lesley Stahl, "You know why I do it? I do it to discredit you all and demean you all, so when you write negative stories about me no one will believe you."[59] But something more complex and dangerous is going on as well.

"Organized lying," as Arendt termed it in her 1971 essay about *The Pentagon Papers*,[60] can have a specific goal in politics: it removes the stable ground from under people's feet, leading the public to be cynical about any news they encounter: "In an ever-changing, incomprehensible world the masses had reached the point where they would, at the same time, believe everything and nothing, think that everything was possible and nothing was true."[61]

What purpose does this destabilization provide? The totalitarian leader, Arendt argues, satisfies the need for logic and order by providing a coherent, usually fictitious narrative that explains the world as it is. For the Nazis, the narrative was that a cabal of Jewish bankers wanted to rule the world, subjugating Germans in the process. Trump's world, in which a "deep state" works to thwart him and his only defense is his personal leadership, provides his supporters with a similar narrative.

It's uncomfortable to invoke Arendt precisely because she was writing about her own experiences with Nazi Germany; a well-known corollary to Godwin's Law suggests that whoever invokes comparisons to Hitler has both ended and lost an argument.[62] Furthermore, by Arendt's definitions, Trump lacks the world-conquering ambitions and philosophical coherence to be a totalitarian. He is likely a mere autocrat. But Arendt offers useful insights to explore the unfamiliar and dangerous territory that unfolds when a political leader systemically works to undermine reality as we know it.

The trick of the totalitarian, Arendt explains, is that his internally consistent, fictitious world is one in which his prophetic knowledge and leadership lead him to win, again and again. So long as he wins elections, consolidates power, and weathers scandals, his fiction is proven right to his adherents: "It is not the truthfulness of the Leader's words but the infallibility of his actions which is the basis for the structure. Without it and in the heat of a discussion which presumes fallibility, the whole fictitious world of totalitarianism goes to pieces, overwhelmed at once by the factuality of the real world which only the movement steered in an infallibly right direction by the Leader was able to ward off."[63] Certain realities—those that challenge the leader's infallibility—have to be denied. Fortunately, "in a totally fictitious world, failures need not be recorded, admitted, and remembered. Factuality itself depends for its continued existence upon the existence of the non-totalitarian world."[64]

Arendt's analysis of the totalitarian leader suggests fragility; his infallibility can shatter if it is exposed to the truth. But contemporary disinformation campaigns can be much more resilient than the disinformation Arendt studied.

In Russia, Peter Pomerantsev had a front-row seat to Vladimir Putin's rise to power, working as a television producer between 2001 and 2010. A Russian speaker, born in Ukraine but raised in Britain, Pomerantsev was knowledgeable enough about Russian society to understand what he was seeing, and he was sufficiently distant from his colleagues to offer a critical view. It's no accident that the book he wrote describing these years is titled *Nothing Is True and Everything Is Possible,* a light rewording of Arendt's famous phrase.

Pomerantsev hoped to make documentaries in Russia that focused on the struggles of everyday citizens to navigate a post-Communist reality. He quickly discovered that it was nearly impossible to get the films onto the air. Russian audiences fell hard for reality television, and the stations he worked for wanted stories of love and riches, not of loss and suffering. For Pomerantsev, reality television became a metaphor for modern Russia: a narrative that's compelling and that everyone knows isn't true but is engrossing and ultimately important nevertheless. His book explores the ways in which Russian politics is scripted, with fake opposition parties controlled by the Kremlin, monitored by government-controlled nongovernmental organizations and a farcical judiciary. "This isn't a country in transition," Pomerantsev concludes, "but some sort of postmodern dictatorship that uses the language and institutions of democratic capitalism for authoritarian ends."[65]

A critical control mechanism of the Russian state under Putin is the news media, argues Pomerantsev, which are more than a government mouthpiece. RT, the government's English-language network designed for broadcast abroad, is an odd mishmash of conflicting perspectives and extreme views, featuring everyone from Julian Assange of WikiLeaks to Larry King, formerly of CNN. The station also provides generous time for European far-right leaders, antiglobalists, and Occupiers and other leftists, and a healthy dose of conspiracy theory—one of the first stories RT ran after launching RT America in 2010 was titled "911 Reasons Why 9/11 Was (Probably) an Inside Job."[66] The network's slogan is "Question More," and Pomerantsev observes that RT's job may be to get people to question everything they encounter, domestically and internationally. While domestic television devotes substantial time to praising Putin's efforts, Russian television focuses heavily on rumormongering, inventing a forthcoming fascist takeover in Ukraine to justify annexing Crimea, or undermining opposition candidates.

Pomerantsev's savvy media industry friends have lived for years in a media environment they don't trust. After sustained exposure to the unceasing mix of opinion, misinformation, and disinformation, they are untroubled. " 'Over the last twenty years we've lived through a communism we never believed in, democracy and defaults and mafia state and oligarchy, and we've realized they are illusions, that everything is PR.' 'Everything is PR' has become the favorite phrase of the new Russia; my Moscow peers are filled with a sense that they are both cynical and enlightened."[67]

While Pomerantsev's enlightened friends don't believe anything they read or see, they know with perfect certainty who's in charge in Russia. An opposition leader like Alexei Navalny can challenge Putin on corruption, lawbreaking, election rigging, and other sins, but in an environment where everything must be questioned, some Russians have questioned his very survival—at least until his apparent poisoning in August 2020. What remains in Russia is a sense that individual citizens lack any control and a simultaneous sense that it is all part of Putin's grand plan, that the leader holds all the strings and is a superlative genius manipulating every aspect of the political, media, and social system.

When former US secretary of state Madeleine Albright invokes fascism to express her concerns about the rise of authoritarians in Europe and of Trump in the United States, she is careful to moderate her comparisons. Albright notes that North Korea, which exists in a highly militarized state of constant emergency, is probably the only true fascist state in the world today: for all her concerns, the United States, and even Russia, are far from Nazi Germany or Mussolini's Italy.[68] But considering the patterns of fascist states is helpful, if only because we know so little about what consequences sustained attacks on truth might have. Can a nation that can't agree on reality govern itself democratically?

What Comes After Mistrust

Whether the United States, Britain, and other high-mistrust nations are heading toward a future that looks like Russia or like Sicily, high mistrust has serious consequences for civic life: disengagement and possibly authoritarianism and ethnonationalism. The obvious question is how people who are committed to open societies should react.

And here the situation gets tricky, especially for those on the political left. If leaders like Trump are gaining ground due to mistrust, isn't the logical response to oppose any attempts to denigrate and weaken institutions? If the right is benefiting disproportionately from insurrectionism, isn't the wisest response to become passionate and effective institutionalists?

Embracing institutions would be the answer if Trump, Johnson, and others had *precipitated* mistrust in institutions instead of merely benefiting from it. The conservative commentator David Brooks has suggested that Trump is the wrong answer to the right question. That question, Brooks believes, is how Americans should deal with upheavals and social shifts like globalization.[69] More broadly, the question is how people should react when faced with institutions that appear to be both ill-equipped to cope with contemporary realities and unable to reform themselves. Rebellion, whether it takes the form of exiting the European Union or electing an unqualified narcissist to the presidency, seems like an answer to the question of widespread mistrust, even if it's a bad answer. Asking people to respond to the contemporary moment by redoubling their commitment to institutions that they mistrust, and that sometimes have failed them, seems like wishful thinking.

At the same time, these institutions are best positioned to sustain what remains of democracy. The challenge is to support and celebrate those doing the hard, and increasingly reviled, work within bureaucracies to protect rights and deliver services, without losing track of how we got here. We can't just work to help people recover trust in institutions. The slide in confidence is a generational one, and we can't wait a generation or two to begin to engage with institutions. We know that mistrust leads to disengagement, and we cannot afford decades in which people choose to disengage from democracy.

Instead, we must transform the institutions we have, even as we build new movements and new approaches to tackle the challenges our societies face. What the consequences of mistrust make clear is that we need a new toolkit for some very old problems.

Sicily, where we began this chapter, isn't a bad place to start exploring this new civics. While generations of Sicilian governments have tried unsuccessfully to combat organized crime, and many individuals have paid with their lives, the Mafia may be starting to lose its grip over the islands. Addiopizzo—"Goodbye, protection money"—is a grassroots organization formed in Palermo in 2004 by a group of youth who were considering starting a restaurant. As they built projections for their enterprise, someone pointed out that they would need to budget for protection money. Their conversation turned to frustration with the Mafia, and they launched an anonymous protest, covering the city with stickers that read *Un intero popolo che paga il pizzo è un popolo senza dignità,* "people who pay the protection money are people without dignity."[70]

More than a decade later, you can take Addiopizzo tours of Palermo, led by guides who steer you to stores and attractions that have stopped paying protection. These stores advertise with a red X marked "Addiopizzo" in their windows. Remarkably, the Mafia has realized that intimidating businesses that have joined the campaign would be counterproductive and has left most of them alone. Members of the movement work closely with hundreds of businesses and have started their own ventures to broaden the work. When restaurants realized they needed a *pizzo*-free supermarket to shop at, a movement member invested his life's savings in launching Punto Pizzofree. The Addiopizzo movement itself has no visible leaders or spokespeople, just dozens of activists working to change both the economics and the culture of Palermo. The expanded toolkit that Addiopizzo is using, focused on markets and norms as much as on law, suggests that one response to pervasive mistrust is to broaden your mind about what constitutes civics and change.

Chapter 4

THE LEVERS OF CHANGE

ON OCTOBER 15, 2017, THE ACTOR ALYSSA MILANO TWEETED, "If you've been sexually harassed or assaulted write 'me too' as a reply to this tweet." She replied to her own tweet a moment later, with the phrase "me too."[1]

Within a day, there were over forty thousand responses to that tweet, many of which Milano responded to:

@brearei23: "#MeToo and I'm still not ok. And it's affected me with everything I do. It has broken me and I'm trying to pick up the pieces still"

@alyssa: "I understand. I'm standing with you."

Milano posted her tweet ten days after her fellow actor Ashley Judd accused Hollywood producer Harvey Weinstein of sexually harassing her. Judd reported that Weinstein had invited her to his hotel room for a meeting and subsequently asked her to give him a massage and to watch him shower. Her account, along with those of several of Weinstein's former employees and actors he worked with, was published in *The New York Times* on October 5. The coverage of Weinstein's behavior led to a wave of accusations from other women he had worked with. Weinstein's ouster from the company he had founded with his brother followed soon after, as did a lifetime ban from film and television production bodies in the United States within a month of the *Times* article.[2]

In the next few weeks, dozens of famous and powerful men—actor Kevin Spacey, sports doctor Larry Nassar, comedian Louis C.K., Senate candidate Roy Moore, radio host Garrison Keillor, television host Matt Lauer, record executive Russell Simmons, Senator Al Franken—were publicly accused of sexual harassment, and many lost their jobs. Judd's accusations against Weinstein had opened the floodgates in the entertainment industry, but Milano's tweet opened the movement to women everywhere.[3]

The #MeToo movement started well before Milano, Judd, and Weinstein. Milano credits a friend on Facebook with urging her to use the phrase "Me too," but it had been coined over a decade earlier. In 2006 the activist Tarana Burke founded #MeToo as a grassroots movement to provide "empowerment through empathy" for survivors of sexual violence in underprivileged communities "where rape crisis centers and sexual assault workers weren't going."[4]

Burke's motivations for Me Too went back to 1996, when she had been working as youth director of a camp that served underprivileged children. After an all-girls bonding session at the camp, a thirteen-year-old girl asked to speak with Burke privately. She told Burke about the sexual abuse she was suffering at the hands of her mother's boyfriend. Burke felt intensely uncomfortable and directed her to another female counselor who could "help her better." In that moment, Burke saw the vulnerability and openness that the girl had offered her close down, and she realized this girl might never reveal these experiences to another person again.[5]

What Burke had wanted to tell the girl was: "Me too." Ten years later, as an experienced activist who had launched a health nonprofit, Just Be, Inc., Burke launched Me Too as a movement, focusing on helping young women of color tell their stories about sexual abuse, assault, and harassment, then expanding it to support grown women when it became clear they needed to be heard as well.[6] For years, Burke had toiled in obscurity, musing that she'd had trouble even giving away T-shirts that said "Me too." Milano's tweet thrust her into the spotlight, and she wasn't initially thrilled: "'Social media,' she says, laughing at the understatement, 'is not a safe space. I thought: this is going to be a fucking disaster.'"[7]

As #MeToo gained momentum, it looked like the grassroots movement Burke had built might be forgotten as Milano and other celebrities took up the banner, but Burke and Milano appeared together on the *Today* show after *Time* magazine featured the #MeToo movement as 2017 Person of the Year. Still, many have pointed out that the *Time* cover featured mostly white actresses and not the movement's Black progenitor. Burke has focused less on this exclusion and more on the ways that attention is a form of privilege: "'Now that I have it, I'm trying to use it responsibly,' she says. 'But if it hadn't come along I would be right here, with my fucking Me Too shirt on, doing workshops and going to rape crisis centers.'"[8]

#MeToo is a different kind of movement. Sexual assault and harassment have been illegal for years, so its main demands are for changes not in law but in norms. Both Milano and Burke articulated an experience that many—possibly most—women have had, of being sexually abused, assaulted, or harassed and afterward remaining silent. As the case against Weinstein unfolded, it became clear that women have powerful reasons for their silence, including threats of lawsuits, restrictive nondisclosure agreements, and a practice of "catch and kill" in which news organizations pay women for their stories, then fail to publish them to protect powerful men. But powerful cultural norms come into play as well. The movement that Judd, Milano, Burke, and others launched encouraged women to share their experiences, even if the only detail they could share was the phrase "Me too." That phrase alone helped people understand how pervasive the problem of sexual harassment and assault is.

Americans of my generation have a tendency to compare contemporary social movements to the pivotal movements of the 1950s and '60s, the civil rights and antiwar movements. In this calculus, contemporary movements inevitably come up wanting. Criticizing online activism in 2010, Malcolm Gladwell concluded that civil disobedience—as exemplified by the 1960 sit-in at a Woolworth's lunch counter in Greensboro, North Carolina—was the product of strong ties between close friends. Since the ties that the Internet builds are weak, he argued, Internet activism is necessarily impoverished: "Fifty years after one of the most extraordinary episodes of social upheaval in American history, we seem to have forgotten what activism is."[9]

For Gladwell, activism is about individuals subjecting themselves to the risk of arrest or assault to support their beliefs. Activism takes place in public, in the street or at the lunch counter. Movements are hierarchically organized, with visible leaders and clear responsibilities for all participants. It's a long, slow process of challenging oppression until those in power recognize the righteousness of the cause and are forced to do something, usually by repealing or passing a law.

What if that's not how activism has to work?

#MeToo moved fast. Days after Judd made her accusations, Weinstein lost his company. Less than a year later, he was criminally indicted and lost his freedom. The movement unfolded in the media, in public, but in a very different way than demonstrations and marches. The women involved took massive risks in sharing their stories, but the risks were different than those Gladwell celebrated: retraumatization, humiliation, embarrassment, attacks in the press and on social media.

The women who launched the movement did not become hierarchical leaders—indeed, it's hard to find people who are willing to identify as leaders of the movement. And while some of the changes that #MeToo is seeking are occurring through law—

legislators in the House of Representatives introduced the ME TOO Congress Act, hoping to get the nation's highest legislative bodies to be transparent about payments made by legislators to settle sexual harassment claims.[10] The impacts may be greater in offices, factories, boardrooms, and classrooms, as people realize that social norms have changed and behavior that would once have been ignored will now be called out.

The most dramatic impacts of #MeToo may be the ones experienced by crisis counseling hotlines. The Rape, Abuse and Incest National Network (RAINN) reports that it received a roughly 30 percent increase in call volumes from 2016 to 2017, leading it to hire forty new crisis counselors. For many women and men, the most important impact of #MeToo is that they're telling stories they would otherwise have never told.[11] It's hard to quantify what this shift will ultimately mean, but a reasonable guess is that bravery will lead to bravery. When Rachael Denhollander called Michigan State University in 2016 to report a sexual assault she'd suffered from Dr. Larry Nassar sixteen years earlier, she opened the floodgates for more than three hundred women to report similar horrific stories.[12]

At a moment of general frustration with politics and lack of interest in conventional civics, amazing power and energy are behind large-scale social movements. Movements like #MeToo, Black Lives Matter, and Never Again, the gun control movement launched by survivors of the Marjory Stoneman Douglas school shooting, are challenging our understanding of what it means to launch, lead, and participate in movements, as well as shifting the parameters for success.

To understand the strengths, weaknesses, and workings of these movements, I've found myself reflecting on a brief moment in 2018 legal history that, on its surface, couldn't be much further from sexual harassment in Hollywood: *United States v. Microsoft Corporation.*

Lessig's Levers

Before Facebook, Google, and Amazon became dominant players, Microsoft was the most powerful company in the global technology landscape. Throughout the 1990s, Microsoft faced legal challenges alleging that it used its power over the personal computer operating system market to favor its own software and hardware products, including the software applications later known as Office, and hardware including Microsoft's mouse. By 1996, the focus of these antitrust suits had moved to the graphical browser, the software that allowed Internet users to interact with the early World Wide Web. Microsoft's Windows 98 operating system included the Internet Explorer web browser as part of its package of software. Netscape, maker of the popular browser Netscape Navigator, saw this as an existential threat to its product and sought relief from the Federal Trade Commission and, eventually, the Department of Justice.[13]

Judge Thomas Penfield Jackson, who heard the suit, appointed a "special master" to advise him on the technical issues of whether the Internet Explorer browser was an integral part of the Windows operating system or an application competing unfairly with Netscape's browser. Lawrence Lessig, a professor at Harvard Law School specializing in cyberlaw, was given six months to research the issue and report back. Ultimately, he lasted only fifty-four days in the role, before Microsoft's lawyers persuaded the federal court of appeals that Lessig was biased against their position. Jonathan Zittrain, who had served as Lessig's supremely overqualified law clerk, quipped to me, "What a week that was!," remembering the scant time the professors had to explain these issues to the court.

Lessig ultimately advised Judge Jackson in an amicus curiae brief that directly addressed an objection that his critics had advanced: "the apparent feeling among a number of courts and commentators is that code is different: that the task of evaluating design decisions involved in technological products is uniquely beyond the ken of federal courts." Lessig continued, "I believe it is a mistake to fetishize code in this way."[14] Lessig's earlier work had made the point that code, in fact, did the work of law in some cases. Writing about software to censor the Internet under the Communications Decency Act, Lessig wrote, "By shifting the burden of censorship from online publishers to individual users, the legal code won't be the censor anymore; instead, software code will do the censorial dirty work."[15]

Not long after his dismissal as special master, Lessig published a book, *Code,* that put matters more simply: " 'Lex Informatica,' as Joel Reidenberg first put it, or better, 'code is law.' " By this, Lessig meant that technological systems can regulate our behaviors as effectively as laws do. To illustrate, he used an example from his own life. While he was teaching at the University of Chicago, he would plug his computer into the Ethernet jack in his office and automatically connect to the Internet. After moving to Harvard, he plugged the same machine into a similar jack, but instead of connecting, he had to register his machine with Harvard's IT department before it would let him connect. While the University of Chicago believed in anonymous, open access to the Internet, Harvard favored being able to trace the behavior of Internet users. Embedded within the network configuration was code, Lessig explained, acting as law.

Code and law are only two forces that regulate individual behavior. Lessig proposes a framework where behaviors of all sorts are regulated by four forces: law, code, norms, and markets. Consider cigarettes, Lessig asks us. Laws in the United States prohibit the sale of cigarettes to people under eighteen, and many local ordinances prevent smoking in certain places. But norms constrain behavior as well—light a cigarette in the car of a nonsmoker without asking permission, and you're likely to get yelled at. Cigarettes are more expensive in places that impose taxes on them, a case of using markets to regulate behavior. And the technology of the cigarette itself—the move to flame-free vaping, for instance—can open up new opportunities or new restrictions to smoking. Lessig explains, "Norms constrain through the stigma that a community imposes; markets constrain through the price that they exact; architectures constrain through the physical burdens they impose; and law constrains through the punishment it threatens."[16]

Implicit in Lessig's understanding of these regulatory forces is the idea that regulations don't just constrain us—they can also free us. He references the Americans with Disabilities Act as a set of laws that demand architectural (code) changes to make buildings and public spaces accessible to all. And if we push Lessig's framework a little further, something interesting happens: the four forces that regulate human behavior become four levers that we can push on to make change.

#MeToo is a movement that sees norms as the most important lever to move. We have laws on the books to prohibit sexual abuse, but those laws often aren't brought to bear. Victims are discouraged from talking about their experiences, and police, courts, and the press often fail to listen. By encouraging a change in norms, #MeToo asks victims to speak and demands that the rest of us listen and take action. That action doesn't always unfold in the courtroom. For many of the men exposed by #MeToo, the consequences were economic and social, not legal. A norms-based strategy for change recognizes that sometimes we need a widespread change in belief and practice before new laws can pass or existing laws can do their work.

In *Code*, Lessig was concerned that law wasn't seen as powerful enough to stand up to the other regulatory forces: how could lawyers hope to govern systems as far from their areas of expertise as computer code? "Many speak as if law must simply take the other three constraints as given and fashion itself to them." Lessig's argument centered on the idea that law had a role in shaping the regulations and affordances put in place by code.

When we invert Lessig and see these four forces as levers for change, we encounter a different problem: the centrality of law as the preferred lever for activists. This, too, is a legacy of the civil rights movement. The victories that civil rights advocates won in the 1960s protected the rights of people of color at a moment when norms had been shaped by decades of segregation, as mandated by racist Jim Crow laws.

The case of *Loving v. Virginia,* in which Richard and Mildred Loving sued the state of Virginia for the right to marry after being sentenced to a year in prison for "miscegenation," illustrates the gap between changes that American courts were willing to make and public opinion. In 1967, the Supreme Court unanimously ruled that "marriage is one of the 'basic civil rights of man,'"[17] forcing sixteen southern states to overturn their bans on interracial marriage. A Gallup poll in 1968, a year after the *Loving* decision, found that only 20 percent of Americans approved of "marriages between whites and non-whites."[18] Furthermore, a 1965 poll (before *Loving*) showed that 48 percent of Americans supported legislation to ban intermarriage, and only 46 percent opposed laws like the one that imprisoned Richard and Mildred Loving.[19]

Throughout the civil rights movement, courts backed changes that many Americans—and often, in southern states, the majority of Americans—vehemently opposed: the desegregation of public schools that began with *Brown v. Board of Education of Topeka* (1954), the prohibition of discrimination in public facilities, in government, and in employment under the Civil Rights Act (1964), the instituting of affirmative action in federal hiring (1965), and the prohibition of housing discrimination (1968). The brutal murders of college students registering Black voters during Freedom Summer (1964), the attacks on peaceful marchers by police mounted on horseback in Selma on Bloody Sunday (1965), and the assassination of Martin Luther King, Jr. (1968), revealed deep and widespread resistance to racial equality in certain parts of America. Had civil rights advocates decided to wait for norms to change before pushing for legal changes, they might still be waiting now.

We can see the ongoing power of law as a lever for change in the more recent struggle for marriage equality. After the Supreme Court ruled in *Obergefell v. Hodges* (2015), the fourteen states that had not previously issued marriage licenses to same-sex couples quickly moved to comply. This is why law is such a powerful lever in making social change: win one court case, and you can move the entire governmental infrastructure. Kim Davis, the clerk for Rowan County, Kentucky, who briefly became a conservative icon for her refusal to issue marriage licenses, is the exception that proves the rule. We know who Davis is only because she was the sole public official to defiantly fail to honor the change in law.

The social climate in which the Supreme Court protected equal marriage with *Obergefell* was radically different from the climate surrounding intermarriage and *Loving,* almost half a century earlier. Gallup polling in 2015 showed that a 60 percent majority of Americans supported treating same-sex marriage identically to "traditional marriage," as opposed to the small minority that had supported intermarriage when *Loving* was settled.[20] The rapid acceptance of equal marriage is sometimes seen as evidence supporting the contact hypothesis—the idea that people are more likely to support equal marriage after having a positive encounter with a homosexual friend or family member. Because homosexuality seems to be evenly distributed within communities, and because American society remains deeply segregated, with only 60 percent of white Americans reporting they have a friend of another race,[21] it's possible that more Americans have gay people within their friends and family than have close friends of another race, leading to more rapid changes of opinion on equal marriage than on intermarriage.[22]

But notably, advocates for gay rights saw a change in norms

as a critical part of their struggle. They developed strategies for changing attitudes toward gay people that paralleled and often preceded legal cases. The steady introduction of gay and lesbian characters into television series—*Will and Grace, Queer Eye for the Straight Guy, Glee, Modern Family, Orange Is the New Black*—has been an activist-supported strategy to give viewers contact with gay people through "parasocial contact," the indirect experience of friendship with a gay television character.[23] As the *Obergefell* case headed into court, the Human Rights Campaign took to social media, asking supporters to turn their Facebook picture to a pink "equals" sign on a red background to show their support for same-sex marriage. The campaign didn't expect Justice John Roberts to count "equals" signs on Facebook before issuing a decision.[24] But it was aware that in launching the most widely adopted social media campaign in history, it was offering proof that a change in norms preceded and likely enabled this change in law.[25]

During the civil rights movement, when law was central to activist theories of change, trust in government was very high. It peaked at 77 percent in 1964, the same year the Johnson administration passed the Civil Rights Act. Today, when less than 20 percent of Americans express strong trust in the government, the ultimate efficacy of law-based theories of change is in question. Not only do approaches like the *Loving* and *Obergefell* cases require confidence in the Supreme Court to make a fair ruling and in the executive branch to enforce the law, they raise questions about who can be involved in making change through law. While the civil rights movement involved thousands of people in protests and boycotts, the core changes in law involved a small number of plaintiffs and the lawyers who argued their cases. For most people, direct involvement in making change through law can feel inaccessible and distant.

Only a few highly professional people have their hands on the legal levers of change, and those levers can feel stuck when

Congress seems paralyzed and the Supreme Court appears political and polarized. It's unsurprising that the other three levers—
markets, code, and norms—are so popular with insurrectionists.

Change Through Markets

Shortly after Donald Trump was elected president, it became
conventional wisdom that his victory was due, in part, to the
influence of a far right-wing news network, Breitbart. Described
by the antiracist Southern Poverty Law Center as offering "a safe
space for anti-Semitic language while its news coverage served
as *The New York Times* for neo-Nazis," Breitbart embraces a
nationalist worldview that critics see as hateful and dangerous.[26]
Research by Yochai Benkler and colleagues confirms that Breitbart's focus on immigration as the central issue of the 2016 campaign appears to have influenced newsmaking decisions at other
media outlets,[27] and Donald Trump's decision to invite Breitbart
chairman Steve Bannon into the White House as his chief strategist supports the idea that Trump, at least initially, saw Bannon
as central to his victory.

The activists behind activist group Sleeping Giants saw Breitbart's importance as well. On November 16, 2016, a new Twitter
account—@slpng_giants—alerted the consumer-lending start-up
Social Finance that it was advertising on the Breitbart site.[28] Half
an hour later Social Finance responded, telling Sleeping Giants
that it would pull its ads.[29] The people behind Sleeping Giants
were anonymous, but even before the conservative blog *The Daily
Caller* outed ad copywriter Mark Rivitz as one of the organizers behind the movement,[30] it was clear that the organizers were
highly knowledgeable about digital advertising. They were able
to explain to companies that even though they didn't choose to
place ads on Breitbart, ads were running there due to "programmatic buying," an inexpensive way to purchase ads so they run on

sites consumers have visited previously. To prevent their ads from appearing on the site, companies had to blacklist Breitbart.

Eighteen months into its campaign, Sleeping Giants reported that more than 3,700 companies had removed their ads from the Breitbart site. The campaign organizers weren't directly responsible for most of those removals—Sleeping Giants relies on its quarter-million Twitter followers[*] to identify ads being shown on Breitbart and to alert advertisers, asking them to add Breitbart to their campaign blacklists. The movement appears to be impacting who is willing to advertise on the site. MediaRadar, a site that tracks what ads appear on what websites, reported that the number of advertisers on Breitbart fell from 242 in March 2017 to 26 in May of the same year, in part due to the Sleeping Giants campaign and an audience for far-right media that Fox News has been increasingly effective at capturing.[31] Breitbart is unlikely to go under—the publication is primarily bankrolled by outside donors—but Sleeping Giants' campaign makes it increasingly expensive for those donors to support the site's mission.

Traditional boycotts are centrally organized and require widespread support and discipline to have an effect. The Montgomery Bus Boycott, which began in December 1955, lasted more than a year and required civil rights leaders to effectively build a parallel transportation system based on carpools and to mobilize the city's African-American taxi drivers to charge only ten cents— the bus fare—to transport boycotters. It was an enormously heavy lift for activists to organize, made possible only through the power of churches to mobilize their parishioners to take part in the action.

By contrast, actions in the style of Sleeping Giants can unfold with surprising swiftness today. High school student David Hogg, a survivor of the 2018 shooting at Marjory Stoneman

[*] 302,000 in August 2020

Douglas High School and a visible organizer of antigun protests, has been a bête noire for some American conservatives. The conservative TV host Laura Ingraham taunted Hogg on Twitter when he posted about being rejected from four colleges he had applied to, apparently forgetting that her political opponent was a teenager who'd recently suffered the loss of classmates in a horrific act of violence. Hogg responded simply. "I'm not going to stoop to her level and go after her on a personal level," he said. "I'm going to go after her advertisers."[32]

Hogg's campaign against Ingraham was remarkably simple, beginning with the tweet "Soooo @IngrahamAngle what are your biggest advertisers . . . Asking for a friend. #BoycottIngramAdverts."[33] Later that day he tweeted a list of twelve companies that advertised on her show and their Twitter handles.[34] That tweet was shared fifty-five thousand times, and within twenty-four hours, nine of Ingraham's major sponsors had pulled ads from her show.[35] Ingraham apologized to Hogg, whose sister used Twitter to observe that the apology would have been more convincing if it had been offered before the boycott cost the host her advertisers. Three days after the boycott began, Ingraham announced she was taking a week off from the show. When she returned, only a few of her advertisers did: during the first week of May 2018, the show featured twelve ads per night, down from thirty-five a night before the boycott.[36]

Market-based change may be most powerful when it leverages consumers to bring about better futures. Elon Musk is celebrated for SpaceX, one of several start-ups that promises to transform space exploration from something nation-states do to something corporations and individuals can participate in. But Tesla, his electric car company, may be leading a more profound change, away from fossil fuels and toward highly efficient autonomous vehicles. Whether or not Tesla ultimately survives as a company—or whether it could have launched without massive government subsidies—Musk's repositioning of the electric vehicle as an object of desire, rather than a manifestation of consumer piety, is a major shift.

Until recently, electric cars generally have not been popular with consumers, in part because manufacturers didn't really want to build them. California's Air Resources Board has administered a zero-emissions vehicle mandate since 1990. To be able to sell cars in California—a state that represents roughly 12 percent of the entire American auto market—manufacturers are required to make an increasing percentage of their cars battery powered or otherwise emissions free.[37] For most auto manufacturers, these cars—sometimes called "compliance cars"—amount to a tax they pay in order to sell other, more profitable vehicles in California. Chrysler, for instance, sold an electric version of the Fiat 500 that was almost twice as expensive to purchase as a conventional Fiat, even with tax breaks, and Fiat lost $10,000 for every vehicle sold. In 2013 Chrysler CEO Sergio Marchionne explained that he has no plans to mass-produce these vehicles: "Doing that on a large scale would be masochism to the extreme."[38]

When Tesla entered the electric car market in 2008, the company's goal wasn't to grudgingly comply with California law but to build a revolutionary sports car. The Model S, Tesla's first large-production vehicle, featured "ludicrous mode," which allowed the car to accelerate from 0 to 60 miles per hour faster than any other car in production.[39] Features like a driver-assist autopilot and the use of touch screens for all internal controls made the car desirable to luxury enthusiasts. Having captured the attention of the luxury car market, Tesla proceeded to build an SUV and an affordable sedan, the Tesla 3, which sold 190,000 cars in the United States between 2017 and 2019, dominating the domestic electric car market.[40] The company has also announced plans for a Tesla semitruck designed to challenge the diesel tractor trailer market and a "cybertruck" to enter into the lucrative American pickup truck sector.

Musk's ambitions for Tesla go far beyond the electric vehicle market. He envisions a fully solar-powered lifestyle, in which your solar roof powers your battery wall and charges your car, dropping your net emissions toward zero. Musk endlessly frustrates industry analysts, who would prefer that he focus on solving Tesla's notorious production problems rather than on a grand strategy for solarizing America. But Musk is not a conventional CEO—he's an activist masquerading as a CEO to use the full power of the market lever to make change.

The California Air Resources Board tried to make change through law, mandating that manufacturers create zero-emissions vehicles and hoping to spur innovation. But it wasn't until Tesla demonstrated that electric vehicles could be more exciting than their gas-powered competition—and that hundreds of thousands would line up to purchase them—that firms including Nissan and Chevrolet were persuaded to invest more heavily in them. Companies like Tesla use markets as mechanisms to scale up clever ideas. If all goes well, Tesla will help normalize the electric car, the solar roof, and the off-the-grid home, and individual consumers will pay for it, making a profit for the company and for its investors.

Recent attempts by the Trump administration to change California's emission laws suggest another way in which markets might be stronger than laws. Even if California is forced to adopt much less stringent national emissions regulations, the market for electric cars will certainly continue to grow, spurred by consumers who see them as highly desirable and manufacturers who want to meet that need.

Making Change Through Code

In late May 2013 a contractor to the National Security Agency, Edward Snowden, flew to Hong Kong, where he checked into a room at the Mira Hong Kong and waited for journalists Laura

Poitras and Glenn Greenwald to arrive. In her resulting documentary, *Citizenfour* (named for the pseudonym Snowden used when he first contacted her), Poitras shows Snowden hiding under the covers of his bed as he enters the passwords to decrypt the files he'd copied from some of the US government's most secure computers.[41]

The files Snowden shared with Poitras and Greenwald were both stunning and totally unsurprising. They revealed what the most paranoid of American technology experts had believed for decades: that the US government was intercepting communications of any Americans who communicated with people outside the country; and that large communication companies were helping them intercept this data. The Department of Justice accused Snowden of espionage and theft of government property, and Snowden fled to Moscow, where he remains.

Snowden hoped that his revelations would lead to an international debate about privacy, surveillance, and what rights private citizens should retain in the face of transnational threats like terrorism. Instead, he sparked a debate about whistleblowing, patriotism, and treason, becoming a deeply divisive figure in the eyes of the American public. Unfortunately, very little has changed in terms of US surveillance law and practice, and as recently as 2015, fully 46 percent of Americans described themselves as unconcerned or not very concerned about US government surveillance.[42] Unsurprisingly, the Trump administration has taken no meaningful action to limit government surveillance of US citizens, particularly since Trump has suggested that Snowden should be executed as a spy.[43] And as COVID-19 forces governments to begin contact tracing to limit the spread of the disease, tech giants Google and Apple have joined efforts to introduce cellphone-based apps that can trace users' movements and alert them if they've been in contact with an infected person, a prospect that raises serious privacy concerns. Yet more than half of Americans polled said they thought it was acceptable for the government to track the movements of those who've tested positive for COVID-19.[44]

Despite this cavalier attitude toward privacy, in April 2016 hundreds of millions of Internet users around the world began encrypting their personal communications, making the practice of intercepting and analyzing them vastly more difficult for officials at the NSA or other intelligence agencies. Responsible for this spontaneous flowering of encryption were two socially conscious billionaires and a skinny, dreadlocked anarchist who goes by the *nom de code* Moxie Marlinspike.

Marlinspike is the founder of Open Whisper Systems, the makers of a powerful secure communications program called Signal. Easily installed on a mobile phone or desktop computer, Signal uses layers of encryption to protect SMS messages and voice calls from snooping. The program is popular with journalists, human rights activists, and whistleblowers—Snowden says he uses the program every day[45]—but it hasn't reached a mass market. In late 2019 the iPhone app store listed it as the forty-fifth most popular social media app, equaling the popularity of niche dating apps like Grindr and Kinkoo.

Enter Jan Koum and Brian Acton, the founders of WhatsApp, a messaging service with over one and a half-billion users worldwide today. In 2014, Koum and Acton sold WhatsApp to Facebook for almost $20 billion but retained day-to-day control of the company. Fierce defenders of user privacy—by 2018, both Acton and Koum had left Facebook over the company's policies regarding user data[46]— in 2016 the WhatsApp founders worked with Marlinspike to integrate Signal's encryption into their application. While Signal encryption is now available as an option within Facebook and Google's messenger products, it is turned on by default in WhatsApp. Once Signal was integrated, hundreds of millions of WhatsApp users around the world began encrypting messages without consciously choosing to do so. Not even WhatsApp can uncover what's being transmitted in those messages, which means that the company can't comply with a court order to wiretap a WhatsApp call or collude with a government to collect messages, as several large US companies did with the NSA. (Recent stories suggest that WhatsApp may have been compromised by Israeli spyware, and Internet security experts strongly recommend using Signal to ensure security of communications.)

Snowden and Marlinspike both consider themselves activists focused on surveillance and privacy. While Snowden is vastly better known, Marlinspike is arguably more successful. This is the power of code as a lever of change—an activist programmer can change tools used by millions of people without them realizing that a change has been made. (Of course, this power can be used for evil as well as for good, whatever definitions of good and evil you prefer.) Venture capital investors have historically invested in software because of its scaling properties: WhatsApp had only fifty employees when it became the third-largest social network in the world; had you bought shares in the company when it had only a few thousand users, you would have made a great deal of money when it sold for $20 billion. These same dynamics make code a powerful lever for activists—individual creators have been able to build technologies that get adopted by millions of people, changing what's possible for people to do.

While Signal and WhatsApp are literally pieces of computer code, Lessig's original definition of code is broad and includes all sorts of technical and nontechnical architectures. For Lessig, code includes physical architecture, like the wheelchair ramp that helps a disabled patron enter a library, or a steep curb that prevents her from navigating a sidewalk.[47] What's true for code as a constraint is true for code as a lever for change. Changing physical infrastructures is a social change strategy that can affect thousands of people, for better or worse. Consider curbs that separate bike lanes from automotive traffic, protecting bike riders but compressing auto traffic into fewer lanes, or armrests in the middle of park benches that make it harder for people to sleep on them. Code-based theories of change are often nuanced, inviting us to look closely into the politics behind design choices. Are systems designed purely for efficiency and cost, or are they working to shape our behavior?

Code-based changes can have complex and unpredictable social effects. While Facebook initially responded to concerns about misinformation on its platform by agreeing to increase transparency around political advertising, it has subsequently announced a "pivot to privacy," which promises to make all communications on Facebook platforms as resistant to scrutiny as WhatsApp is, through widespread adoption of encryption. While this is a victory for privacy advocates, it may make it impossible for governments, activists, or Facebook itself to understand the spread and influence of misinformation, as encrypted conversations are impossible to analyze. It seems perhaps too convenient that the adoption of privacy-protecting technologies absolves Facebook of responsibility for monitoring and controlling conversations on its systems.

Making Change Through Norms

In August 2014, when Officer Darren Wilson fatally shot eighteen-year-old Michael Brown after an altercation in Ferguson, Missouri, the killing sparked protests, marches, clashes between police and protesters, and nonstop media coverage for months. As the story broke, media outlets were left with a choice of how to portray the deceased man. They turned, as reporters do, to Facebook and chose a photo of Brown standing on the porch of his house. The photo is shot from below, making him look even taller than his six-foot-four-inch frame. He wears a Nike Air basketball shirt and is flashing a peace sign while scowling.

I've shown this photo in dozens of talks around the world, and

I always ask my audiences to describe how Brown looks in the photo. After a long pause, someone will eventually offer, "Like a thug." As many eighteen-year-olds do, Brown shared a photo of himself in which he looks strong, dangerous, and tough. But he shared other photos on Facebook, including one taken head on, where he's wearing a varsity letter jacket and looks more like a child—which he was when Wilson shot him. The question isn't why Brown chose to share a picture in which he looked "like a thug"—it's why American media outlets chose that photo to represent a young man who'd tragically been killed.

Watching the events in Ferguson from Jackson, Mississippi, was the thirty-three-year-old defense lawyer C.J. Lawrence. Lawrence couldn't get over the images he was seeing. One that circulated on Twitter showed Brown's dead body, and one Twitter troll had tweeted, "Look at him with his pants sagging," implying that Brown was gang-connected. The images that news organizations had selected to portray the young man were not much better. Wondering about the hundreds of self-portraits he himself had uploaded on social media, Lawrence posted two—one in which he's wearing a graduation gown, speaking at a podium to an audience that includes a laughing Bill Clinton, and another in which he's wearing sunglasses and holding a bottle of Hennessy cognac—and asked Twitter "Which photo does the media use if the police shot me down? #IfTheyGunnedMeDown"[48]

C.J.'s followers knew the answer to the question. So did thousands of others, who posted the tag 186,000 times in the week after Brown's killing, alongside pictures that juxtaposed people looking their most and their least respectable: a Marine in full dress uniform next to the same man flipping off the camera; a saxophone player in tuxedo at a concert and another time wearing a do-rag. Collections on the blogging platform Tumblr assembled hundreds of examples of the meme and hosted debates about whether white kids should participate in the phenomenon. (The overwhelming opinion: no.) Three days after Brown's death, *The New York Times* ran a front-page story titled "Shooting Spurs Hashtag Effort on Stereotypes," explaining the hashtag campaign and the larger use of activist hashtags on "Black Twitter," observing that the social network was more widely used by Black people under thirty than by white people.[49]

C.J. says he did little to promote the hashtag besides sharing it with his followers. Black Twitter did the rest. He credits the actors Reagan Gomez and Jeffrey Wright, both active on Twitter, with amplifying the meme. "I think that it was just right on time, because all of us were feeling rowdiness from seeing Michael Brown's body on the ground," he told me in an interview in 2020. "It was literally just us still trying to make sense of what had occurred . . . that was my way of responding."

What's remarkable about the campaign is not how little organizing was required to get hundreds of thousands of people to pay attention; it's how effective the hashtag was in changing media behavior. The majority of media stories published about Brown more than a week after the campaign used the image where Brown looks less intimidating, and once the family released his high school graduation photo, most stories used that image. A Google image search for "Michael Brown" primarily yields Brown's graduation photo.

It's a long walk from challenging the image used to represent a young man killed by the police to creating racial justice reform, but it helps us understand the logic behind norms-based activism. Michael Brown's death helped galvanize the Black Lives Matter movement, started by Alicia Garza, Patrisse Cullors, and Opal Tometi when George Zimmerman was acquitted of killing Black teenager Trayvon Martin the year earlier. While Brown was killed by a police officer and Martin by a private citizen, the killers' perception of both young men as a threat is a common thread between the two tragedies. Black Lives Matter and successors like the Movement for Black Lives have worked on a wide range of racial justice issues, but their primary focus is on how policing disproportionately affects communities of color.

Challenging racial inequities in policing is hard to accomplish by passing new laws: it's long been illegal for police departments to treat citizens differently based on race. Rather than changing laws, campaigns like #IfTheyGunnedMeDown aim at exposing and changing the attitudes and biases that can lead to use of excessive force.

Black people represent 13 percent of Americans but 31 percent of people killed by police. That disparity is even higher in cases where people killed by police were unarmed.[50] Studies tested in simulators suggest that police (and civilians) are quicker to shoot Black suspects than white ones.[51] A study that asked police officers to estimate the ages of white, Black, and Latinx children suspected of crimes showed that officers overestimated the age of Black boys by 4.5 years, routinely identifying fourteen-year-olds as adults.[52]

This disparity in perception helps explain the tragedy of Tamir Rice, a twelve-year-old boy who was playing with a toy gun. Rice was killed by police officer Timothy Loehmann, who opened fire two seconds after exiting his police cruiser. Loehmann might have taken a few more seconds to assess the situation if he hadn't held biases that led him to identify a twelve-year-old boy as a threat. But how do we change the biases of a society as a whole?

You take on the media, as C.J. Lawrence did. By urging media organizations to think carefully about what photographs they use in cases like Michael Brown's, C.J. and thousands of others are working to reverse the social norm that Black people should be perceived as a threat. C.J. Lawrence is now CEO of Black With No Chaser, a digitally native activist news outlet focused on an African-American point of view on racial justice issues. He told me, "I certainly saw a need for narratives to be controlled by the people that are most impacted by those narratives. I saw a responsibility to not let the power of something like #ifthey-gunnedmedown die."

Changing norms is a slow process, and #IfTheyGunnedMe-Down isn't the only effort aimed at changing America's racial biases. This makes it hard to evaluate the impact of any individual campaign. But norm change is a lever that's used a great deal today, primarily because it's one young people feel especially well-equipped to use. Whether you're a celebrity like Alyssa Milano or a Mississippi lawyer like C.J. Lawrence, your hashtag can become a movement.

Using the Four Levers Together

Very few successful approaches to social change use only one lever. Black Lives Matter focused on law as well as on norms, producing a set of proposed legislation for states to adopt. Ultimately, the group helped to pass more than forty laws in twenty-four states addressing racial bias in policing, mandating body cameras for police officers, and limiting the flow of surplus military equipment to police departments.[53] Tesla has leveraged markets to scale its reach, used new technologies (code) to make novel vehicles available, and benefited from government subsidies and mandates (law) that encourage electric vehicles.

The adoption of rooftop solar panels offers lessons in how the four levers can complement each other. Ten years ago, having photovoltaic panels on your roof usually meant you were a deeply committed environmentalist or a technological early adopter. Now solar panels have become so mainstream that new homes constructed in California after 2020 must have them.[54] The rapid shift in adoption shows how effective the four levers can be when used together.

In the past decade, solar panels have become much more efficient and much cheaper. The solar panels that President Jimmy

Carter put on the White House in 1979 cost roughly forty dollars per watt. Newer panels today cost less than a dollar per watt, and prices continue to fall as manufacturers design panels that will be affordable in low- and middle-income countries, where rooftop solar's impact is even greater than in the United States and Europe. Manufacturers have created easy-to-assemble aluminum mounting racks for panels, which makes installation quicker and cheaper and requires less expertise. While these changes have made solar systems cheaper, they reflect changes in code—they're technological tweaks made by a small number of engineers that changed the larger dynamics of the solar industry.

Market forces have also been at work. Realizing that most homeowners couldn't spend $30,000 to invest in rooftop solar systems, solar companies became lenders, offering financing for projects or leasing panels to homeowners, recovering their costs by replacing the homeowner's electric bill with a bill to pay off the solar panels. Law played a major role as well. A massive tax benefit allowed taxpayers to deduct 30 percent of the cost of a solar system from their federal taxes, until it expired in 2016. The tax credit clearly appealed to homeowners, as installations surged in 2016 and decreased in 2017. Solar's appeal varies from state to state depending on whether local laws permit homeowners to sell excess power to the electric grid, "running your meter backward." In my state, Massachusetts, local law makes it so easy to recover the costs of solar installation that, despite scant sunlight, there have been more rooftop solar installations here than in sun-drenched Texas or Florida.[55]

Rooftop solar has leveraged a powerful norms effect as well. The installations are advertisements—it's easy to see when your neighbor has installed solar panels. My decision to put solar on my own roof had more to do with the sinking feeling that I'd be the last person in my neighborhood to help the environment than with any financial calculations. If the technical, market, and legal innovations that make rooftop solar affordable and attractive had not been available to me, my guilt would likely have been counterbalanced by practical concerns. Multiple levers used in tandem provides a more powerful impetus to change than a single strategy used in isolation.

There's nothing new about seeking change through complementary tactics. The civil rights movement of the 1950s and '60s masterfully used market, norm, and legal strategies in concert. The Montgomery Bus Boycott cost the city's bus company more than 65 percent of its revenue for over a year, as activists used the economic lever to push for legal social change.[56] On the legal side, the boycott ended when the NAACP brought *Browder v. Gayle* to the federal district court and won a judgement that Alabama's racial discrimination laws for transportation were unconstitutional. Decades later, we remember the Montgomery boycott because leaders of the civil rights movement were acutely aware of the power of the press. Organizers used the nonviolent action of protesters and the violence of segregationists (who attacked Black riders on the buses when they returned at the end of the boycott) to make the normative case that integration was the peaceful and moral stance for the nation to take.

In our current moment, mistrust in institutions makes an expanded toolkit for social change more critical than ever. People will choose the tools they find most familiar and easiest to use. More important, they will gravitate toward levers they think they can move. The key ingredient in contemporary social change is efficacy: the sense that you, personally, can have an impact on the world.

Many contemporary critiques of youth disengagement from politics assume that young people suffer from low internal efficacy—they don't understand how political institutions work—but if they could be made to understand how powerful youth could be within these institutions, they'd support them and seek change from within.[57]

But David Hogg and Moxie Marlinspike certainly don't seem

to suffer from low internal efficacy. They also appear to know how political and social systems work. In fact, they've got high internal efficacy and low external efficacy. They understand how to make social change, and they understand that the institutions they want to change are highly resistant. In 1968 the social movements scholar William Gamson suggested that historical moments like this are pregnant with the possibility for change: "a combination of high sense of political efficacy and low political trust is the optimum combination for mobilization—a belief that influence is both possible and necessary."[58] This is the combination of factors that animated the civil rights movement: disciplined, creative, and thoughtful activists working to change a highly resistant political and social system.

Even if these new tactics are a sign of high efficacy—people embracing the tools they are best able to use—any shift from law-based theories of change to a broader repertoire of civic action presents challenges. While new approaches to social change hope to make civic engagement more broadly inclusive, they are often equal but inequitable. You and Alyssa Milano are equally able to post on Twitter, hoping to start a social movement. But Milano has over 3 million Twitter followers, and you most likely do not. Similarly, Elon Musk's campaign to popularize green energy is made possible in part by wealth he received from his involvement with PayPal. And Marlinspike's code-based activism is built on his skills and talent as a programmer, skills that are not equally distributed around the world. When we embrace theories of change that disproportionately favor those positioned to move levers of norms, markets, and code, we need to acknowledge these pitfalls.

In theory, strategies that focus on legal levers should be equitable as well as equal—we each have one vote, whether we're rich or poor, famous or unknown. But in practice, the ability to make change through law has become deeply inequitable. As politics has become professionalized, holding office now requires having specialized skills. Meanwhile political contributions may be shaping politics in ways that give more power to the wealthy. Equitable participation in elections should be our goal, but we have to recognize that gerrymandering, voter suppression, and other barriers can make change through law more inequitable than change through the other three levers.

I thought of the levers of change when I heard Larry Lessig speaking on the podcast *Criminal*, not about Internet law but about sexual abuse. As a young man, Lessig had been a student at the residential American Boychoir School. There he was repeatedly molested by the choir director. Lessig represented another student, John Hardwicke, in his lawsuits against the school. That suit opened the door to additional legal action and indirectly led to the school's closure. When I heard Lessig on *Criminal,* he was talking about his personal experiences of abuse, adding his voice to thousands of others who are speaking out. Like Milano, and like Burke, Lessig was making these discussions more normal as a way to make abuse less frequent.[59]

Chapter 5

INSTITUTIONALISTS TO THE RESCUE

JEN PAHLKA DOESN'T LIKE IT WHEN I CALL HER AN INSTITU-tionalist. "You make me sound like a bus driver." She pauses for a moment, then allows, "I'm a Capricorn. We're supposed to be bus drivers."[1]

Pahlka worked alongside technologists for more than a decade, running a gaming magazine and planning technology conferences before coming to some uncomfortable realizations: the people she worked with thought the government was impossibly broken, and those who'd given up on government knew very little about how it worked and what it did. We pay an enormous amount of attention to politics, Pahlka explains, but "government is like a vast ocean, and politics is the six-inch layer on top." The organization Pahlka founded, Code for America, uses technology to improve that layer below politics, the complex bureaucracy that serves as our interface to services from federal, state, and local governments.

Since 2009, Code for America has trained and deployed hundreds of tech-savvy volunteers to work inside government agencies for a yearlong fellowship. Thousands more volunteer for Code for America "brigades" that help local government agencies evaluate and implement technology projects. In the process,

Pahlka has become one of the most visible advocates of technologists engaging with government, on city, state, and federal levels. In 2013 she became deputy chief technology officer for government innovation, working to establish the US Digital Service within the office of the president, and 18F, a digital agency within the General Services Administration.

Code for America places geeks in government offices not because Pahlka naïvely trusts in our institutions. She's a fierce critic of government shortcomings, opening a recent essay much as I opened this book: "Public trust in government is at historic lows in the United States. The most obvious culprit is partisan gridlock in Washington, but perhaps as important is government's difficulties delivering on its promises."[2] Her volunteers work to modernize the distribution of food stamps or to make school choice comprehensible precisely because they see the broken and dysfunctional aspects of government. Helping to fix broken systems has at least three benefits: it increases trust in government, it helps the techies involved get a deep understanding of the systems they want to transform, and potentially, it saves a lot of money.

Social-safety-net programs, like Medicare and Social Security in the United States, represent a massive share of the federal budget, as much as two-thirds of government spending, or more than $2.7 trillion.[3] By contrast, all philanthropy in America, including gifts from individuals and foundations, totals $390 billion.[4] "When we talk about making government more effective, realize that a 15 percent increase in the effectiveness of government social-safety-net programs would represent as much money as all of philanthropy. What are the chances we're going to double all philanthropic spending? Quite low."[5]

The potential victories that come from making the government a little less broken are so compelling, Pahlka argues, that we must engage with flawed systems precisely because they're broken. Explaining her decision to participate in a discussion of the American Technology Council convened by the Trump White House, Pahlka wrote, "Our federal government lately seems like a building on fire; if we want to save it, we must run towards it, not away from it."[6]

There's more than one way to run into a building on fire. The naïf who believes they will be able to do great things once they've gained power within the system, only to become cynical and disillusioned in the process, is a trope that runs from *Heart of Darkness* through *Mr. Smith Goes to Washington* and into David Simon's celebrated television series *The Wire*. Some people turn to institutionalism because proximity to power is attractive. Others fail to understand that institutions can be in such bad shape that there's no effective change from within that doesn't involve reinventing how the system works.

By contrast, effective institutionalists have overcome their naïveté—they understand that the institutions they're supporting are often badly flawed, and they have a strategy for how to keep them from total collapse.

Pahlka believes that she can help government institutions learn to become "user-centered, iterative, and data-driven"—in short, to build citizen-facing services the way they're built in Silicon Valley, not the way they're currently built, by defense contractors and other businesses whose primary strength is their ability to follow government procurement policies. The benefit, she hopes, is not only that citizens will benefit from better tools but that government will do a better job of learning what citizens want and need. "One thing Silicon Valley is actually pretty good at is paying attention to what people actually want and need. For some people in government, it's almost like that's beneath them." Part of Pahlka's battle is to persuade people in government who build technology to think differently. But a first step in that process is respecting the importance of the work people within institutions currently do.

In Defense of the Deep State

After Donald Trump took office in 2017, a wave of Twitter accounts associated with the US government "went rogue." On the day the president was sworn into office, the official Twitter account of the National Parks Service retweeted Binyamin Appelbaum, a *New York Times* correspondent who'd shared images of the spotty crowds for Trump's inauguration, comparing them to those for Obama's ceremony.[7] The new administration responded by temporarily banning all Department of Interior employees from using Twitter. The following day the offending tweet was removed and an apology was posted on the National Park Service feed. But three days later, the account of the Badlands National Park in South Dakota began tweeting out climate facts, including "Today, the amount of carbon dioxide in the atmosphere is higher than at any time in the last 650,000 years. #climate."[8] Later that day @AltUSNatParkService, which claimed to be run by current and former park rangers, launched with a flurry of two hundred tweets critical of Trump, gathering more than half a million followers in its first day online.[9] "Alternative" accounts for NASA, the EPA, and other government agencies followed, creating the impression of a massive bureaucratic rebellion against the incoming president.[10]

It's impossible to know whether these new "alt.gov" accounts were actually run by rebellious government bureaucrats, or whether activists simply realized the value of reminding anyone who was listening that the government was filled with people who believe in science and accuracy over spin. This is, in fact, a deeply important reminder. While a small percentage of government jobs change hands as political leadership changes—the six-inch layer on top of Jen Pahlka's ocean—the vast majority of people who work in an agency like the National Park Service or the EPA are there because they believe in preserving national lands or prosecuting environmental crimes. While the Trump administration has taken aim at weakening or eliminating government departments, and sometimes appointed cabinet secretaries who have expressed an interest in shuttering the corner of government they've been entrusted with overseeing, thousands of people show up for work every day and do more or less the same jobs as they did before the presidency changed hands.

An agency like the EPA will not be replaced with anything better under the Trump administration, so working to preserve the values and importance of the existing institution is a perfectly reasonable—and downright noble—thing to do. Consider the impact that federal justices have had in ruling against the Justice Department's increasingly xenophobic immigration policies: by doing their jobs and maintaining the strength of the institution they represent, they've been able to slow some of the worst excesses of the Trump administration's executive orders. While the administration's response to COVID-19 has essentially stopped immigration in mid-2020, a Ninth Circuit ruling that ordered the "remain in Mexico" policy to be overturned suggests that once the immediate response to the pandemic is ended, courts will continue to check executive power on issues of immigration.

What neither the EPA nor the federal courts have done— whether or not it is needed—is eliminate or reform their institutions. Indeed, at a moment when the existence of their institutions is threatened, it may be unrealistic to ask these institutions to address their shortcomings. Their challenge now is to survive in an increasingly hostile environment.

Effective institutionalists have theories for why their participation within an institution is important: they believe the institution is the best positioned to tackle a problem and requires support, or they believe they personally are positioned to transform the institution by their very presence.

On July 11, 2016, a group of four men were skinning dead

cows outside the village of Una in Gujarat, India. The men were Dalits, a group excluded from Hinduism's four Brahminic castes, historically considered "untouchable," and excluded from villages by many Hindu communities. A group of vigilantes, members of the far-right Hindu nationalist political party Shiv Sena, accused the men of killing the cows, a deeply controversial practice in India. The men protested that they were skinning cows that had died of natural causes, a traditional profession left to Dalit men. But soon they were stripped, tied to cars, and beaten with sticks and iron pipes. The vigilantes documented their attacks on the men and shared the video on social media, leading to a wave of protests.[11]

Jignesh Mevani, a Dalit lawyer and social activist, led a massive march of Dalits from the Gujarati capital of Ahmedabad to Una, the village where the beatings took place. Mevani's intentions in organizing the march went beyond calling attention to extremist violence. He asked the tens of thousands of Dalits who marched with him to pledge that they would no longer take on the work of skinning and butchering cattle, the task they'd performed for three thousand years and the nominal reason they were considered untouchable by some Hindus. In return, he demanded that the Gujarat government redistribute five acres of land to each Dalit family so they would have both the economic and the status benefits from being landowners.[12]

Mevani's success as a movement leader led to success at the ballot box, and he was elected to the Gujarat legislative assembly with a strong showing in one of the state's poorest constituencies. While there are many Dalits in government throughout India—the result of a compromise, struck by Mahatma Gandhi and Babasaheb Ambedkar, the Dalit father of Indian independence, that created reserved seats for "scheduled castes"—the presence of a Dalit activist within government is a radical development. When I interviewed him in August 2018, Mevani explained that his path to politics gave him an unusual degree of power: "They're forced to take me seriously, because they know I can bring people into the streets again." From this privileged position, Mevani sees his role as bringing the issues of Dalits and other poor constituents to the state government.

I didn't understand how controversial and visible a figure Mevani had become until a colleague pointed out how careful she'd had to be in setting up our meeting, choosing a location that couldn't be traced to her or her family, and that Mevani never travels alone, after past confrontations with police. While Mevani focuses now on serving his constituents, his presence in government is a statement in itself that Dalits can advocate for their rights and will use the tools of the Indian government to do so. For Dalits who want to see discrimination end, Mevani's loud and visible voice is proof that change is possible.

Mevani's presence in Indian politics offers some of the same hope that Alexandra Ocasio-Cortez provides to American progressives. As a twenty-eight-year-old *puertoriqueña* from the Bronx, she unseated a powerful Democratic leader, challenging him from the left by running on a platform of democratic socialism. The sheer presence of a working-class woman—Ocasio-Cortez worked as a bartender and a waitress in a taqueria before launching her legislative career—advocating for workers' rights suggests a hope that America's least-trusted institution could be transformed by the presence of young leaders. The danger, both for Mevani and for Ocasio-Cortez, is that they will find themselves frustrated by the inability to change the institutions they've fought to join.

The real power of Mevani and Ocasio-Cortez will be realized when their ideas, not just their presence, become central to their chosen institution. Both might find inspiration in an unlikely locale for institutionalist revolutionaries: the district attorney's office.

The Radical Institutionalists
in the DA's Office

In the spring of 2008, Adam Foss graduated from Suffolk Law School in his native Boston. Before starting as a prosecutor in the Suffolk County district attorney's office, he spent his summer touring with his band, a decision he remembers as an easy one to make, "as there weren't any programs to teach me how to become a prosecutor—it was just assumed that I would go straight from law school into the courtroom." As a result, Foss didn't know how to do very much other than seek prison terms for young defendants he was supposed to bring to justice. "Five thousand years ago, the first doctors conducted surgery with stone tools. Fortunately, the medical field has made tremendous progress since then. But in the prosecutor's office, we're still dealing with our favorite stone tool: prison."[13]

During his years prosecuting mostly young Black men in Boston, Adam realized there had to be a better way to achieve justice than to contribute to "a system that has put more African Americans in prison right now than were enslaved at the start of the Civil War." As Foss learned his trade, he discovered that prosecutors in the United States have enormous flexibility in their choices about defendants: they can send them into drug treatment, diversion programs, community service, and other ways to rehabilitate and to address the damage they've caused. Foss likes to tell the story of a young man who'd stolen dozens of laptops from a Best Buy store. Rather than prosecute the culprit, leaving him with a lifetime felony record, Foss worked with him to recover the stolen laptops, pay for the ones he couldn't recover, and perform community service. The young man now works as a banker in Boston "and makes a lot more money than me," Foss quips. That's a good thing: instead of costing Massachusetts money, the man Foss worked with has become a taxpayer and a contributing member of society.[14]

The key, Foss now believes, is showing prosecutors around the country that they have another way to work. With his nonprofit organization Prosecutor Impact, he conducts trainings he wishes he'd experienced before starting his job, introducing prosecutors to the communities that many defendants come from, and showing them the full toolkit at their disposal, from counseling and community service to criminal prosecution. My former lab at MIT, Center for Civic Media, has worked with Foss to develop metrics for district attorneys' offices that track progress toward healthy, just communities, rather than the number of criminals incarcerated. It's a move similar to one that public health advocates are making; to track "wellness" instead of the number of patients a doctor or hospital sees.

Foss is part of a national movement toward decarceration that's seen New York and New Jersey drop their prison populations by over 25 percent since 2000.[15] The city of Philadelphia recently elected Larry Krasner, a civil rights attorney with years of experience, to head its district attorney's office. Krasner stunned even his most passionate supporters with the sheer scope and pace of changes he put into place, firing thirty-one DAs who weren't comfortable with his new direction for the office and placing twenty-nine police officers on a "do not call" list because of indications that they had lied under oath to seek convictions. More stunning was a five-page memo Krasner sent to those reporting to him, setting new guidelines that demanded approval from a superior before prosecuting for possession or sale of marijuana, prostitution, or possession of an unlicensed weapon.[16] Inspired by Krasner, Foss, and others, activist lawyers who've worked on issues like housing discrimination are mounting campaigns for the DA's office. They see a chance to transform outcomes through their presence and their commitment to a new way of using a powerful institution.[17]

Neither Foss nor Krasner is changing the purpose of the prosecutor's office. The purpose of that important, though often broken, institution remains to provide justice to the community. Foss acknowledges that one of the hardest parts of his job is explaining his approach to the families of crime victims. But these prosecutorial reforms aren't changing laws—they focus on changing norms within the prosecutor's office, helping bring an institution back to its original purpose. I consider Foss and Krasner to be radical institutionalists. They look and sound like radicals, but their approaches are about strengthening institutions, bringing them back to their original purposes, not eliminating them like insurrectionists, or working outside them, as in counterdemocracy (see Chapter 6).

Send Lawyers, Scratch Tickets, and Money

Because radical institutionalists seek power within existing institutions, their success often depends on hacking the rules that govern institutions. In other words, a lot of radical institutionalists are lawyers. (Try not to hold that against them.)

One of the most frequently lambasted institutions in the United States today is the Electoral College, a peculiar process for selecting a president that has, in two of the five presidential elections this century, resulted in sending the candidate who won fewer votes to the presidency. In an attempt to strike a balance between popular will and the excesses of populist zeal, the framers of the Constitution created a system in which each state has electors proportional to its number of senators and representatives, ranging from 3 (two senators and one representative) in the smallest states to 55 in California, the largest. Wyoming, the least populous state, has 3 electors for roughly 574,000 citizens (1 to 191,000) while California has 55 electors for 39,770,000 (1 to 723,000). As a result, it's theoretically possible to win a presidential election by winning only 23.1 percent of the popular vote.[18] Trump won in 2016 with 46.1 percent of the popular vote as compared to 48.2 percent for Clinton, in part because sparsely populated—and electorally overrepresented—states like Wyoming tend to support Republican candidates.

In the wake of the 2016 election, California senator Barbara Boxer introduced legislation that would eliminate the Electoral College, saying, "This is the only office in the land where you can get more votes and still lose the presidency. The Electoral College is an outdated, undemocratic system that does not reflect our modern society, and it needs to change immediately."[19] Boxer knew her bill would not succeed—it was a plea for attention to the problem—as abolishing the Electoral College requires amending the Constitution, a process that the document's authors intentionally made difficult.

Perhaps the most likely method for hacking the Electoral College comes from a computer science professor who transformed the world of gambling. Dr. John Koza is known in computer science circles for his work on genetic algorithms, systems that can optimize their performance by creating slightly mutated "children" and holding competitions between them to see which perform a task most efficiently. But before applying natural selection to computer programming, Koza founded and ran a company called Scientific Games that produced huge print runs of randomized game cards. Originally used by supermarkets to give customers a fun, variable reward, Koza convinced the State of Massachusetts to try a scratch-off lottery ticket that allowed players to win instantly instead of waiting for a weekly drawing. These "instant win" tickets were an instant hit, selling $2.7 million in the first week and quickly making Koza rich.[20]

Since 2006 Koza has dedicated a significant fraction of his wealth to popularizing an end run around the Electoral College called the National Popular Vote Interstate Compact. The idea is simple: states that sign on to the compact agree to pledge their electors to the winner of the total popular vote in the presidential election. The compact has a trigger clause, which means it doesn't come into effect until states with a combination of 270 electoral votes—enough to win a presidential election—sign on to it. Thus far, ten states and the District of Columbia, representing 165 combined electoral votes, are on board. But finding the next 105 electors will be a challenge, as the states that have signed on are all safe Democratic strongholds, and no Republican or battleground states have agreed yet.

If enough states sign on to the compact, they would commit their electors together and control the outcome of the election, irrespective of any other state's voting outcome. The result of such an election would almost certainly be appealed to the Supreme Court. Koza's proposal is a compact on purpose: a binding contract between states that state governments use to coordinate behavior on issues like cross-border pollution. Koza learned about compacts from the lottery business; an interstate compact underlies Powerball, the massive multistate lottery drawing. But the Constitution gives Congress some authority over interstate compacts that impact the federal government, and passing the Popular Vote compact would inevitably lead to a showdown in court between state and federal powers.[21]

There's a cleaner solution to the problem of the Electoral College than Koza's end run, but it's much less likely to come about and is vastly more radical, despite being entirely within the original intent of the Constitution. The inequities of the Electoral College reflect the fact that Americans are not equally represented in Congress. Each of fifty states has two senators and a set of representatives proportional to its population, but the nature of that proportionality is a complicated beast.

George Washington, the general who led the American rebellion against Britain and become the first US president, was notably reluctant to weigh in on the drafting of the Constitution. One issue where he expressed an opinion was the ratio between citizens and representatives, opining that one representative for thirty thousand citizens was a more appropriate apportionment than one for forty thousand.[22] Throughout the nineteenth century, Congress was reapportioned following the decennial census, which determined the population of each state and expanded the House of Representatives to deliberate on behalf of their growing populations.

This system came to a halt in 1920, when Congress failed to reapportion seats in the wake of the census. Between 1910 and 1920, populations had shifted significantly from rural to urban areas. This shift had implications for the pressing political issue of the day—Prohibition—as urban populations generally favored keeping alcohol legal, while rural populations did not. Prohibition advocates refused to honor the new population figures, fearing that they'd lose the ability to enforce the recently passed Eighteenth Amendment, which prohibited the sale of alcohol.[23] In 1911 the size of the House of Representatives was fixed at 435 members as a result of the reapportionment after the 1910 census, and except for a brief period after Alaska and Hawaii joined the union in the late 1950s, it has barely changed since.

A current member of the House of Representatives represents roughly 750,000 people, vastly more than Washington had prescribed and more than three times the ratio when the limit of 435 members was implemented. In other developed countries, the population represented by a member of the lower house is far smaller: 97,000 to 1 in Britain, 114,000 to 1 in France, 135,000 to 1 in Germany, and 147,000 to 1 in Australia.[24]

If we reapportioned Congress based on 1911 ratios, the United States would have 1,509 representatives. If we got more radical and returned to George Washington's ratio, it would have almost 11,000. In either case, Congress would need to operate in a very different fashion. The Capitol doesn't have enough room for offices for 11,000 representatives, or even 1,500. Congress might need to become a virtual organization, meeting and debating via the Internet, perhaps, with representatives spending more time in their communities than in Washington. In the process, both lobbying and campaign financing, two of the factors most often identified as flaws in American representative democracy, would likely be transformed. Representatives scattered around the country are harder to lobby than those that attend the same cocktail parties in the same city, and buying the legislative loyalty of thousands of representatives through campaign contributions might prove economically infeasible even for wealthy corporations. And since candidates running for seats in Congress would have to reach tens of thousands of voters, rather than nearly a million, campaigns might come to rely less on expensive television advertising and more on face-to-face campaigning.

At 1911 ratios, Wyoming would have 4 electoral votes, while California would have 186 (contrasting to 3 to 55 today). In an enlarged House, Democrats would likely have an advantage, as states with large urban populations—which generally vote Democratic—are currently underrepresented. Michael G. Neubauer and Joel Zeitlin, political scientists at California State University, Northridge, have demonstrated that had the House of Representatives been larger than 597 members in 2000, Al Gore would have beaten George W. Bush.[25] Due to the size of Congress, states with small populations have more representatives per capita than large states—remember the disparity between Wyoming's 3 electoral votes and California's 55. As long as less populated states lean the same way politically, those states can sway elections if the size of the House of Representatives is small. Increase the House size, and the effect goes away. This idea, called the House Size Effect, suggests that American elections are a function not only of popular will but also of the size of the House of Representatives,[26] a consequence that feels somewhat undemocratic.

Congress could change its size on its own, by overturning the laws that enshrined 435 as the number of representatives. It wouldn't require a constitutional amendment, just a majority in both houses. But it's unlikely to happen, because it would utterly transform how Congress works, weakening the powers of every individual representative. Oddly, though such a change would almost certainly benefit Democrats, the two most prominent proponents of movements to expand the size of Congress are Republicans, Bruce Bartlett who worked for the Reagan and George H. W. Bush administrations, and the conservative columnist George Will.[27]

The point is not that a much larger House of Representatives would reduce mistrust in America's least-trusted institution, though it certainly might. The point is that institutionalists can advocate for radical change without overthrowing existing institutions. Sometimes enforcing laws as originally written would be enough to thoroughly transform an institution.

The idea that George Washington, were he alive today, might prefer a "Big House" of ten thousand representatives is a clue: debates over the intent of rules that govern our institutions are a significant challenge to radical institutionalism. Politicians have justified dramatic rule changes by claiming that they maintain the intent of long-dead founders. *Citizens United*, the Supreme Court decision that supported the right of individuals and corporations to pour nearly unlimited funds into political campaigns, is based on an "originalist" interpretation of the Constitution that understands money as speech. Much of what seems so dysfunctional about current institutions in fact emerges from incremental institutionalist changes.

Institutionalist approaches to social change, radical and otherwise, require a balance between what's accomplishable now and the animating power of a larger vision. Proposals to expand the House of Representatives or eliminate the Electoral College are animated by a vision of bringing the United States closer to a "pure" democracy, where majority will equals electoral victory. The argument to leave these systems unchanged—and there is a legitimate argument—is animated by the desire to protect the interests of people in small, rural states so their perspectives aren't erased. When we see attempts to interpret existing rules and to modify them to meet contemporary needs, we must always see the animating vision and values as well. Rules, like all systems, have values and agendas embedded within them.

In India, Jignesh Mevani's short-term goal is to use his position as a legislator to provide services to the poor and increase the visibility of Dalit activism. But his animating vision is ambitious: the annihilation of caste, an idea put forward by Babasaheb Ambedkar in his 1936 book of that name. "This isn't a victory we win legislatively," Mevani explains. "It comes when Dalits and so-called 'high caste' Hindus marry and have kids. It comes from progressive Hindus who are willing to ignore three thousand years of history that have separated us. At some point, this whole absurd system becomes unsupportable." In other words, his position within the Gujarat legislative assembly allows him to use law as a lever to make change, but his longer struggle will require a massive societal shift in norms.

When we resolve to change an institution from the inside, we face a singular danger: despite our best efforts, we can end up supporting systems that are fundamentally flawed and broken, keeping them standing longer than they might without our assistance.

In 2010 Noah Kunin joined the US government, working for the Consumer Financial Protection Bureau before signing on as infrastructure director for 18F, the digital services agency that Jen Pahlka helped establish within the General Services Administration. When Donald Trump won the 2016 election, Kunin published a brief blogpost affirming his decision to remain at 18F: "My oath to this country was not to a particular office, or person, and certainly not to a political party. It was to the Constitution and to the people."[28]

Less than a year later, Kunin published another post, this time explaining why he decided to leave 18F. He referenced Pahlka's idea of running into the burning building, explaining that he'd often used the same metaphor to explain his decisions: "This time is different. The people with the matches are inside the house. The house is not burning down (this time) because it was struck by lightning, or the wiring was shoddy. It's now on fire because the people in charge want to burn it down."[29]

Chapter 6

COUNTER-DEMOCRACY AND CITIZEN MONITORING

IN 1966 IN OAKLAND, CALIFORNIA, BOBBY SEALE AND HUEY
Newton began policing the police.

Oakland's police department was notorious for harassing
Black motorists, using unnecessary violence to enforce the law.
Half of Oakland's population was Black or Latinx, and Seale and
Newton collected five thousand signatures from those communities, demanding that the Oakland City Council establish a police
review board to investigate reports of brutality against Black and
brown citizens. The council ignored their demand.[1]

Seale and Newton organized groups of young men to follow
the police as they conducted traffic stops. The men dressed in
leather jackets, sunglasses, and black berets—a uniform designed
to be affordable. Stanley Nelson, who produced the documentary
Black Panthers: Vanguard of the Revolution, explained: "Every
young Black man has a black leather jacket or can get one or can
borrow one if they can't buy one."[2] The Panthers were armed.
California law permitted open carry of handguns, and the Panthers exercised their rights: when police stopped a motorist, the
Panthers would stop as well and observe the interaction, guns in
hand, from about twenty feet away.

The Oakland police found this tactic sufficiently intimidating that Republican assemblyman Don Mulford introduced a bill that would ban the open carry of firearms. Thirty Panthers, armed with pistols and shotguns, responded by "occupying" the California state house. Republican governor Ronald Reagan hastened to sign Mulford's bill, commenting that he saw "no reason why on the street today a citizen should be carrying loaded weapons."[3]

While the police patrols were short-lived, they helped build the Black Panthers into a national movement and called attention to the Panthers' broader ambitions, a ten-point platform that sought economic and social justice for Black people.[4] The patrols also demonstrated that counter-democracy—taking civic action by monitoring existing institutions and holding them responsible— is a powerful strategy for social change. The Panther patrols forced a conversation about a phenomenon—police brutality— that was widely known but not widely discussed. By adopting the language of an institution—"policing" the police through "patrols"—the Panthers recovered the idea that the police are an institution that answers to the people. We have a right to review and document their work.

The performative, symbolic nature of the Panthers protest is part of what gave it power, notes Nikhil Pal Singh in *The Black Panther Party (Reconsidered)*: "The 'shadow of the gun,' moreover, was far more important for the Panthers than real guns could ever be."[5] Seale and Newton knew they couldn't reverse America's endemic racism with a handful of revolutionaries and a small cache of weapons. But the highly visible act of holding police accountable was an action with lasting symbolic weight.

Quis custodiet ipsos custodes? The 2014 murder of Eric Garner by Staten Island police brought the ongoing problem of police violence against unarmed people of color back to the forefront of American consciousness and reminded people of the importance of watching the watchers. We know what happened to Garner only because his friend Ramsey Orta recorded the arrest and sub-

sequent death on his cellphone as Officer Daniel Pantaleo held
Garner in a proscribed chokehold.

Much as the Panthers recognized that many people owned or
could buy a leather jacket, today's monitors of power leverage
ubiquitous cellphones more often than guns. In 2015 in North
Charleston, South Carolina, police stopped Walter Scott for a
broken taillight. The arresting officer tased him and, when Scott
fled, shot him in the back five times. Michael Slager, the officer
who shot Scott, was sentenced to twenty years in prison based
on video footage recorded by Feidin Santana, a young immigrant
from the Dominican Republic who heard taser fire and began
filming what became a murder.[6]

Monitoring the abuse of power may be easier today because of
mobile phones, but it is seldom safe. Walter Scott's family hailed
Santana as a hero, and Black Lives Matter activists celebrated
him, but supporters of Officer Slager sent him death threats, so
he returned to the Dominican Republic.[7] Ramsey Orta, who
had filmed Garner's death, was arrested on unrelated drug and
domestic violence charges and jailed for four years. He reports
being abused and kept in solitary confinement in prison in retaliation for filming Garner's death.[8]

Before his incarceration, Orta promoted an organization,
Copwatch, that since 1990 has helped communities monitor
local policing. Copwatch distributes guides and runs trainings,
explaining citizens' rights under US law to record police activity
on public property and clarifying the lines between documenting police activity and interfering with arrests. A guide, developed by Copwatch and the human rights organization Witness,
for Water Protectors, people seeking to block the Dakota Access
oil pipeline, offers legal advice and strategies for effective documentation: "Documenting arrests is crucial because it's the point
when police make physical contact with Water Protectors. It is
also often when false charges are made against activists, such as
assaulting an officer or resisting arrest."[9]

The language used by Copwatch organizers can be rough and confrontational—their websites and Facebook groups sometimes use the term *pigs* to refer to police officers. Certain activists involved with the organization have no trust for the police and heckle officers, while others work more closely with authorities, sharing footage with police internal affairs divisions in hopes of taking abusive officers off the streets.[10] The movement is chaotic and many-headed and can be confusing to understand. It is also, according to the French political theorist Pierre Rosanvallon, a critical ingredient in contemporary democracy.

Rosanvallon is one of France's most respected political theorists and historians, whose scholarship engages with the past and present of French democracy. One distinctive aspect of his work is his insistence that understanding democracy involves understanding not only institutions like parliaments and presidents but also people outside the system who watch, influence, and pressure those in power. He calls this idea *contra-démocratie* but is careful to explain that these forces buttress democratic institutions, strengthening them by pushing against them rather than seeking to topple them.

Rosanvallon traces the roots of counter-democracy back to the French Revolution, when citizens, after achieving the end of the monarchy, held their new government accountable through oversight (surveillance) of elected officials, mobilization to protest poor decisions, and sitting in judgment over officials accused of corruption or other crimes. He finds antecedents for these tendencies even further back, in Athenian juries and other ancient institutions. While counter-democracy is not always as clearly described and documented as a system like voting, Rosanvallon sees it evolving in parallel, as a necessary component to the systems we understand as core to democracies. Indeed, it's a known bug of democratic systems, "the inability of electoral/representative politics to keep its promises [that has] led to the development of indirect forms of democracy."[11]

Once we understand that counter-democratic structures are part of a healthy democracy, Rosanvallon believes we will conceive of democracy not as a political system in decline but as one that is changing its form. The mistrust many feel for democratic institutions can be seen as greater "social attentiveness," fuel for engagement in efforts to hold elected and bureaucratic powers responsible. This "ethos of democratic oversight" animates not only individual activists but also nonprofit organizations and monitors within the government itself, like the Government Accountability Office, which was founded as a nonpartisan monitor of federal spending,[12] or the inspector general corps, established to oversee corruption within the executive branch in the wake of Watergate.[13]

The Italian designer and programmer Luigi Reggi was working for the European Union when he discovered the power of counter-democratic practice. He had spent over a year building a website that allowed citizens to see precisely how much money their community had received in EU funds and how it had been spent. While his site won design awards, unfortunately, virtually no one used it. So Reggi tried a different model: he invited friends to audit the projects the European Union had funded, running Monithons—hackathons for monitoring public works projects like senior centers and new transportation projects by visiting them and documenting what had worked and what had failed.

Citizens who weren't interested in reading about how EU funds were spent were excited by the possibility of discovering corruption and malfeasance. Their "social attentiveness" was activated not by the chance to learn passively but by the chance to evaluate using a method that's closer to confrontation. Monithons offer citizens the possibility of uncovering a scandal, something that benefits society less than it lines the pockets of those involved. But many Monithon participants discovered that the projects they examined had in fact been carefully conceived and were well carried out; as they began to understand the challenges and constraints, including budgeting, involved in public works projects, their skepticism eased.

Reggi discovered a truth inherent in a high-mistrust world: people who are alienated from democratic institutions will often find a home in counter-democracy, keeping democratic institutions honest, accountable, and in check. But Monithon also suggests that counter-democratic projects can quickly become institutions of their own. Most participants in Monithons today are high school students, who complete the project for civics classes, beginning in the classroom and ending in field trips to evaluate local projects and discuss the outcomes. Reggi had initially hoped to help interested adults better understand how EU funds work—instead, he's helped redesign Italian civics education.[14]

Contemporary technology is custom-made for counter-democracy. The smartphone, with its ability to capture and transmit images, is a perfect tool not only for documenting police violence but also for *sousveillance,* the practice of watching powerful institutions from a ground-up perspective.

Dr. Steve Mann coined the term *sousveillance* more than thirty-five years ago as a way of explaining his practice of wearing a head-mounted camera and recording everything he saw, a practice now called life-logging. Security guards and other authority figures often objected to him entering buildings, demanding to know if he was recording. Mann noted that these buildings almost invariably had security cameras, which meant that he was being subjected to surveillance—why couldn't he respond with recordings of his own: sousveillance? Anticipating a world where cameras were omnipresent, trained by authorities on people, and vice versa, sousveillance helps explain the dynamic at play when citizens begin monitoring those who traditionally monitor them: anger, followed by a recognition that power dynamics have shifted, often followed by a change in behavior.[15]

Five years ago I found myself in Brazil, explaining Dr. Mann's work to a group of community activists, high school students, and at least one former drug dealer, standing on a wire-fence-enclosed basketball court in the favela of Santa Lúcia. Located on a steep hillside in Belo Horizonte, Brazil's sixth-largest city, Santa Lúcia is a pocket of intense poverty between two wealthy neighborhoods. I'd come with my students from the MIT Media Lab to test a prototype system we'd built called Promise Tracker that invited members of a community to document neighborhood problems using mobile phones. Emilie Reiser from our team had built an app that let people take photos and GPS readings and combine the two into annotated, illustrated maps that community leaders could show to local government officials, documenting and analyzing what was wrong with local infrastructure.

I assumed it would take a while to sell the community on the power of sousveillance as a tool for social change, but most of the audience immediately embraced the project. Rejecting the cheap phones we'd brought in for them from the United States, they pulled out Android phones and loaded our app onto them. What surprised me even more was the issues they wanted to monitor. The Santa Lúcians I worked with chose *corrimãos*—handrails—a topic that made sense only when we started walking through the neighborhood.

A single traffic-snarled road snakes through Santa Lúcia—almost all travel and commerce in the favela takes place on steep stairways that run through the neighborhood. As we took photos and mapped locations of these stairways, we noticed that only those that connected Santa Lúcia with its wealthier neighbors had railings. The deeper we got into Santa Lúcia, the more broken and dangerous the stairways became. As we worked, locals who'd stopped to ask what we were doing shared stories. An old man pointed up a stairway that climbed thirty meters: "I helped build that fifty years ago. And last year, I fell down it. I wish I could tell my younger self that we needed a railing for the old people."

After our group developed and tested Promise Tracker, we handed it over to a committed team of Brazilian activists and academics. Working in nine states around Brazil, they've discovered that some of the tool's most passionate users are, again, high school students. After discovering it in workshops about addressing local environmental issues, they bring it into the classroom to document problems ranging from unreliable Internet access to bathrooms without toilet paper. The most widespread deployment of the Promise Tracker app monitors a complaint that's nearly universal: the poor quality of school lunches. Since 2010, Brazil has included a right to food in its constitution, which guarantees students at least one nutritious meal a day, sourced in part from local farmers.[16] Students documented it when lunch wasn't provided, or when it fell short of nutritional guidelines.

Watching from afar, we wondered whether students would be able to turn the data they'd collected into action, or whether local authorities would brush them aside. But the students have been embraced by local public prosecutors, who've started using the reports to identify and diagnose problems with the school food system. Sometimes the problems signal corruption, where someone has stolen food meant for students and sold it. Far more often, the problems have to do with failing infrastructure: the meat is delivered on Monday, but the school has no refrigeration, so there's no meat for students by Wednesday. In Rosanvallon's spirit of counter-democracy, critical surveillance by the students is improving existing institutions.

Promise Tracker works in large part because it allows people to identify the issue they want to pay attention to. Michael Schudson, the journalism scholar who reminds us that the shape of citizenship in America has changed significantly over the years, proposes that "monitorial citizenship" is a dominant form of citizenship in the modern age. Instead of expecting citizens to be interested in every aspect of politics or civics, Schudson argues, it's more reasonable to ask them to monitor issues they're concerned with and knowledgeable about. Monitorial citizens are neither disengaged nor uninterested, but they may not take action unless they feel they are directly affected by an issue. Schudson distinguishes monitorial citizenship from "informed citizenship," the model he sees as dominating contemporary theories about civics, in which ideal citizens are broadly knowledgeable about civic issues, informed about current developments in the news, and capable of weighing in on a wide range of topics.[17]

For Schudson, the Informed Citizen model—advanced by the American progressive reformers of the early 1900s—is too optimistic about citizen capabilities and expects far too much from people who have full and busy lives. By contrast, the Brazilian students' engagement with school lunches exemplifies citizen monitoring, a productive selfishness that increases an individual's sense of efficacy. Citizen monitoring also has the advantage of pre-existing expertise. It requires some work for the average voter to become knowledgeable about agricultural policy, for instance, but most high school students have a deep, intuitive understanding of how school lunches succeed and fail. At its best, citizen monitoring leverages knowledge that citizens already have about an issue, encourages them to learn about the deeper causes, and proposes original solutions.

On March 11, 2011, a massive earthquake off the Pacific coast of Japan led to a catastrophic tsunami that sent waves of up to forty meters high as far as ten kilometers inland. The earthquake and tsunami killed over fifteen thousand people and displaced hundreds of thousands more. One of the numerous crises that the Japanese government faced was the level-seven meltdown of three nuclear reactors at the Fukushima Daiichi nuclear power plant. The only other level-seven meltdown in history was the catastrophic accident in 1986 in Chernobyl. As the Japanese government mobilized to react, many citizens in Tokyo, 150 miles away, began to worry about radiation contamination from airborne particles.

A group of hackers with ties to Japan, including the legendary programmer Ray Ozzie (creator of Lotus Notes and former chief technical officer at Microsoft), began working to create an affordable mobile Geiger counter that could store time and location information as well as radiation readings. The instrument the team built was stored in a bento box, a waterproof box used to carry lunches to work or school, and the device became known as the bGeigie.[18]

The hackathon project became the nonprofit organization Safecast, which designs and builds high-quality instruments for environmental monitoring, deploys instruments to people affected, and communicates its findings to governments and the general public. With more than 40 million readings submitted by thousands of volunteers over seven years, Safecast is one of the largest citizen science projects in history. It maintains a public map of radiation readings that cover Japan thoroughly, and the network is starting to provide robust coverage in parts of Europe. In the process, the Safecast core team have become deeply knowledgeable about radiation monitoring and effects, meeting regularly with the Japanese government to advise it on recovery from Fukushima and on communication with the public around radiation and other environmental health indicators.

Members of the Safecast team were drawn into radiation monitoring because they were concerned about their families and their health in the wake of Fukushima, much as the people involved with Copwatch tend to be young people who have lived with the effects of overpolicing. And much as the activists involved with Copwatch have become deeply knowledgeable about their rights to document the police, and about the circumstances where police-citizen interactions can go off the rails, Safecast's team have become expert on the differences between alpha, beta, and gamma radiation. This particular form of citizenship, at the intersection between expertise and engaged knowledge, is very different from traditional informed citizenship. The informed citizen can become sufficiently knowledgeable about a topic to have an opinion by reading the newspaper and staying engaged in her community. But citizen monitors become experts on the issues they study, capable of understanding them to a level of detail that's unreasonable to expect from average citizens, and they are often capable of mobilizing fellow citizens to the cause.

But knowledge of an issue and of the communities it affects isn't always sufficient to be an effective citizen monitor. Sometimes you need to be an expert.

In 1986 an eighteen-year-old dry cleaning clerk, Ronda Morrison, was murdered in Monroeville, Alabama. Walter McMillian, a Black logger and small businessman with no felony record, was accused of the murder, despite the fact that at the time the crime was committed, dozens of witnesses attest that he was at a church fish fry. While there was no physical evidence tying McMillian to the murder, the jury chose to ignore the evidence of the eyewitnesses who provided alibis for McMillian and sentenced him to life in prison. The judge, Robert E. Lee Key, Jr., used a uniquely Alabamian procedure—the judge override—to convert McMillian's life sentence to a death sentence.

The override caught the attention of Bryan Stevenson, a twenty-eight-year-old Black lawyer who had recently graduated from Harvard Law School and the Kennedy School of Government. Stevenson visited McMillian on death row and brought an appeal to the Alabama Court of Criminal Appeals, offering new evidence including the fact that key witnesses against McMillian recanted their testimony and admitted to having been paid to give false testimony. The Alabama Court of Appeals turned down Stevenson four times.[19]

Realizing that he was unlikely to find justice within the Alabama court system, Stevenson complemented his lawyering with storytelling. McMillian's home town, Monroeville, was the hometown of Harper Lee and the likely setting for *To Kill a Mockingbird,* the famous novel in which a Black man is falsely accused of raping a white woman. Pointing to the irony that a town that claimed to celebrate Lee's moving book was now railroading an innocent Black man to execution, Stevenson brought the story to the national television newsmagazine *60 Minutes*. After the *60 Minutes* piece aired, Stevenson took the case to appeal for the fifth time, and after six years on death row, McMillian was exonerated.

His experience with McMillian led Stevenson to form the Equal Justice Initiative (EJI), a remarkable nonprofit organization that provides representation to poor and indigent defendants, particularly those facing prosecution for capital crimes. While EJI has been successful in challenging the worst excesses of the criminal justice system, reversing decisions or gaining release of more than 125 prisoners wrongly sentenced to death, Stevenson's advocacy has accomplished structural changes as well. Starting in 2006, EJI led a litigation campaign that challenged the practice of sentencing people to life without parole for crimes they committed as minors. Two Supreme Court decisions in 2012—*Miller v. Alabama* and *Jackson v. Hobbs*—established that mandatory life without parole sentences for minors were unconstitutional, forcing twenty-nine states to change their laws.[20]

In his use of the court system to seek sentencing reform, Stevenson looks like a radical institutionalist, using the rules of the system to evolve and correct it over time. But a recent project suggests EJI has a focus on counter-democracy. In 2018 it opened the National Memorial for Peace and Justice, a memorial to 4,400 Americans killed extrajudicially between the end of the Civil War and World War II, a period Stevenson refers to as an "era of racial terrorism." Visitors entering the monument pass between a series of massive metal blocks. As they follow a ramp leading down into the museum, they realize that the blocks are suspended, hanging above the ground, roughly human-sized, one for each of the men, women, and children executed during a period of history when the murder of Black Americans was not only accepted but something families took their children to watch, like a parade or a picnic.

Stevenson seeks to exonerate the wrongly convicted, yes, but his wider goal is to expose and transform the intricate system of biases and injustices that stem from one of America's original sins: slavery. The lynching memorial stands as a counterpoint to the history of the civil rights movement in America, often taught as an example of how a society could admit its failings and find a new way. The steel blocks hanging like Black bodies in trees remind us that a society that tortured and killed people does not shed the legacy of white supremacy overnight. It is no accident, Stevenson reminds us, that one of three Black male babies born today will end up in jail or prison. It is the logical outcome of a system that started with slavery and has still failed to address the consequences of this original sin.

Stevenson's work with EJI uses law as a lever for change, relying on litigation to challenge systemic injustices. But EJI also focuses on norms-based change, recognizing that we have broken laws because we've failed to deal with some of the most horrific aspects of our collective past. While Copwatch monitors and challenges individual acts of police brutality, EJI challenges the complex of laws, beliefs, and attitudes that makes such abuse possible. Like many counter-democratic organizations, EJI relies on naming and shaming—Rosanvallon would recognize its work as "denunciation"—action critical to restoring trust in institutions by calling out and forcing the removal of bad actors. As a result, EJI is not only a legal organization but also a media one. Rosanvallon notes that activist organizations frequently become media organizations when they begin exposing and denouncing fundamental social wrongs: "the media are the routine functional form of democratic oversight, while militant civil society groups are the activist form. The two are thus functionally complementary. This complementarity is the basis for the well known slogan, 'Don't hate the media—become the media!' "[21]

For Americans, the most familiar counter-democratic institution is the press, sometimes elevated to a "fourth estate" or
"fourth branch" of government, signifying an equivalency of
power with the legislative, judicial, and executive branches. The
press is often able to force examination of issues that the government would prefer not to address. In April 2018, when the Trump
administration implemented a "zero-tolerance" immigration
policy, sharply constraining avenues to asylum and imprisoning
anyone who entered the country without proper paperwork, the
shocking consequence was detention camps for children. Courts
had previously decided that US authorities could not incarcerate
children for a parent's alleged immigration crimes. But under
the zero-tolerance immigration policy, authorities also could
not release these children to stay with family members or return
them home. Instead, children were removed from their parents
and sent to government-run camps while their parents were pro-
cessed or deported.

Zero-tolerance was meant to be a victory for Trump's most
earnest supporters, many of whom favored strong restrictions
on immigration. But investigative journalists, led by Spanish-
language media outlets like Univision, quickly revealed that
the children were being held under horrific conditions. While a
government spokesman described the conditions "like summer
camp,"[22] photos of children being held in chain-link fence cages
quickly countered that narrative. Subsequent stories revealed that
children were being sexually assaulted while in custody and that
some were being tranquilized with powerful psychiatric medi-
cines. The Trump administration was forced to back away from
the policy of family separation after a public outcry and a ruling
from a federal court in California.[23]

Rosanvallon sees the press as a way of organizing public opinion and creating power that can challenge the power expressed
by the voting booth: "Thus the [elected] deputy and the journalist are potential rivals." Citing dialogues contemporaneous with

the French revolution, Rosanvallon reminds us of a tension that's very much alive today: questions of the democratic legitimacy of the press and other counter-democratic institutions.

While Donald Trump's criticisms of the press have more to do with his thin skin and his desire to create a unified enemy than with legitimate critiques, there is reason to question the power of the press. Elections grant legitimacy to representatives—the will of the people put them in power, and our vigilance and denunciation can remove them from power if appropriate. Who legitimates the power of counter-democratic institutions?

Rosanvallon offers three paths toward legitimacy, both for democratic and for counter-democratic institutions. First, an institution is legitimate if it enjoys majority support. This reads as an extension of electoral democracy: if the majority of people voted for a candidate, she should hold office; if a similar majority believe in a free and independent press, it should survive. Legitimacy can also derive from impartiality: institutions like the judiciary are supposed to be immune to the vicissitudes of politics and to gain legitimacy by treating all those in society alike. Finally, institutions—democratic or counter-democratic—are legitimate if they reflect a widely held value or aspiration.

The Equal Justice Initiative likely doesn't have the support of the majority of Alabamians, given their tendency to continue electing judges who disproportionately incarcerate Black Americans. (Judge Key, who sentenced McMillian to death, was reelected to his seat every six years over three decades on the bench.) EJI also is far from an impartial institution. It advocates particularly for the indigent, the disadvantaged, and people of color. Its legitimacy comes from its values and its aspirations to create a justice system that works for all Americans.

Questions of legitimacy are increasingly challenging for the American press. Only 24 percent of Americans express strong or moderate trust in newspapers, and even fewer trust broadcast television. Recently, a majority of Republicans surveyed agreed with President Trump's characterization of the media as the "enemy of the people,"[24] a chilling phrase that dates to the Terror, Robespierre's eighteenth-century purge of French counterrevolutionaries. While American media have defended the idea of impartiality with a vigor that's disconcerting to Europeans—who are used to news organizations having an identifiable political slant—there's little or no consensus on what US news organizations could be considered impartial. (A recent study asked Americans to identify an impartial news organization. Some identified *The New York Times* or CNN, both frequent targets of the president, who sees their coverage as biased against him. The largest plurality identified Fox News, an outlet those on the left see as little better than pro-government propaganda. The majority of those surveyed could not identify an impartial organization.)[25] Press legitimacy in America rests on the value our democracy has placed on the press as an independent monitor of power. If that norm shifts as a result of attacks by the president and his party, it may fatally undermine the legitimacy of the press as a counterdemocratic force.

If counter-democratic forces face one set of problems defending their legitimacy, another set of problems arise from their position outside traditional forms of institutional power. While traditional institutions are supported by clear revenue models—taxation for government, profit making for corporations—counterdemocratic institutions often depend on volunteer efforts and individual largesse (in the form of donations) for their survival. Until recently, US newspapers were a powerful profit-making institution that dominated most local advertising markets. With a shift from "print dollars to digital dimes," many newsgathering organizations now find themselves struggling for their continued fiscal viability. This sets up a challenging asymmetry of power: news organizations that are fiscally fragile may be the chief force checking powerful, well-funded institutions. In this sense, the press may be becoming like other counter-democratic institutions, gaining its legitimacy ultimately from the fact that it is able to marshal funding and volunteer effort toward the work of questioning and countering power. Organizations like Copwatch and Safecast take lessons from the Black Panthers and other militant civil society groups, using the asymmetric nature of their struggle as a source of legitimacy and power.

This asymmetric power is at its strongest when institutions are open and willing to change. Not every institution is susceptible to counterpressure—some cannot be effectively named and shamed. Institutions that are willing to change often end up seeing counter-democracy advocates much as Rosanvallon sees them: buttressing institutions and making them stronger in the long run. Those that resist counter-democracy are often the most brittle and subject to disruption—consider the Catholic Church's initial refusal to address sexual abuse allegations, and the losses in membership and prestige it has since suffered.

The most fundamental limits to counter-democracy as a strategy for effective citizenship are questions of neither legitimacy nor sustainability. Because counter-democracy focuses on existing institutions—and often a single institution—it can be only as powerful and effective as those existing organizations. Counter-democracy can help transform institutions, allowing them to more fully realize their potential. But while removing racial bias from the US justice system would be a profound achievement, a reformed judicial system won't address other areas of structural racism in American life: economic disparity, educational inequities, unequal distributions of property and capital. Counter-democracy and monitorial citizenship can give us stronger, more accountable institutions. But what can it do with institutions that may have outlived their usefulness?

Chapter 7

PRODUCTIVE DISRUPTION

TAXIS DON'T GET A LOT OF LOVE.

In many cities around the world, taxi driving is a dangerous and low-paid profession, a job often held by recent immigrants. In the United States, the cultural image of taxis is shaped
by films like *Taxi Driver,* in which an unstable Vietnam veteran
who drives a taxi descends into vigilantism, and *Taxi,* a sitcom
in which a range of down-on-their luck characters drive taxis
because they can't find other work. American taxi drivers are
twenty times as likely to be murdered on the job as the average
worker—and taxi and limousine drivers die via homicide more
than twice as often as police officers.[1]

In London, taxi driving is an honored and carefully regulated
profession—cabbies must pass a legendarily difficult test on London geography called "The Knowledge." But London taxis also
suffer under the pressure of market forces. Their high cost per
ride has led to the rise of minicabs. This less expensive option,
piloted by drivers who have had less rigorous training and have
less understanding of the city they navigate, threatens to undermine the existing regime.

It's hard to find many defenders of the current American taxi
system. Arguing against the spread of ride-sharing services like

Uber, the law professor and civic technologist Susan Crawford doesn't bother arguing that the current taxi system is worth saving. She agrees that "taxis aren't viewed as expressions of the public value of clean, safe, city-validated, superior, inexpensive transport for everyone involved—and as a vehicle for good jobs." But she hopes that we could imagine a good, safe, affordable taxi system provided by someone other than a private company.[2]

Today's taxis aren't an especially good deal either for riders or for drivers. Many cities provide a limited set of taxi licenses, which tends to concentrate power in the hands of "medallion holders," who make money renting that limited monopoly out to drivers. Conservatives and libertarians don't like taxis because they're a tightly controlled, government-regulated system with an artificial monopoly on the market. Progressives aren't big taxi fans because they're far from the affordable, accessible, environmentally sound models of public transportation they advocate for.

In other words, taxis are an institution—a system of interchangeable parts that we interact with as an entity rather than as a set of individuals—ripe for disruption.

When Uber was founded in 2009, it aimed to reduce the cost of renting luxury cars with drivers, the chauffeured "black cars" that serve a higher-cost part of the on-demand transportation market than taxis fill. By 2014, Uber's controversial founder and then CEO, Travis Kalanick, announced, "We didn't realize it, but we're in this political campaign, and the candidate is Uber, and the opponent is an a—hole named taxi." As Uber decided to challenge the taxi industry as well as car services, his rhetoric grew blunt: "We have to bring out the truth about how dark and how dangerous and evil the taxi side of things is."[3]

As Uber grew from disrupting black cars to disrupting taxis and delivery services—promising ultimately to disrupt public transportation as a whole—its business model has emerged as a new paradigm. In the 1990s and early 2000s, technology firms in Silicon Valley focused on putting offline information online, from scholarly papers to product catalogs, an innovation that made companies like Amazon possible. In the next wave, social media invited everyone to become a content creator, and advertisers mined the information we shared to sell ever more refined ways to target us. The current wave of innovation centers on "disrupting" existing offline businesses, and Uber and Airbnb, which began challenging the vacation rental and hotel business in 2008, are the multibillion-dollar companies seen as the pioneers in the field.

The premise of disruption is that the world is filled with dysfunctional systems that can be replaced with ones that work vastly better for customers and, perhaps, for workers. Until COVID-19 replaced venture-capital-backed "disruption" with a very real disruption of existing systems, Silicon Valley was pursuing the Uberization of everything. Producthunt, a service that tracks start-up companies, has a category of "on-demand" services called Uber for X, including Lugg ("it's like Uber for movers"), Wag! ("Uber for dog walking"), Minibar ("Uber for alcohol"), and Washio ("Uber for laundry and dry cleaning").[4] Uber and Airbnb were two of the most valuable "unicorn" companies globally (privately held technology companies valued at more than $1 billion), and fifteen other on-demand companies, disrupting everything from jet plane rental to grocery stores, have attracted ten-figure valuations before going public.[5] Very few of them actually make money, and the crash of WeWork, which sought to disrupt office rental, may have soured some investors on the category. But venture capitalists, who provide much of the money to keep these businesses running at a loss, see these disruptive businesses as potentially dominant players in their sector—Airbnb's valuation of $38 billion makes more sense when you imagine it can dominate the hotel space, a sector that earns $200 billion a year, globally.[6] (At least it did, before the idea of letting a stranger sleep in your house seemed like a great way to catch the novel coronavirus. Or when travel was something people did for work and for fun.)

There's a dark side to disruption, of course. Participants in the gig economy—the people who drive, walk dogs, and deliver groceries and laundry for Uber and its kin—are shouldering much of the risk associated with their businesses. Companies like Uber are "asset light"—drivers own their cars, not the company—and if Uber revokes a driver's ability to use the platform, the driver will be the one saddled with debt. Drivers for Uber are not covered by their personal car insurance once they're on the job, because they are "hauling others for a fee," a category considered more dangerous that driving yourself. Uber provides some insurance for drivers, but that coverage varies as to whether you have a passenger. Insurance coverage is sparse during times when drivers are waiting for the next client—accidents during that period can easily bankrupt a driver, as that time is not covered either by a driver's personal insurance or by Uber's insurance.[7] And like taxi drivers, ride-sharing drivers are on the front lines of exposure to COVID-19 and other diseases.

In the United States, the gig economy is sometimes called the 1099 economy because workers are independent contractors (who receive a 1099 form rather than the W-2 that employees receive), which means they're generally ineligible for health benefits. That's a hardship in a country where uninsured medical expenses are the largest cause of bankruptcy.[8] Most Uber drivers, even if they're not risking financial calamity, aren't making much. A study by economists at MIT's Center for Energy and Environmental Policy Research surveyed over eleven hundred American drivers and determined that Uber and Lyft drivers made an average hourly profit of $8.55, earned after paying for gas and depreciation of their vehicles. Forty-one percent of drivers made less than the minimum wage for their states.[9]

The story gets uglier. These disruptive new services often suffer serious problems of racial bias. A recent randomized control trial that tested ride-sharing services in Boston and Seattle found that riders with African-American-sounding names faced 35 percent longer wait times than those with white-sounding names and that they were more than twice as likely to have their rides canceled by drivers.[10] Airbnb guests have experienced mistreatment and canceled reservations when hosts discovered they were African-American, leading to an investigation by the State of California into housing discrimination and a popular social media hashtag #AirbnbWhileBlack.[11] A Harvard study of 6,400 Airbnb listings found that users with traditionally African-American names were 16 percent less likely to have their lodging requests accepted than were users with white-sounding names.[12] While traditional taxi services still reflect racial bias among drivers—and some studies suggest that ride-hailing services discriminate less than taxi drivers—these new tech-driven models are hardly racism free and may be enabling racist providers of lodging and rides to discriminate against clients.[13]

The shift from taxi services to ride-sharing has been economically catastrophic for people who invested their life's savings in buying a taxi medallion, a common retirement strategy for New York City taxi drivers. In 2018, *The New York Times* reported five suicides by taxi drivers and owners in five months, including a man who shot himself outside New York City Hall to protest government inaction and failure to regulate ride-sharing services.[14]

There's a reason we associate disruption with tech-driven companies like Uber and Airbnb. Successful disruption often leverages a combination of technological change (Lessig's "code" lever) to pioneer a new way of doing business, and market mechanisms to scale up their impact. Technology by itself is rarely enough to drive these profound shifts. But when technology is able to use a market to reach billions of users, changing behavior patterns (norms) in the process, disruption can happen with disconcerting speed.

Throughout most of the twentieth century, providing phone service, especially over long distances, was an attractive business. Most countries had a single phone provider that often charged extortionate rates because it had a "natural" monopoly: ownership of the network of copper telephone lines. In the United States, the Justice Department broke up the monopoly in 1982, forcing competition between different regional phone companies. In much of the world, existing phone monopolies collapsed when mobile phone companies emerged as competitors to wired telephony, and people began abandoning their wireline phones. Still, revenue from voice calls, particularly international voice calls, has remained lucrative. Mobile phone businesses have emerged as powerful economic players in the countries where they operate, though it's easy to imagine those profits disappearing as IP telephony like Skype and voice chat like WhatsApp undermine those businesses.

Existing institutions don't fold without a fight—mobile phone companies employ millions of people worldwide and have massive marketing and promotional budgets. Many will successfully transform themselves into Internet service providers, selling us the mobile connections that our Internet-connected devices rely on, and dropping phone calls from their marketing documents with as little sentimentality as AT&T showed when it stopped delivering telegrams. When markets and code offer a superior product at a superior price, disruptive change is hard to stop. Institutions seeking to block this sort of change turn to law and norms to protect their existing businesses. If Uber fails, it's likely because cities decide to strengthen their laws to protect existing taxi businesses. If Airbnb fails, it may be because hotels convince customers that they aren't ready to give up the reliability of a traditional hotel to stay in a stranger's house, or to adopt new norms about how they travel and do business. Of course, both could fail because neither drivers nor hosts want to take the risk of opening private spaces to strangers who might have COVID-19: disrupting existing industries becomes more complicated when the entire economy is disrupted by a pandemic.

Businesses are easier to disrupt than other institutions because they are inherently vulnerable to market pressures: if you offer a better product or service at a better price, the market will do much of the work for you. Institutions like churches and governments won't necessarily change because someone's found a way to do something better or cheaper. It took the Catholic Church until the 1960s to endorse priests saying mass in the vernacular instead of in Latin. (You might think of the rise of Protestantism as the missed market opportunity in the process.) To disrupt most institutions, you need two things: a better way of doing something and the power to ensure your new way of doing things survives.

I had never heard of Mazdoor Kisan Shakti Sangathan (MKSS)—the Association for the Empowerment of Workers and Peasants—until I met one of the movement's co-founders, Nikhil Dey, in a Bombay hotel. He'd brought me a book, a history of the organization's campaign for the right to information in India. It wasn't a gift, he explained sheepishly. All founders of the organization had pledged to pay themselves India's minimum wage, around 280 rupees ($4) a day, and the cost of the book was several days' wages.[15] I happily bought the book and expressed my admiration for his decision to live at the minimum wage for more than two decades. "Many of the people we work with make much less," he explained.

MKSS was founded in 1983 by Nikhil Dey, Shankar Singh, and the civil society activist Aruna Roy, who moved into a mud hut in Madhya Pradesh and began the work of researching rural poverty in India. They were trying to understand the problems local farmers were facing. Mostly they freaked out their neighbors: Why were the men cooking? Why did the men carry water, which everyone knew was women's work? In 1987 they moved to Rajasthan, which was several years into a brutal drought. With crops failing, villagers were desperate for government work, projects designed to pay workers minimum wage to avoid starvation. But there wasn't enough work to go around, Dey explained. In many cases a thousand people would show up to apply for fifty jobs. And while the jobs paid minimum wage—at that point, eleven rupees per day—the lucky farmers who received a job were paid only between one and seven rupees, while local officials pocketed the rest. Often people would work and never receive their pay.

The activists of MKSS began leading sit-ins and hunger strikes to demand pay for their communities. The hunger strikes worked, but only long enough to get the local government to pay back salaries. The underlying pattern of corruption continued. "We ultimately realized that hunger strikes are your last nonviolent weapon: it's turning violence on yourself," Dey told me. "We did hunger strikes, some long ones, before we realized we were not Gandhi."

As Dey and his colleagues led demonstrations, they started receiving key pieces of information—the public administration rolls—from sympathetic government workers. They soon held public meetings where they read aloud these government ledgers, which often included people being paid three times, cows and other farm animals being paid, and dead people receiving salaries. MKSS's supporters, many of them illiterate, realized that government records were being used to rob them. A song they began singing at rallies included the words, "The thieves of lore lived in the jungles, the thieves today live in bungalows; The thieves of yore would kill with the gun, the thieves today kill with a pen."

In the course of fighting for the right to meaningful, remunerative work for India's citizens, MKSS ended up creating two new institutions. The first is the right to information, which started with state efforts and ultimately became national law. In many countries, the establishment of the right to information is a battle

fought by newspapers and journalists who want access to government records to report on current events. In India, the right to
information became a rallying cry even for people who could not
read the records they were demanding access to, because revealing records demonstrated the corruption of India's bureaucratic
institutions and the ways they were being used to rob the poor
and enrich local politicians. The meetings MKSS ran where it
read off public ledgers and citizens learned that payments were
being made to livestock or dead people turned into a new, powerful institution: public audits of government spending.

I had asked to meet Dey because MKSS has achieved something that seems like a dream to progressives globally: a national
right to work law, called the Mahatma Gandhi National Rural
Employment Guarantee Act, which provides at least one hundred
paid days of work a year for every household where adults volunteer for unskilled manual work. Dey acknowledges that the law
seems almost unbelievable, even in India, but he explains that
it would be meaningless without the right to information and
the novel mechanism of the community audit. Before MKSS's
actions, India had institutions that were supposed to protect
the poor, but they were corrupt and needed to be replaced with
something that served communities. To regain trust, this new
institution had to be built around transparency and audits.

Like Silicon Valley–style disruption, technology has a role
in overthrowing institutions. Dey insists that public meetings
and microphones are technologies that deserve as much respect
and as careful consideration as digital tools. And as with
Airbnb and Uber, unseating institutions also requires a change
in norms. Airbnb has run ads designed to convince customers
that the world is a welcoming and inviting place that they can
really explore only if they stay in other people's homes, challenging a suite of norms about stranger danger. Dey explains
that the critical part of MKSS's struggle was helping citizens

move from an attitude of "It's government money, let it burn" to "Our money, our accounts."

"Radical politics argues we need to replace the state," Dey told me. "We believe we need to reclaim the state and truly own it."

Disruptive change within government organizations often requires more than changes in technology and norms matched with market forces or political power. You also have to get lucky. India's right to work resulted from one of the strangest moments in Indian politics. Sonia Gandhi's party won the 2004 elections, but Gandhi wasn't able to become prime minister because she had been born in Italy. She named a different prime minister and became leader of the National Advisory Council, a new body with high visibility and unclear responsibilities. She named Aruna Roy to the council, and when searching for legislative proposals that would acknowledge the needs of the *aam aadmi* (ordinary man), Roy suggested enshrining the right to work and guaranteed employment as a gift to the rural communities that had elected Gandhi. Once issued, this right is politically impossible to pull back, much like Social Security in the United States. Campaigning against the right to work would be political suicide in rural districts. The right to work in India is a reminder that disruption sometimes happens because someone had a brilliant idea up their sleeve and encountered a unique set of circumstances.

But while commercially backed disruptions can rely on market forces to do the heavy lifting, disruptive social change requires power. The MKSS activists gained only limited traction through their hunger strikes. They began achieving real change once local bureaucrats felt threatened by the hundreds of people assembling to audit accounts and demand wages. Demonstrating power through marching or occupying doesn't always lead to significant social change. The Occupy protests that swept across the world in 2011–12 dissipated without major legislative or structural change within the United States. But citizen power, when creatively harnessed by organizers and paired with norms change and technological innovation, can lead to the permanent disruption of institutions.

The Sunflower Student Movement in Taiwan achieved global visibility in 2014 when students and NGOs occupied the Taiwanese parliament for five days, protesting the passage of a trade agreement with China that had not received adequate review by citizens and by opposition lawmakers. When more than a thousand police raided Parliament and threw the protesters out, hundreds of thousands of supporters occupied downtown Taipei from March 30 to April 10. The movement weakened the KMT, the political party that had supported the trade deal with China, which went on to lose elections in 2014 and 2016. More critically, a generation of activists who participated in the protests have emerged as the authors of Taiwan's g0v movement, a radical rethinking of how citizen participation works in Taiwan.

The leaders of g0v include an open-source hacker who goes by the handle "Ttcat" and a transgender programming prodigy who became Taiwan's digital minister at age thirty-five. They speak of their work as "forking the government." This open-source terminology refers to modifying a piece of existing code so that it takes on new functions and may be incompatible with the existing project. G0v works to fork how Taiwan's government works, trying new systems and practices, and then merges the best ones back into the government's operating system.[16] Its most successful experiment blends offline and online consultation to ensure citizens have a voice in policy making.

Allowing the voices of individual citizens to be heard by their government is one of the great unsolved problems of civics. Representative democracy, as in the United States, recognizes that thousands of citizens can't effectively deliberate about policy issues. Managing a conversation at that scale, and educating all participants about the issues at hand, are huge challenges. Instead, we elect a small set of designated deliberators to represent citizen interests. But what happens if your issue isn't being addressed by your representative, or your representative disagrees with your perspectives? Even very modern governments fall back on very old methods.

The Obama administration's much-touted mechanism for citizen participation was We the People, an online iteration of the ancient technology of the petition, which originated in China during the Han dynasty as a way subjects could bring matters to the emperor's attention through letters called 章表 or "Memorial to the Throne." The dynasty's system was far from open and required petitioners to write in careful, classical Chinese—which limited its applicability to the educated and nobility—but the emperor responded to all petitions, sometimes with marks that signified that he had read them. Fast-forwarding fifteen hundred years, petitions in colonial America required governmental hearings and responses, which gave them the power of, in effect, setting legislative agendas.[17]

But by the time the Obama administration dragged the petition into the digital age, petitions were nonbinding. They were a form of speech that, while explicitly protected by the First Amendment to the Constitution, no longer mandated an official response. We the People promised a response from the White House to any petition that received five thousand signatures within thirty days. As Americans got better at mobilizing online, the threshold increased and now stands at one hundred thousand signatures, which basically requires petition authors to become online organizers in order to get a response.

After a wave of excitement, in part due to a humorous petition urging the government to build the Death Star from *Star Wars* and a pitch-perfect response from the White House, the site has seen decreasing levels of engagement. The civics scholar Erhardt Graeff theorizes that this is largely because petitions on the site have not achieved any real change. When petitioners demand a course of action the White House doesn't want to take, it is able to acknowledge the petition and restate the official government position, with no apparent change resulting from a hundred thousand citizens uniting to make a demand. In the first years of Trump's presidency, popular petitions demanded Trump's resignation and his divestment of financial assets while in office, neither of which has transpired. The tenor of the site has changed recently and petitions demand the arrest of House Speaker and Trump enemy Nancy Pelosi for treason and the designation of George Soros as a terrorist. Despite the president's likely enthusiasm for these positions, they're also unlikely to lead to action.

Petitions in the United States coordinate voices but they don't coordinate power. The situation is not so clear in Taiwan. As organizer and digital minister Audrey Tan notes, "We can always occupy again." G0v's efforts at building tools for citizen participation has led to a system with real teeth. Ttcat, Tan, and others have built software that invites citizen conversation and participation in pressing social issues—for instance how Uber's entry into Taiwan should be handled. Thanks to citizen input, Uber was allowed to enter Taiwan, but with restrictions designed to "level the playing field" between the new company and existing taxi companies. G0v's software uses sophisticated techniques to estimate what percentage of Taiwan's citizenry the comments offered online represent, so that single voices don't dominate.

To ensure that online questions get addressed, each government department now has a digital engagement director, responsible for seeking out input online and channeling it into government decision-making processes. As Taiwan began coping with the COVID-19 crisis, the government put price controls on face masks and limited citizens to buying only two a week. Citizens told these engagement directors that they were having trouble finding stores that sold facemasks. The government released a feed of digital information on what stores were carrying facemasks, and members of g0v rapidly built mobile phone apps that let citizens find the masks they needed.[18]

Half a decade after the protests, the systems the g0v team has

built work so effectively that the team tours the world, introducing the technology to other governments that want to institution-
alize online citizen participation and make it part of government
decision making.

Despite successes like MKSS and the Sunflower Movement,
institutions are hard to dislodge and resilient to the departure
of specific individuals. Institutions work toward their goals with
processes that change slowly and gradually. We hope that institutions continue to function even when leadership is weak or
incompetent, but the price for this resilience is inflexibility. Thousands of people's identities and livelihoods are linked to doing
business in a particular way, and they will often be reluctant to
stray from existing paths, even when they acknowledge that institutions need to learn and evolve. As Upton Sinclair observed, "It
is difficult to get a man to understand something, when his salary
depends on his not understanding it."

There's a positive upside to this inflexibility. When an institution is successfully disrupted and replaced with a new way of
doing things, the new system tends to be passionately defended
and rapidly becomes its own institution. Consider Wikipedia,
which represents a massive shift in how knowledge is created and
disseminated. After a decade of controversy, in which it was common to hear arguments about whether Wikipedia was a source
of accurate information, Wikipedia has now been blessed by
Google, frequently appearing as the top search result in response
to queries and populating the vast databases the company uses
to answer user questions. As YouTube, Google's video-sharing
site, received criticism about surfacing extremist content, Google
responded by linking searches to Wikipedia articles to counter
misinformation.[19] Because Wikipedia has a process for resolving
disputes over what factually occurred, using the principle of Neutral Point of View and a process where editors from opposing
viewpoints sand the edges of statements until they have something both can live with, Wikipedia is remarkably well positioned

to provide an anchor of clarity at a time when reality itself seems up for grabs.[20]

In the process, Wikipedia has become an institution. Its charismatic founder Jimmy Wales hasn't been involved with day-to-day operations since 2006, and the organization has moved through multiple presidents with little disruption. But participants in Wikipedia have noted that it's ever harder to become an effective contributor to the site. While the software behind Wikipedia—the code innovation that made it possible for Wikipedia to disrupt existing encyclopedias—remains simple to use, there are thousands of community rules around what content is appropriate and long-running conversations about how new articles should be created. This culture and community give Wikipedia its staying power and resilience, but it also has some unforeseen consequences. While men and women use Wikipedia in equal numbers, less than 15 percent of the contributors are female, and women often report feeling unwelcome and attacked when they do contribute.[21] While Wikimedia, the nonprofit that operates Wikipedias around the world, has launched several efforts to recruit more female editors, the gender disparity remains and appears to lead to bias in who gets included in the encyclopedia. Northeastern University professor Joseph Reagle studied Wikipedia and *Encyclopaedia Britannica*'s biographical coverage and found that *Britannica* is far more balanced between biographies of women and men.[22]

Wikipedia grew from, and inherited the views of, an open-source software culture that's primarily male and that appears to systemically discriminate against female contributors, accepting their contributions at a lower rate than those of males when gender is revealed.[23] As Wikipedia grows in importance, it may become harder, not easier, to solve its problems with gender and representation. Now that people rely on Wikipedia to debunk misinformation, disruptive changes to the site's culture and process would have consequences for hundreds of millions of users.

This fear of disruption can become a fear of making changes that would address long-standing inequities and that might eventually lead to institutional collapse. The number of people editing Wikipedia regularly is shrinking, even as the project becomes ever more important. In the long run, Wikipedia may not be able to survive alienating 50 percent of its potential editors.[24]

As disruptive institutions cement their culture, they begin to attract their own counterpower-based projects. Drivers who feel Uber is an unaccountable institution rely on services like Sherpa-Share, an app that lets drivers track their earnings and make decisions about what clients, routes, and employers will make them the most money.[25] The ethnographer Stuart Geiger calls such tools "successor systems," tools that help users navigate systems that have power over them and allow them little control. Geiger points to Turkopticon, a system that helps workers on Amazon's Mechanical Turk system share information about employers and tasks to improve their income, as an example of a successor system.[26] If people are building successor systems to allow users more power and agency within your system, it's a pretty good indication that your institution has become rigid. Geiger and his colleagues have built a successor system called Snuggle designed to help Wikipedia editors coach people who've just joined the community instead of scaring them away by deleting their first attempts at edits.[27]

Sometimes institutions have good reasons for seeming bureaucratic and clunky. Often policies have been put in place over years to ensure that they serve populations equitably. Disability advocates in New York City sued the city's taxi system for failing to provide sufficient cabs to carry passengers using wheelchairs. The city ultimately agreed to a settlement in which half of all taxis will be ramp-equipped by 2020, though only 1,800 of nearly 14,000 medallion cabs had ramps by May of that year.[28] The same group of advocates are now suing Uber, which offers ramp-equipped cars, but so few that advocates argue Uber is not a viable transportation option for them.[29] Disruptive approaches will almost always marginalize some populations as they introduce new ways to operate. At present, Taiwanese citizens who aren't comfortable participating online aren't experiencing the benefits of the changes the g0v movement has realized. And as disrupters adapt to serve a broad landscape of people, they often gain a complexity that sometimes offends and alienates early adopters and the original innovators.

To move from disrupting old institutions to building new ones in their place requires careful, iterative change. Often the people who lead disruptions are personally ill-suited to carry out these slower, more gradual processes. It's no accident that Travis Kalanick, the founder and former CEO of Uber, is (by most accounts) an asshole. It helps to be a deeply passionate person, convinced that you're right and the world is wrong, to successfully disrupt an existing institution. That same passion, so helpful for starting a revolution, can be a liability once a disruption is under way and the key job is to ensure that the disruption helps society broadly rather than reinforcing existing barriers and biases.

The gospel of disruption is particularly influential at engineering schools like MIT, where I taught undergrads and grad students from 2011 to 2020. Students are keenly aware that technology can be profoundly disruptive, and many are working simultaneously on their degrees and their own inventions, which they hope will unseat established corporate players or tackle unsolved social problems. While they've gained experience as technical thinkers, they're often not nearly as experienced at thinking through the social implications of the changes they want to bring about. As we look toward disruption as a path for change, we need to do a better job of studying and teaching the social context that institutions operate within, the many populations they serve, and the unintended consequences that can come from change.

It's too early to tell whether the gospel of disruption will survive the rapid and painful disruptions of the coronavirus pandemic. Disruption is more fun when you target brittle, moribund institutions and much less fun when you discover your ongoing dependence on essential institutions to predict pandemics, produce tests to diagnose new diseases, and provide coherent public health advice to a scared nation. One outcome of the shock of COVID-19 on Americans might be a wave of gratitude for functioning institutions, much like what Britons are expressing for the country's National Health Service. But I suspect otherwise. Even as General Motors was contracted to build ventilators and Google and Apple announced a partnership to develop contact tracing software, hundreds of young engineers were launching projects to build these essential technologies themselves, faster and cheaper.

At some point in the future, a young engineer will decide that ride-sharing services like Uber and Lyft are so broken, they will demand a rethinking from the ground up. Taiwanese youth will despair that they don't have any influence over the system that the g0v innovators put in place and will find a way to protest and demand change. Disrupters become institutions, and institutions attract counterpowers designed to make them more accountable, transparent, and fair. Radical institutionalists will arise within these new institutions, attempting to steer them in different directions and adapting them to new demands. Eventually disrupters will propose an entirely new way of solving a problem. This can be a virtuous cycle, leading us toward a world in which systems better suited to the current moment replace those that have aged into obsolescence. But such a world demands a profound openness, a sense of antifragility that understands that anything we create will be replaced.

Or of course, we could simply try to ensure we never create any new institutions again.

Chapter 8

DECENTRALIZATION

FOR FORTY-TWO YEARS, MUAMMAR GADDAFI RULED LIBYA IN a deeply idiosyncratic fashion. While the government used its oil wealth to provide education, health care, and subsidized housing for some of its population, Libya was also a one-party state where books were burned, private enterprise was illegal, and dissenters were routinely disappeared or killed. While Gaddafi was legendary in international circles for his rambling speeches at the United Nations, his entourage of female bodyguards ("Revolutionary Nuns"), and his habit of pitching an opulent nomad's tent in foreign capitals, he ran a brutal police state that tortured political opponents, supported terrorist organizations around the world, and was shunned by many nations.

In February 2011 the Arab Spring spread from Tunisia and Egypt into Libya, where citizen uprisings against Gaddafi morphed into a civil war. NATO forces helped opposition fighters seize the capital. During the battle, Gaddafi was captured and killed. Years after his death, Libya remains a failed state: a UN-based government controls only part of the country's vast territory and competes for authority with two rival governments and a wide array of armed groups, including an offshoot of ISIS.

In other words, Libya is not a place where most people look to find inspiring models of governance.

On the other hand, Susanne Tarkowski Tempelhof is not most people.

Tempelhof spent much of her twenties as a government contractor working on reconstruction in postconflict countries, first in Afghanistan and later in Libya. Her experience in Libya after the fall of Gaddafi's government was transformational. Even though the country, in the early stages of the civil war, had neither a functioning government nor rebel leadership, "everything worked amazingly well. Volunteers were doing everything from trash collection to traffic policing, neighborhood watch and cell tower engineering." While Benghazi, where she worked,[1] was initially an example of how a practical anarchism could provide key services ad hoc, the situation didn't last long: "As layers of government got added, security deteriorated."[2]

Frustrated by the apparent inability of foreign governments to achieve peace in conflict zones, Tempelhof looked to the Internet. She studied Facebook, which she hoped might reduce conflict by increasing routine contact among people who might otherwise come into conflict. But she found her calling when she was introduced to Bitcoin.

Bitcoin is a digital currency whose operations are not controlled by a government or central bank. Computation and distributed participation maintain the currency and payment system. A small set of software developers work on the system's code, while a much larger set of participants—miners—rent computational power to the network that powers the currency. The miners work together to maintain a ledger of transactions that prevent the currency from being spent multiple times or otherwise abused. Miners are rewarded, in turn, with a chance to discover new bitcoins, which are released such that those who contribute the most to the operation of the system are most likely to win one.

No one gave Bitcoin permission to launch in 2009. One can easily imagine regulators and legislators who would have denied permission. Yet millions of people have been willing to trade cash—called "fiat money" in cryptocurrency circles—or services for bitcoins, and the entire cryptocurrency market is valued in the hundreds of billions of dollars.[3] For a certain breed of thinkers, Bitcoin and the vision of bold, permissionless innovation it promises is both a metaphor for how things could be done differently and proof positive that anyone can and should invent the future.

Specifically, Bitcoin inspired many, like Tempelhof, who see nation-states as increasingly obsolete and dangerous governance structures. Tempelhof's father was stateless for part of his life, and she's told reporters, "I believe the nation state system represents the greatest apartheid in the world."[4] This perspective on states and decentralization led her to the experiment she's best known for: Bitnation, a "decentralized borderless voluntary nation" or DBVN.[5] As Bitnation's white paper explains, "We wish you to be able to create, opt-in or opt-out of the Nation of your choice on your mobile phone."[6]

If this is hard to swallow, it helps to understand Bitnation's definition of a nation. It's not about land, territory, or flag. At first, at least, it's not about passports or the ability to cross borders. According to Bitnation's founders, "the core function of any nation is to protect its citizens and their assets through an enforceable jurisdiction (the practical authority to administer justice within a defined area of responsibility). Security and justice ensure that our assets, including our bodies, are safe from violence and dispossession. Increasingly security and justice are merging as more of our assets become digital."[7]

Put aside for the moment the idea of keeping our bodies safe from violence: Bitnation neither has, nor imagines, armies or police. What it promises is legal jurisdiction for contracts, including financial contracts, marriages, legal identities, and the notarization of agreements between willing parties. Instead of maintaining a court system to arbitrate these agreements—and potentially a criminal justice system to arrest and detain those who harm others—Bitnation relies on an "algorithmic reputation token" (XPAT) designed to be accumulated through conducting contracts. If you participate in lots of successful contracts, you'll accumulate XPAT tokens that speak to your reputation, Bitnation theorizes, and you'll be rewarded by people's willingness to do business with you. You'll also be protected from deception by people's unwillingness to break contracts and ruin their reputations. What happens when people realize they can decamp to a virtual nation after being run out of town? Or what happens to people who've burned enough online jurisdictions that they're virtually stateless? The good news is that these problems don't need solving until sufficient Bitnation dwellers adopt the system in the first place.

Underlying Tempelhof's vision is the "smart contract," an idea that's gained popularity as cryptocurrencies like Bitcoin have become prominent. Ethereum, one of the most popular successors to Bitcoin, goes beyond sending money to someone over the Internet (a simple form of contract), allowing users to build complex arrangements and rely on computer code to carry them out. Say I decide to rent a vacation home with four friends. I don't want to get stuck holding the bag if my friends back out, so I create a smart contract with the property's owner that will rent the house if, and only if, my three friends commit as well. I escrow my payment, and when three friends do the same, the contract executes itself and the house is rented.

If you're noting that code often has bugs, that contracts sometimes benefit from ambiguity and interpretability, and wondering whether such an enterprise is all that smart, you're in good company. In 2016 fans of smart contracts created a Distributed Autonomous Organization, a pool of funds designed to act as venture capital investment in cryptocurrency and smart contract projects. The DAO, as it came to be known, collected over $150 million in investments, which swelled to $250 million as Ethereum increased in value. But before the group could make a single investment, a hacker discovered a bug in the smart contract code and used it to steal $70 million from the pool. This bug undermined the notion that smart contracts would be safer for conventional investors, and it forced the developers behind Ethereum to "undo" a set of transactions, something that's supposed to be impossible for a cryptocurrency.[8]

Not only were investors upset by the hacking of a smart contract: the US Securities and Exchange Commission also was not thrilled. Investigating the DAO hack, the SEC determined that the entire setup constituted the offering of a security and had to be regulated in the same way that a stock sale would be under US law. Whether the United States can or should claim jurisdiction over schemes like the DAO is a worthwhile question for lawyers to tackle. But for projects like Bitnation, jurisdiction is the essence of the matter.[9]

The nations Tempelhof and colleagues want to create consist of sets of rules for these contracts, along with the reputation and mediation systems designed to enable them. Tempelhof doesn't want a single digital nation—she wants a whole set of them, with different, competing rules and regulations that people could choose from. In some, the DAO would be legal, while in others, it would be banned; in some, investors would have gotten their money back, in others, the hackers would have kept their spoils. The tyranny of the nation-state that Tempelhof worries about is counterbalanced by the ability to pick the digital nation you want to participate within. Don't like the nation you're in? Pick another one that meets your needs better, for any specific purpose.

This ability to pick and choose the nation whose rules you are subject to is already reality for the very rich. Limassol, the second-largest city in Cyprus, has become 20 percent Russian-speaking in the past decade after a steady influx of Russian émigrés.[10] The town's beautiful beaches aren't the draw. Cyprus is a member of the European Union, and holders of a Cypriot passport travel visa-free to anywhere EU citizens are similarly welcomed. Russian investors are able to purchase a "golden visa"—permanent residency, which includes a passport—in exchange for making an investment of €2 million in local real estate.

Over twenty countries offer golden visa programs, including thirteen in Europe. And while golden visas can attract legitimate businesspeople to a country, they're also popular with corrupt government officials. For them, an alternative nationality offers an escape valve should their thefts become visible to authorities in their home countries, and an opportunity to purchase real estate with stolen funds in more desirable markets.[11] In addition to providing a service for corrupt officials seeking to stash money abroad, golden visas are horribly unfair. You gain the right to free movement if you can afford to purchase an attractive citizenship. (It's worth noting that birth citizenship, where you can end up with an attractive immigration status because you were lucky enough to be born in the United States or the European Union, instead of Nigeria or Indonesia, is also deeply unfair.)

In a less dramatic way, the tiny Baltic nation of Estonia offers "citizenship as a service" along the lines of Bitnation's theories. In the wake of its independence from the Soviet Union, Estonia invested heavily in e-government systems, building a system of digital identity cards that citizens could use to vote, access their health records, file their taxes, or start a business. The system, x-road, has won international awards and helped rebrand the nation of 1.1 million as "e-Estonia," attracting investment in technology start-ups like Skype.[12] Now over thirty thousand non-Estonians have signed up as e-residents. They are permitted to open bank accounts, start companies, sign documents, and pay tax under Estonian jurisdiction and law. But Estonia's e-citizenship is not a golden visa. There's no right to residency or to any government services. As Primavera di Filippi, a scholar of decentralized systems, observes, Estonia has unbundled the services commonly offered by a government and offered a subset to its e-residents, just as Tempelhof hopes to sell digital jurisdiction to hers.

In that sense, Bitnation and e-Estonia are competitors: both seek people who wish to transcend geographic jurisdiction and choose governance that's fit for their purposes. Tempelhof believes that digital nations could be more convenient, secure, and cost-effective in providing governance services than traditional geographic nations. Perhaps a network of voluntary, competing service providers, rather than geographic monopolies or the efforts of multinational organizations like the UN, would serve citizens better. In the process, Tempelhof hopes "to free humankind from the oppression and sanction of pooled sovereignty and geographical apartheid and the xenophobia and violence that is nurtured by the Nation State oligopoly,"[13] presumably even from forward-looking nations like Estonia.

I simultaneously have little confidence that the Bitnation experiment, as it is, will take off, but also great confidence that Tempelhof's intentions are sound. The cryptonation's Initial Coin Offering, basically a stock offering of XPAT tokens, was a bust, and as of the drafting of this chapter, the 42 billion tokens issued had a total value of less than $100,000. But despite investors' disinterest in its cryptocurrency, Bitnation has tried to demonstrate the value of voluntary citizenship. It issued a blockchain emergency ID, a digital identity card designed to help refugees who've fled without papers reestablish identity through a web of trust, in which friends and relatives vouch for an individual's identity.[14] While it's unclear whether these identities will ultimately be accepted in the nations where refugees are fleeing, the logic of ensuring identity despite displacement echoes Hannah Arendt's reminder that citizenship is "the right to have rights," a right that's often targeted by governments to marginalize and disenfranchise populations.

Bitnation sounds radical in part because so few of the institutions we are used to are ones we choose.

Institutionalism is built in part on the assumption that we should work within the institutions we're born into and make them fairer and stronger. Insurrectionism believes we can choose to work outside of those institutions, transforming them or replacing them with something more effective. Decentralization proposes that we build a world where we are unconstrained, where we choose from a world of competing institutions the ones that are the most fair or the most fit for purpose. If only for their sheer audacity, it's worth engaging ideas like Bitnation.

Of course, it's possible to share enthusiasm for the goals of Bitnation and be deeply skeptical about the details of their execution. In practical terms, implementing distributed currencies like the bitcoin has proven to be damned complicated. Distributed systems are orders of magnitude less efficient than centralized systems, at least in terms of the number of transactions they can process. A common comparison, much disputed by cryptocurrency adherents, points out that Visa, the credit card processor, processes on average 150 million transactions a day, or roughly 1,700 per second. Bitcoin processes three to four a second, and Ethereum as many as fifteen per second.[15] These are different transactions inasmuch as Visa has central control of its system— should someone within Visa decide to divert a few cents from any transaction into her personal account, it would be difficult to detect that fraud, whereas such theft by a single actor should be impossible within a cryptocurrency. But by investing in robustness and decentralization, cryptocurrencies have incurred a huge energy bill. By one estimate, Bitcoin uses five thousand times the energy of a transaction with a centralized system like Visa, leading many critics to see the spread of Bitcoin as an environmental catastrophe.*16 I stopped experimenting with Bitcoin when I found a credible estimate that the energy used by a single Bitcoin transaction was enough to power my electric car to travel over 2,500 miles.†

Bitcoin may also be failing in its most basic value proposition: a currency not controlled by anyone. A well-known vulnerability of Bitcoin is that if a single group controls more than 51 percent of the mining pool—the group of computers that verify transactions on the shared ledger—they can conspire and change the ledger, giving bitcoins to whomever they want. The system's distributed nature is supposed to solve this problem; since anyone can mine bitcoins, it seems unlikely that someone could control over half the network. But Chinese bitcoin miners have taken advantage of the country's very cheap electricity to build massive bitcoin mines, and since 2015, between 60 and 80 percent of the world's bitcoin mining capacity has been based in China. Scholars have identified several ways that China's government could influence domestically-based bitcoin miners to either disable

---

* It's impossible to write about cryptocurrencies without incurring the wrath of those who strongly believe in their potential. Some legitimately point out that the incredible energy appetite of Bitcoin is directly connected to "proof of work," the system used to validate transactions on the network. If cryptocurrencies were to refocus around the less expensive "proof of stake," the energy costs of the system might drop, though the concentration problems would remain. Others have argued that the freedoms provided by Bitcoin are so important that it matters little if the system's energy demands exceed those of some small nations. For me, that argument is evidence that for many users, cryptocurrencies are more a belief system than a technology, that the underlying idea of the system is more important than any practical engineering propositions.

† The energy estimate from Digiconomist.net is 646 kilowatt-hours per Bitcoin transaction. My Chevy Bolt travels around 240 miles on a 60 kilowatt-hour charge.

the currency, decrease trust in it, or execute fraud on a massive scale.[17] The ability of Bitcoin to create a postnational currency may be compromised by the power of existing nation-states.

Putting aside the technical questions of whether distributed currencies will work at scale and whether smart contracts will take law out of the hands of lawyers and put it in the hands of programmers, it's worth interrogating whether the future that Tempelhof and others imagine is desirable. Bitnation's idea of nations as voluntary associations, in which we might choose to participate to gain some benefits, is radically libertarian. It rejects the idea that we have obligations to fellow citizens that we did not choose to take on. But governments do vastly more than provide jurisdiction for transactions, and Tempelhof and others may be thinking about the social contract as too much like a literal financial contract.

People in advanced nations benefit from having good educations, meaningful work, and strong social safety nets to fall back on. These benefits are hard to price: what is it worth to live in a society that meets people's basic social needs and makes it less likely that they will be robbed by someone who needs money to survive? It's unclear how many people would be willing to enter into the contracts necessary to support those most in need of a social safety net. Tempelhof might argue that the constructive anarchist approach in Libya suggests that people are naturally inclined toward these arrangements, but it's not hard to imagine rich people's voluntary nations where they have no obligations to the poor.

Peter Thiel is a libertarian billionaire, one of the founders of PayPal and a board member at Facebook. He's unabashedly an insurrectionist. With a portion of his vast wealth, he funds an organization that urges entrepreneurs to reject college, opt out of the institutions of traditional education and certification, and go ahead and build their projects. One of his obsessions is the ability of humans to exit the nations they live in and explore new frontiers. As journalist Jonathan Miles observed in a profile of Thiel, "Forget start-up companies. The next frontier is start-up countries."[18] Speaking with Miles, Thiel explained that he was obsessed with the importance of frontiers and unexplored territories: "We're at this pretty important point in society where we can either find a way to rediscover a frontier, or we're going to be forced to change in a way that's really tough."[19]

Where are these new frontiers? Thiel's 2009 essay "The Education of a Libertarian" lays out three directions: online spaces, outer space, and seasteading, or building new nations that float in international waters.[20] The first idea is so much a part of our current business and political culture that it no longer seems radical. Escape to outer space, Thiel concedes, is decades away, though worth researching and funding. He's a major investor in his friend Elon Musk's SpaceX, which is building reusable rockets to challenge national governments' monopoly on space travel. But the quirkiest—and perhaps most revealing—of Thiel's plans for exits involve seasteading.

You might think of seasteading as Bitnation on boats. Independent, floating micronations anchored in international waters would be able to maintain the jurisdictional independence that Tempelhof seeks with Bitnation but would also—in theory—have control over all aspects of law in their tiny territories. (Bitnations are still located within existing geographic nations, as only Antarctica is a nationless territory.)

Thiel has funded former Google engineer Patri Friedman's Seasteading Institute, which initially followed the model of the X Prize, offering a Poseidon Award for the first city with fifty permanent residents, real estate for sale, and "de-facto political autonomy."[21] As the initial deadline for the prize—2015—drew near, Friedman refocused on a new vision, the Floating Island Project, a projected $10–$50 million initiative to create floating real estate in French Polynesia, complete with a special economic zone independent of much of the nearby nation's laws.[22] While

Thiel is no longer contributing to the project, the Seasteading Institute's executive director Randolph Hencken says that a thousand other donors have contributed.

It's possible to see seasteading as merely finding an exit from taxation. One of the earliest seasteading experiments, MS *The World*, is a luxury cruise ship launched in 2002 on which a small population of travelers live full time. The ship is collectively owned by the passengers, all of whom have bought apartments ranging in size from studios to three bedrooms. Because the ship is at sea most of the year, many full-time residents pay no taxes to terrestrial nations.[23] But Thiel, Freidman, and others seem to be seeking exit in a much grander sense.

Friedman has described exit as "the one universal human right" and suggested that other human rights can be derived from Article 13 of the Universal Declaration of Human Rights, which documents freedom of movement. Friedman suggests a single universal human right:

(1) Everyone has the right to leave any country, as long as they are not fleeing significant outstanding obligations
(2) Everyone has the right to create a country, as long as joining it is voluntary.[24]

Much as Tempelhof imagines choosing between different nations to pick the package of contract law that best suits us, Friedman imagines a multiplicity of governments with different configurations of rights that we choose among. So long as our right to movement is unencumbered, so long as governments cannot "lock us in" to certain sets of rights and practices, Friedman posits that we will see healthy competition between governments to attract productive citizens and that new nations will emerge to compete if existing nations treat citizens badly. As a result, Friedman is not interested in more traditional human rights, like speech and safety (though he'd probably allow a right to be protected from violence, especially the violence of the state), believing that people will choose states that provide the rights they need and forsake "unnecessary" rights like a right to health care or to be free from starvation.

This focus on the ability to exit as a primary form of political expression seems central to Thiel's thinking, at least in his early writings on libertarianism:

> In our time, the great task for libertarians is to find an escape from politics in all its forms—from the totalitarian and fundamentalist catastrophes to the unthinking demos that guides so-called "social democracy."
>
> The critical question then becomes one of means, of how to escape not via politics but beyond it. Because there are no truly free places left in our world, I suspect that the mode for escape must involve some sort of new and hitherto untried process that leads us to some undiscovered country; and for this reason I have focused my efforts on new technologies that may create a new space for freedom.[25]

Intentionally or not, these conversations about exit invoke one of the great thinkers of the twentieth century, Albert Hirschman, who might have been bemused by a conversation about a world beyond nations. That he fought fascists in the Spanish Civil War and Nazis with the French—supporting powerful democratic states in challenging nondemocratic ones—would be only part of his bemusement. The great economist's 1991 book *The Rhetoric of Reaction* critiques reactionary thought, and one can imagine Hirschman analyzing arguments made by Thiel and others through the lenses of perversity, futility, and jeopardy, which he identifies as the argumentative methods of reactionaries.[26]

Hirschman is now best known for his 1970 book *Exit, Voice and Loyalty,* which examines a fundamental conflict in how economists and political scientists think about organizations (firms, clubs, or countries) that are struggling or in decline. For economists, the response to a decline in quality by a manufacturer is easy to model: customers will switch to a superior product from a rival firm. But that's not what happens, Hirschman observes: often loyal customers will raise their voices before exiting, complaining about a decline in quality and trying to help a firm improve its performance. To understand this behavior, Hirschman explains that voice is especially prominent in cases where it is difficult to find a replacement good—that is, it would be difficult to get me to exit Diet Pepsi for Diet Coke. Voice also comes into play where entry and exit are costly (an exclusive club with an initiation process) or where exit is impossible (for Hirschman, nations). Further, voice is often economically rational for Hirschman. If you are more likely to achieve your goals by shaping an organization via voice than via exit, loyalty makes economic sense.

Thiel's and others' abandonment of voice—essentially, giving up on influencing existing institutions in favor of decentralization— would have disappointed Hirschman. Hirschman wrote the book because, as an economist, he saw many situations where exit alone failed to explain economic behavior. While exit happens in a commercial sense—people do leave a failing firm for a better one—we normally can't exit political systems. Hirschman explains that full exit is more complicated than moving to an island in Polynesia:

In other words, *full exit is impossible*; in some sense, one remains a consumer of the article in spite of the decision not to buy it any longer, a member of the organization in spite of formal exit. . . .

The distinguishing characteristic of [public goods] is not that they *can* be consumed by everyone, but that there is *no escape* from consuming them unless one were to leave the community by which they are provided. Thus he who says public goods says public evils. . . .

A private citizen can "get out" from public education by sending his children to private school, but at the same time he *cannot* get out, in the sense that his and his children's life will be affected by the quality of public education. There are many ostensibly private goods of this sort that one can buy or refrain from buying; but they have a "public good dimension" (often called "externalities" by economists) so that their mere production and consumption by others affects, ennobles or degrades the lives of all members of the community.[27]

Hirschman was sympathetic to the problem that Thiel and others later identified, acknowledging that one person's public good could be another's public evil. He noted that Americans afford exit a special primacy in their politics, in part because the nation was created through the literal exit from England. But Hirschman saw exit from the United States as almost unthinkable, inasmuch as it has become a homeland for those—like him—who exited their previous homelands: "As a country's central bank is the lender of last resort, so has the United States long been the 'country of last resort.' To most of its citizens—with the important exception of those whose forefathers came as slaves—exit from the country has long been peculiarly unthinkable."[28]

It's a mark of this mistrustful moment that exit from jurisdiction of the United States—the country of last resort—is an obsession of interesting and creative thinkers. For one thing, the United States is no longer a viable country of last resort. The Trump administration has made it clear that this is a dangerous country for people with legitimate refugee claims. The European Union, which might have adopted the mantle of land of last resort, is now being torn apart by debates over immigration, leading to Britain's anticipated departure and the rise of ethnonationalism as a dominant force in Hungary and Poland. The spread of the novel coronavirus means that all borders are being tightened, and it is unclear what will happen when it comes time to loosen again.

Beyond the racist, nationalist, and public health impulses associated with the closure of national boundaries, the interest in decentralized nations reflects the ways people are looking for exit from systems they perceive to be failing them. For those for whom other insurrectionist strategies are insufficiently radical or complete, creating a new nation, digitally or otherwise, is a way of throwing out the failing institutions and building a de novo, de minimis set of institutions in their place.

It can be a challenge to look beyond the many ways micronations, digital or otherwise, can fail, and lingering suspicions that the motivations behind these projects are often selfish, to see what's intriguing and powerful within this line of thinking. The importance and potential of decentralized institutions is sometimes clearer when examining projects that have a narrower scope.

Social media platforms like Facebook, YouTube, and Twitter have emerged as a major part of the current infrastructure for democracy. The political philosopher Yochai Benkler refers to these participatory online spaces as the "digital public sphere,"[29] updating Jürgen Habermas's vision of a community "made up of private people gathered together as a public and articulating the needs of society with the state" to the affordances of our contemporary technology and culture.[30]

These platforms provide spaces for discourse, yes, but for 68 percent of Americans, they are also a source of news and, for 49 percent, a significant source of news.[31] Social networks also offer a powerful tool for mobilization. Facebook is widely credited with bringing people into the streets to end Hosni Mubarak's government in Egypt,[32] and Zine al-Abidine Ben Ali's government in Tunisia during the 2011 Arab Spring.[33]

Facebook and others are facing heavy pressure to control the abuse of their platforms by bad actors, including Russian agents who attempted to sway the 2016 US presidential election through disinformation campaigns across social networks.[34] While there are widespread calls for platform owners to take a more pronounced role in editing what appears on those platforms,[35] there's an opposite push from those who believe these large companies already exert too much power and control over public discourse.

Instead of giving social media platforms more control over speech, an alternative would be to work toward a plurality of social networks, each with its own rules, practices, and missions. Much as Tempelhof imagines people choosing between nations, advocates for an ecosystem of social networks—and I am one— hope for a diverse landscape in which people can speak under different rule sets and for different purposes, and can move to a new platform if one isn't meeting their needs.

The project that's made the most progress in achieving this vision is Mastodon, an alternative to the Twitter social media service that can run on a stand-alone server. If you are reasonably technically competent, you can start your own instance of Mastodon and invite people to join you there. Even if very few people join you, you can still have a conversation, because Mastodon is a federated network: your server can share posts with other servers on the network. With a little work, you can not only follow people on different Mastodon servers but share your posts on Twitter as well.

This vision of federated decentralization has an interesting wrinkle. Different servers allow different kinds of content, and administrators of individual servers reserve the right to design and enforce rules. Some servers make clear that rude or harassing behavior will lead to being banned, while others choose not to impose this rule. But servers can also decide whether to federate with one another, which means Mastodon can look like a different network depending what server you're sitting on and whether it accepts posts from other servers with different rules.

The implications of that wrinkle became visible in the summer of 2017, not long after Mastodon received a wave of publicity and new users in the technology press.[36] Usage numbers for the network rose sharply, but the growth was centered in Japan. Researching the phenomenon, I found that many users had joined Mastodon servers built by a popular image-sharing site, and that they were using Mastodon to share "lolicon," illustrations that depict underage children in sexualized ways. Lolicon is not child pornography—it's drawn, not photographed—and it is treated very differently within Japanese culture, where child pornography draws the same disgust as in North America. In Japan, lolicon is widely accepted as part of the anime-manga community.[37]

Twitter, wildly popular in Japan, had been the platform of choice for Japanese lolicon fans, but after the company decided to start removing users who shared sexualized images of minors, many users switched to Mastodon servers, which offered much the same functionality with a rule set they liked better. Administrators of North American and European Mastodon servers soon saw controversial imagery passing through their systems and refused to federate with servers hosting the content.

While it's uncomfortable that a key use case for Mastodon has involved content that many people find objectionable, this is exactly how decentralized social networks are supposed to function. Want to have conversations free of lolicon? Join a server whose policy is not to federate with servers that support lolicon. In 2018 the passage of the Fight Online Sex Trafficking Act (FOSTA) by the US House and the Stop Enabling Sex Traffickers Act (SESTA) by the Senate made websites criminally liable for hosting content related to prostitution. Sex workers fled the seized site Backpage.com and formed a Mastodon community called Switter.at. Based in Australia, where sex work is legal, the network is a sex-worker-friendly space that's taken the place of banned services.[38] Less inspiring, Gab.ai, one of the Internet's most hateful communities, a gathering place for white supremacists, moved its site onto a customized instance of Mastodon in 2019, leading Mastodon to denounce Gab and its values—but not to block it from using the project's code.[39]

With Mastodon, much as in Tempelhof's utopia, you can pick the rules that work for you.

But very few people are trying these new rule sets. The last reliable estimate of Mastodon's population was made in 2018, when roughly 1.3 million users were registered,[40] a tiny fraction of the 2.5 billion using Facebook and its affiliated Instagram and WhatsApp services each month.[41] Switter boasts 302,000 users, only 25,000 of whom are characterized as active, and the size of Gab's userbase is hotly debated, with estimates of a few thousand to over a million.[42] Facebook is not likely losing sleep over any of these projects.

It's hard to attract people to decentralized social networks because many people are already using centralized ones, and as much as they may complain about them, it's difficult to leave a network once you're entangled in a web of friendships.

In November 2017 my former lab at MIT, the Center for Civic Media, launched a social network aggregator called Gobo (Gobo. social).[43] It allows you to see your timelines on Twitter, Mastodon, and other networks at the same time, lowering the switching cost to trying a new social network. Existing social networks really don't like this idea. Part of their value comes from the large number of users they've "locked in to" their platforms. When another company, Power Ventures, sought to integrate different social networks in a single client, Facebook sued and prevailed in a California courtroom.[44] Producing a fully functional version of Gobo may require policy changes that force platforms to remain compatible. A code solution alone may not solve the problem— we may need help from law as well.

Perhaps the most ambitious project to challenge the existing structure of social networks was one focused on a different institution: the newsroom. Civil.co was a platform and community for news publishers. To join it, publishers had to agree to a set of principles that all newsrooms follow. But they also needed to do something else. They had to stake a set of tokens, cryptographic currencies similar to bitcoins, that they forfeited if the community agreed they were violating Civil's constitution.

Unlike a conventional democracy, you could vote only if you owned Civil tokens, which you could buy as a way of supporting the Civil ecosystem or earn through participating in the community around Civil news sites. (If other users appreciated your comment, for instance, either they or the Civil administrators might award you more tokens.) In the long run, Civil hoped to provide a steady flow of news and conversation on its website and mobile phone client that could challenge the dominance of Facebook's news streams.

Unfortunately, that was not to be. The initial launch of the Civil token in late 2018 was rocky. Civil's token—CVL—was technically a cryptocurrency, though it was designed to be useful not for transactions but only for participation in the system. So fans of independent journalism who wanted to support the experiment had to traverse the complexities of purchasing cryptocurrency. One journalist reported on the forty-four separate steps he had to go through to purchase the tokens.[45] It currently requires a great deal of identity verification to purchase Ethereum, the currency Civil accepted for payment, and even more identity checks were required to validate you as a Civil user. Few users made it through all the steps—I was one of some three thousand people who succeeded in buying tokens, and Civil's initial sale brought in less than a fifth of the $8 million it had set out to raise.[46] Even then most of the money came from another entity that had previously invested $5 million in the company.[47]

Civil regrouped and relaunched in 2019, this time allowing participants to buy tokens using conventional currency, not the decentralization-compliant Ethereum. Uptake remained slow. For the project to succeed, Civil needed thousands of people to buy into it, both for fiscal and for governance reasons. To meet the goal of having a newsroom that's not controlled by a small group of people, Civil tokens had to be widely held, and it was never clear whether enough people would make large enough bets both to fund the project and to ensure that control wasn't centered in few hands. On June 2, 2020, Civil's founder Matthew Iles declared, "It's the end of Civil," and folded the project's remaining assets into ConsenSys, the blockchain company that had invested millions into the venture.[48]

While Civil aimed to weaken the power of a centralized platform like Facebook in controlling our access to news, the organization's utility depended on supporters of one newsroom reading and supporting another newsroom, using the Civil registry of publications as a hub. Civil was less decentralized than it was participatory, though you could imagine rival publishing ecosystems with their own tokens springing up with different constitutions and rules for including newsrooms. That future is even further off.

In other words, whether you're trying to launch a virtual nation or simply provide an alternative to Facebook, decentralization is hard. Decentralization has a lot to prove even in replacing individual institutions, like a social media platform or a newsroom, and the track record of Bitcoin and other cryptocurrencies is not encouraging for a technology that wants to replace central banks and fiat currency. But while it's easy to laugh at the ambitions of a project like Bitnation—or even to find its assumptions deeply problematic—it would be a mistake to ignore distributed institutions entirely as an insurrectionist strategy.

Decentralized institutions have one massive potential advantage over conventional, centralized institutions: they should be far more resilient and capable of change. Decentralization could make them less subject to the calcification that's plagued other institutions, even those once-disruptive organizations that have gradually frozen into place as institutions. But for now, this advantage is only potential. We won't truly know if the promised resilience of distributed systems manifests until more of these ambitious projects actually come to life and take over the province of existing institutions.

Chapter 9

DO SOMETHING

Efficacy and Social Change

BEFORE MARCH 5, 2012, JOSEPH KONY WAS FAMOUS TO MANY people: the populations of Uganda, the Central African Republic, eastern Democratic Republic of Congo, and southern Sudan. He and his band of rebels had been fighting a years-long guerrilla war against the Ugandan government. Kony was notorious for kidnapping children who became either soldiers or sex slaves, and for being crazy in a particularly colorful way, invoking a deeply twisted understanding of Christianity to justify his atrocities.

After March 5, Kony was famous for the same things, but to a very different group of people: American teenagers.

In 2004 the filmmakers Jason Russell, Laren Poole, and Bobby Bailey had founded the nonprofit organization Invisible Children as the outgrowth of a documentary project. Hoping to document atrocities in the Darfur region of Sudan, the three traveled to northern Uganda. When their convoy was fired on by the Lord's Resistance Army (LRA) and they had trouble moving into Sudan, they were forced to stop in the small city of Gulu. There they encountered young people who had walked from the villages surrounding the city into Gulu to sleep in groups, in hopes of avoiding being abducted and added to Kony's army.[1]

The story of the children of Gulu became the organizing narra-

tive for Invisible Children. For years, Russell and colleagues organized Christian youth groups in an event called the Global Night
Commute, which invited supporters in North American cities to
sleep outside in solidarity with children in northern Uganda. The
funds they raised allowed them to build networks of volunteers
in Uganda connected by high-frequency radio, who monitored
movements of the LRA combatants. But Invisible Children's primary focus, accounting for more than two-thirds of its spending
pre-2012, was on "raising awareness," holding events, making
films, and lobbying legislators to support the Ugandan army in
its search for Kony.

In March 2012, Invisible Children launched its most successful
awareness-raising campaign: Kony 2012. Anchored by a slickly
produced half-hour video, the singular and simple idea was to
make Joseph Kony famous. The people who watched the *Kony
2012* video could help do that by sharing it on social media and
asking influencers, people with large media audiences, to share it
as well. The website that accompanied *Kony 2012* included tools
to make it easy to share the video with everyone from President
Obama to Oprah Winfrey to your friends and neighbors.

Within two weeks, *Kony 2012* had been viewed over 83 million times. Invisible Children heavily promoted the video via
its existing mailing lists and urged supporters to tweet about it,
coordinating their actions to make them more likely to appear
on Twitter's trending topics—an early instance of what's now
become the standard tactic of making causes "go viral."[2] At a
certain point, mainstream media attention on Kony 2012 focused
as much on the campaign's massive spread as on the details of
its message.

At the urging of a friend who studies youth culture online, I
jumped into the fray and wrote an essay challenging the narrative that Invisible Children put forward in the video.[3] I was one
of dozens who wrote articles challenging Invisible Children's
strategy, asking whether its campaign focused too much on fund-

raising and awareness-raising and too little on the complexities of actually capturing Kony. Others, including Ugandan friends, wrote asking whether Invisible Children was listening to the needs of the Ugandan people it claimed to represent.

The backlash to Invisible Children was swift and severe, and the organization was ill-prepared for it. While the organization worked closely with lobbyists and advocates who understood the complexities of Central Africa, most Invisible Children spokes-people who were interviewed by media were defensive and dis-missive when asked about the challenges associated with working with Uganda's military, notorious for its human rights abuses. The narrative about Invisible Children quickly changed from describing it as a brilliant and inspiring campaign to one that was overhyped and underresearched.

The strain on Invisible Children's leadership was significant. On March 15, 2012, ten days after the launch of the campaign, Jason Russell was arrested on a street corner in San Diego, naked, talking to himself and masturbating. He was taken in for psychi-atric evaluation and received a diagnosis of reactive psychosis,[4] a brief but intense break from reality brought about by the extreme stress of the attention and criticism that the Kony 2012 campaign had received.[5]

Invisible Children never entirely recovered from Kony 2012. In late 2014 it announced that it would be shrinking to just four staff, with Russell and other key members leaving the team.[6] It continues to function at a much smaller scale than at its Kony 2012 peak. On the one hand, its advocacy had been a profound success. The Obama administration committed troops to support the Ugandan military in searching for Kony despite widespread concerns about Uganda's abysmal human rights record.[7] Visitors to the Department of Defense and congressional offices reported seeing Kony 2012 posters in the offices of many Washington deci-sion makers. On the other hand, Joseph Kony remains at large.

Kony 2012 was an entrancing and baffling moment for people who study social change online. Invisible Children quickly captured an audience that most activists only dream of reaching. However, it reached this massive audience by massively oversimplifying the situation surrounding Kony and by advocating for policies that few experts on Central African affairs supported. In one late-night conversation, a friend accused me of being anti–Invisible Children because I was jealous that they'd garnered thousands of times more attention for African issues than I had in years of writing on international relations.

He was right. The Kony 2012 campaign infuriated me because it gained attention by glossing over all the details that I find so interesting about a figure like Joseph Kony and his impact on Uganda. I was—and I remain—convinced that it is disastrous to try to influence policy halfway around the world without understanding the context. But I also acknowledge that Invisible Children wasn't trying to turn its supporters into Central Africa experts—it was trying to mobilize them for action.

Ironically, the post I wrote on Kony was shared tens of thousands of times, and is probably the most widely read piece of my writing ever, despite the fact that most people who read it hated it and rushed to tell me so.

One of the kinder respondents, Erin, asked a question I've wrestled with ever since:

But . . . what CAN we do? Much of the appeal of Kony 2012 is that it gives us white, American liberals a method to engage and do SOMETHING with our bleeding hearts. I have no doubt of the complexity of the problem, and I appreciate the detailed blogpost you've written. But you've made the same omission as many others who've written truthful narratives about Africa: you've left us with the impression that there is no solution, because all the players are bad and untrustworthy, so we shrug our shoulders, blame the Africans, and turn away. Give us hope; point us toward a solution; give us something specific and achievable to do! This is what Invisible Children has appreciated about human psychology and has done so effectively.

Erin was right. The desire to do something—whether it is the right or the best thing—is a powerful human impulse that we often underestimate. Humans want to be effective. We need to believe we can affect the world we live in, that we can bring about changes that really matter. Understanding the power of this need is one of the keys to understanding how social change unfolds today.

Why Do We Bother to Vote?

This deep into a book on mistrust, you could be forgiven for assuming that I pose this question as a cynical provocation. But the question exposes a deep paradox in democratic government, one that was identified as early as 1785 by the mathematician and social scientist Nicolas de Condorcet: "In single-stage elections, where there are a great many voters, each voter's influence is very small. It is therefore possible that the citizens will not be sufficiently interested [to vote]."[8]

The political scientist Anthony Downs took up the question in a 1957 book, *An Economic Theory of Democracy*.[9] The question of why rational voters participate in elections even when the cost of voting exceeds the "perceived benefit"—the possibility of swaying the election—is commonly called Downs's paradox. The paradox stems not from the import of a given election but from the fact that an individual's particular vote is unlikely to be decisive. If humans were purely rational, it would make sense to vote only in very close elections, or ones where the personal benefits of a certain outcome were massive for the voter.

To explain the paradox, Downs speculates that a lot of voting is motivated by duty, a sense that democracy is the right way to run a society, and the recognition that democracies won't work without widespread participation. Voting legitimates the system. The "I Voted" sticker, ubiquitous on Americans' chests after an election, is a duty-driven way of stimulating electoral participation. It prods anyone who sees it to do their duty and participate in the election too.[10]

At the same time Anthony Downs was linking voting with duty, political scientists at the University of Michigan were poring through surveys conducted after the 1952 US presidential election, trying to understand who had voted and why. In their 1954 book *The Voter Decides,* Angus Campbell and his colleagues offered another factor to explain voter behavior: efficacy. The political scientists asked voters five questions about the complexity of politics, the possibility of having influence through voting, and the voters' personal sense of being able to influence politicians and the government. They defined efficacy as "the feeling that individual political action does have, or can have an impact on the political process, i.e., the feeling that it is worthwhile to perform one's civic duties. It is the feeling that political and social change is possible and that the individual citizen can play part in bringing about this change."[11]

Campbell and his colleagues found wide variability in voters' sense of efficacy. Men felt higher political efficacy than women, wealthy people more than poor people, city people more than rural dwellers. People with college educations had a much higher sense of their ability to bring about social and political change than those who hadn't completed high school, and the survey found a massive gap in efficacy based on race: 48 percent of Black participants felt a low sense of efficacy, compared to only 18 percent of whites.

One way to explain these disparities in perception is that they reflected the actual ability of different people to make meaningful social change at particular points in history. A wealthy, college-educated white man likely had a much better chance of

influencing the US government in 1952 than did a poor, unedu-
cated woman of color. Despite the visible effects of race, gender,
class, and education, Campbell and his colleagues believed an
independent sense of efficacy would also help explain participation. An individual who felt low efficacy had little reason to participate.[12] But someone who felt high efficacy was subject to "an
ascending spiral where participation and efficacy reinforce each
other."[13]

To understand these ideas about efficacy, it may be helpful
to return to the distinction between institutionalists and insurrectionists. Institutionalists believe that working within existing institutions is the likeliest way to make change. They have
a high sense of internal efficacy—that is, they feel confident
about their skills in making change. They also have a high sense
of external efficacy—that is, they believe the systems they operate within allow them to make change. Insurrectionists too have
high internal efficacy—they know how to organize and build a
movement—but they have low external efficacy, believing that
systems resist significant change. The political scientist George
Balch and his team highlight community organizer Saul Alinsky
as an exemplar of someone with high internal and low external
efficacy. Arguably, many American civil rights leaders fit this
same insurrectionist pattern: they were thoughtful and disciplined in their attempts to make change but faced deeply resistant
authorities and regimes.[14]

In 1973 Marsha Bell Puro, a graduate student in political science, conducted a survey of college students that rounds out the
connection between low external efficacy and insurrection. She
found that students with high internal efficacy and low external
efficacy supported insurrectionist movements of the time, including Students for a Democratic Society and the Black Panthers.
Meanwhile students with low internal efficacy and high external efficacy—those who believed in the power of the government, if not in their personal ability to understand or influence

it—inclined toward nationalism and a belief in the importance of sacrifice for the sake of the nation.[15]

Civic education, as celebrated by Justice Sandra Day O'Connor and others, is designed to increase internal efficacy by giving people the tools they need to be effective advocates within governments. But civic education may have another effect. In the early 1970s, educators in Rochester, New York, worked with a cohort of African-American children, teaching a curriculum designed to make students more self-confident and independent. When the students were contrasted with peers who'd not gone through the same program, they had a higher sense of internal efficacy but a lower sense of external efficacy. It's possible that in learning about their own power, they came to the conclusion that many people of color in the United States have come to: that systems are stacked against them.[16]

Our current age of mistrust is one in which many of us are feeling a low sense of external efficacy. We lack confidence in our ability to influence the institutions that affect our lives. In some cases, we may doubt that those institutions are really the ones in control and wonder whether an even less addressable entity holds real power.

A rational response to low external efficacy is to cease participating in public life. Why bother participating if you feel powerless to make any real change? The magic of Invisible Children was that it convinced people they could make change by giving them clear instructions on how to amplify the message and a clear way to measure success, in terms of how often the video had been shared and viewed. The readers who so hated my blogpost were angry in part because my words had decreased their internal sense of efficacy. They knew less about what to do after reading it than they had before they read it.

Throughout this book, I've talked about institutionalists and insurrectionists. To understand insurrectionists, we must realize that they are people who've decided not to give up on making change, even though they have little faith in doing so through existing institutions. Rather than dropping out of civics, they look for ways to make change with new levers of power. In other words, they have high internal efficacy and low external efficacy, much like the pioneers of the civil rights movement. Understanding how and when they engage is key to keeping civic life open for people who've lost faith in conventional forms of engagement.

Thin and Thick

On June 7, 1893, a young Indian lawyer, Mohandas Gandhi, was on a train from Durban to Pretoria when a man of European descent demanded that he leave the first-class cabin. Gandhi refused and was thrown off the train at Pietermaritzburg into a cold winter's night.[17] The experience set the young man on a path of satyagraha, or principled, nonviolent resistance against the racial and ethnic discrimination that characterized South Africa. Beginning in 1906, Gandhi led the Indian population of Transvaal in a campaign of protests and strikes that led, in 1913, to a set of political and civil rights reforms that offered some protection for Indian citizens of South Africa.

In 1914 Gandhi returned home to India, and by 1920 he was the most visible figure in a campaign for Indian independence. Gandhi began spinning and weaving his own simple clothing as a protest against British-manufactured cloth. He and his followers began extracting salt from seawater as a protest against the Salt Act of 1882, which had granted the British a monopoly over the dietary staple. Through these everyday acts of protest, as well as through strikes and marches, Gandhi became an avatar of resistance to the British. He embodied this stance in every aspect of his life and work.[18]

American visions of appropriate protest lean heavily on Gandhi's example in part because civil rights leaders drew guidance from his life story. Martin Luther King, Jr., studied Gandhi's books and modeled his protests after him. "From my background I gained my regulating Christian ideals," he said. "From Gandhi, I learned my operational technique."[19]

Given the centrality of the civil rights movement to the American understanding of social change, it is not surprising that we often expect Gandhi-like commitment from our activists and change makers. Malcolm Gladwell's critique of online activism, which we discussed in Chapter 4, centered on the idea that online activists weren't engaged in "real" activism because they weren't putting themselves at physical risk.[20] Invoking Mississippi Freedom Summer, in which three volunteers were killed, and many were beaten, shot at, and arrested, Gladwell observed, "Activism that challenges the status quo—that attacks deeply rooted problems—is not for the faint of heart."

The danger with demanding Gandhian levels of commitment to social change is that most of us aren't Gandhi. We shouldn't have to be to change our societies for the better. When we make social change into something that requires superhuman courage, the danger is that we feel either inadequate or powerless unless we are able to dedicate ourselves completely to making change.

There are a variety of legitimate ways to work for social change, from methods that demand deep and full conviction, which I describe as "thick," to "thinner" forms that gain their power from widespread participation and significant scale but demand less from each individual participant.

Thin engagement requires little thought on your part because organizers have designed a campaign in which your participation is predetermined. Sign a petition, give a contribution, join a march: in a campaign that uses thin engagement, the organizers know what they want you to do and simply need you to show up and do it. By contrast, in thick engagement, the campaigners ask you for your creativity, your strategic sensibilities, or your ability to make media, carry out research, deliberate, or find solutions.

The campaigners know they want to do something but ask you to shape the strategy.

Thin engagement requires your feet; thick engagement requires your head. At their best, they both harness your heart.

Much as we expect activists to channel their inner Gandhi, we assume that the best forms of engagement are thick and that the goal of thin engagement is to ease people into more involved forms of activism. Make a donation to a political campaign, and you may be asked to put up a lawn sign, then to phone bank, then to canvass door to door. There's nothing wrong with moving people from lightweight forms of participation to more engaged ones, and movements recruit their leadership from within these ranks, asking those who are most engaged in thin activities to take on more leadership for the cause.

That said, the acts of civic engagement we most celebrate— voting in particular—are thin. When voting requires you to undertake careful, detailed planning to ensure you can cast your vote, we describe those circumstances as voter suppression. A healthy democracy lowers barriers to entry to participation, enabling as many citizens as possible to access information about candidates and to vote. Thin engagement works best at scale. A petition with a few dozen signatures gets ignored. But similarly, a census with fractional participation will underrepresent populations who neglect to fill it out or who were intimidated into nonparticipation.

One of the central challenges for social change campaigns is designing actions that are both thin and meaningful. As with voting, it can be hard to feel that your particular contribution is important when you are one of thousands. Especially successful thin campaigns leverage creative ways to help participants feel a personal sense of efficacy.

On March 25, 2013, the Human Rights Campaign (HRC), an American organization focused on equal rights for gay, lesbian, bisexual, and transgender people, launched a social media campaign designed to document support for equal marriage on social networks. In early 2013 the Supreme Court heard arguments about California's Proposition 8, which banned gay marriage, and HRC's campaign encouraged users to change their profile photos to a pink "equals" sign on a red background, a reworking of HRC's iconic logo, a yellow "equals" sign on a blue background. As with the Kony 2012 campaign, celebrities embraced the cause: the actor and gay activist George Takei shared the campaign with his millions of Twitter followers, and his tweet was shared tens of thousands of times.

Critically, HRC embraced people's impulse to personalize and remix the campaign. While most people simply adopted the HRC's new icon, many offered their own spin on the image, turning the "equals" sign into two twinkies, or two pieces of bacon, or superimposing possible gay couples, including children's television characters Bert and Ernie, or the Statue of Liberty kissing Lady Justice. Not all the remixes were supportive—a small number of people turned the image into the "not equals" sign ($\neq$)— but for most, these tweaks took a thin form of participation and made it more personal and meaningful.[21] According to Facebook in-house data scientist Eytan Bakshy, roughly 2.7 million more Facebook users updated their profile photo on March 26 than on an average day, suggesting massive uptake of the campaign.[22]

Other than generating a wave of media attention, did the profile image changes have any effect? One popular Internet meme rubbished the idea, showing an image of Chief Justice John Roberts with the text "Before we make a ruling, did enough people change their Facebook pictures?" My students Nathan Matias, Matt Stempeck, and Molly Sauter offered a different interpretation: the presence of so many changed profile pictures on Facebook helped people see how widespread support for equal marriage had become.[23] For someone passively supporting equal marriage, the presence of these images might make it safe to come out as a supporter of equal marriage. For someone opposed to equal marriage, the campaign might challenge the assumption that their position was universally held.

Using the four levers framework from Chapter 4, we might consider the red "equals" sign as a norms-based approach to change. If enough people change their profile picture, perhaps the social pressure will shift the opinions of those opposed to gay marriage. A more helpful way to think of the campaign, though, is as an example of a voice-based effort.

The four levers we've considered—laws, norms, code, and markets—all make change through instrumental means. Activists have a set of behaviors they seek to accomplish—passage of a law, adoption of a new technology, a shift in social norms—and they seek to persuade people to help them accomplish that goal. By contrast, voice-based activism has as its primary goal the raising of other voices, rather than achieving an instrumental goal.

Before 2010, conventional wisdom in the immigrant rights movement held that undocumented immigrants shouldn't engage in visible activism given their risk of being arrested and deported. In January 2010 three undocumented students launched the Dream Walk, a march from Miami to Washington, DC, to advocate for the Development, Relief, and Education for Alien Minors (DREAM) immigration reform act. In May 2010 five undocumented students, dressed in caps and gowns, staged a sit-in at Senator John McCain's Arizona office, daring police to arrest them.[24] The new spirit of visible defiance on the part of the undocumented was summed up in the slogan "Undocumented and Unafraid."[25]

Search any platform that hosts videos for the phrase "undocumented and unafraid," and you will find hundreds of videos. In these often simple, unscripted pieces, undocumented youth look into the camera, identify themselves as undocumented, and talk about the experience of discovering that they were not legal citizens of the United States. There's a risk associated with these videos: in theory, they could be used to help Immigrations and Customs Enforcement identify them as targets for deportation.

Undocumented and Unafraid videos are clearly a thick form of engagement, requiring personal risk and creativity as well as participation. In instrumental terms, it's hard to know what they're meant to do. It's unlikely that legislators are cruising YouTube to measure public opinion. Yet the videos achieve something. They help undocumented youth deal with the fear and isolation that can come with discovering their immigration status. By coming out as undocumented, a video maker invites friends to understand and support her immigration battle, to talk about it rather than remain silent. And as with the coming out movement for gays and lesbians more than a generation earlier, coming out as undocumented on video makes it easier for other people to identify themselves as undocumented and to begin the process of becoming unafraid.

Thinking of engagement in terms of thick and thin, voice and instrumental, gives us ways of understanding and evaluating activism that doesn't resemble Gandhian protest. Voice-based activism that's thick, like Undocumented and Unafraid, can provide fuel to build and enlarge movements, reminding participants what they're fighting for.

In 2012 the Susan G. Komen Foundation announced that it would stop funding the women's health organization Planned Parenthood under pressure from anti-abortion activists.[26] The digital activism leader Deanna Zandt launched a campaign called Planned Parenthood Saved My Life. She invited women to e-mail her stories of how Planned Parenthood had helped them—from providing affordable women's health services through to providing abortions—and placed the stories on a Tumblr blog. The dozens of stories collected there offered a human face to a policy battle. The site was featured across US media, calling attention to the fact that Komen had been supporting not abortion services but breast cancer screening. In part due to Deanna's campaign, Komen reversed course and resumed funding for Planned Parenthood.[27]

If thick voice-based activism can add a potent layer of humanity to abstract policy issues, thin voice-based activism runs the risk of "slacktivism," the critique that writer Evgeny Morozov and others have offered about activism that's more about virtue signaling and unconsidered participation than about making change. Morozov cites an experiment by the Danish psychologist Anders Colding-Jørgensen, who started a Facebook group implying that the Danish government would be dismantling Copenhagen's beloved Stork Fountain.[28] Colding-Jørgensen seeded the group with 125 friends and watched in amazement as the group ballooned to 28,000 members, ostensibly opposed to a policy decision that would never take place. Morozov sees Stork Fountain as evidence that people support causes as a form of fashion, a way of signaling their social virtue and identity, rather than as a path toward change. But you could read the same example in a different light: Danes who wanted to ensure their fountain wasn't torn down grasped at a thin, ineffective way of making change because they weren't offered anything else.

Ill-considered and ineffective activism is a real thing, but being thin doesn't mean an engagement is meaningless. Voting is both thin and instrumental, and despite making little sense in terms of personal calculus, it's enormously important in determining law-driven change within a democracy. The problem of slacktivism is a problem of efficacy. Whether you're engaged in thick or thin action, or are focused on voice or instrumental outcomes, it's possible to have a lousy theory of change or, worse, no theory of change.

Efficacy is always a problem of perception. People will undertake actions, even deeply demanding actions, if they are persuaded their participation can make a difference. The challenge for organizers of social movements is to create a range of actions, from thin to thick, that let participants feel they're making effective change. Invisible Children did a brilliant job of creating thin actions that helped participants feel powerful. What it failed to do is establish a path for those who asked tough questions about efficacy to get more deeply involved, to understand the complexity and nuances of the problems of violence in Central Africa. Transformative movements understand that some participants in thin actions will want to take thicker steps, owning the movement themselves, using their own stories to encourage the voices of others. Architects of social movements neglect these people at their peril.

Act Locally—Whatever That Means to You

The slogan "Think globally, act locally" has become a mantra for the environmental movement, used to explain the logic of actions like recycling, which have little instrumental impact but allow people to feel a sense of efficacy and participation. The phrase is attributed to the Scottish biologist and urban planner Patrick Geddes, who believed that the character of cities as whole entities relied on the preservation of historic buildings and of public spaces like village greens and public gardens.[29] The larger logic, which encourages people to work on the problems they know best and feel best positioned to address, offers another view on efficacy and motivation.

Despite high levels of mistrust in national institutions, there's a sense that politics at the local level is still salvageable and that local institutions may often be more competent than national ones. Governors in all fifty states, for example, have received higher marks than the federal government regarding their handling of the new coronavirus.[30] Books like *The New Localism* by Bruce Katz and Jeremy Nowak offer examples of how cities are creating economic turnarounds by building partnerships between universities, local organizations, industries, and governments in a way that's deeply optimistic and promising, especially when compared to dysfunction and polarization at the national level.[31]

Cities may be less subject to polarization because the issues they face don't map neatly to political ideologies. As New York City mayor Fiorello La Guardia famously said, "There is no Democratic or Republican way of cleaning the streets."[32] Indeed, only three of the ten most populous cities in the United States have partisan elections, where candidates identify as Republicans or Democrats. The remainder hold nonpartisan elections, hoping to increase cooperation among city leaders across political differences.[33] A less idealistic explanation would point out that most American cities are Democratic strongholds and have no meaningful partisan challengers.

Whether you favor the idealistic or the cynical explanation, among Americans, confidence in state and local governments is significantly higher than confidence in the federal government. In 2018 Gallup asked Americans whether they trusted different branches of government a great deal or a fair amount (a much looser standard than the question I examined in Chapters 1 and 2, about trusting the government entirely or a great deal). Sixty-two percent expressed confidence in local government, and 63 percent in state government, but only 40 percent expressed confidence in the U.S. legislative branch and 42 percent in the executive branch.[34] A different Gallup poll found confidence in local government to be significantly higher than confidence in state government. The two were interchangeable from the 1970s through the '90s but began to diverge in the 2000s, as confidence in state governments dropped.[35] While many Americans have low confidence in government across the board, a significant number of Americans have confidence in the government that's closest to home.

A possible explanation for this disparity is familiarity. Richard Fenno addressed the paradox that Americans dislike Congress but like their individual congressperson in his 1978 book *Home Style: House Members in Their Districts.*[36] Fenno argues that voters know the projects and accompanying spending that members bring to their districts and are grateful, but they see the rest of the governing process in Washington as disconnected from their lives. Gallup polling suggests some support for this theory, finding that people who could identify their congressperson had more positive feelings toward him or her, leading to the theory that people who didn't know their representative were expressing feelings about Congress as a whole, not about an individual member.[37] But the media environment has changed radically since Fenno's book: in 1978 people got news primarily from local newspapers and television stations, which often reported on the policies and votes made by the congresspeople who represented the area. Today, by contrast, twenty-four-hour cable news and social media focus disproportionately on national politics, whose figures are likely more familiar to many citizens than congressional representatives. We are far more likely to know the positions of party leaders than those of our local representatives, in part due to these media shifts.

Another explanation for voter enthusiasm for local politics is efficacy. It can be incredibly hard for citizens to feel a sense of efficacy in national politics, where the effects of one vote, one phone call or one tweet are too small to measure. But the same action in a local context has a greater chance of swinging an election or changing a politician's mind. I sometimes ask students to try an experiment: write letters to a congressperson and to a local politician, like a state senator, about the same issue. In my experience, the congressperson will usually respond with a form letter, if at all, while the state senator will often set up a staff call to discuss the matter further. Local politicians know that an individual voter might sway a few dozen friends and family by sharing either a good or bad experience, and they allocate their time to constituents accordingly.

The efficacy effects of locality apply not only to political geographies. The #MeToo movement is unfolding as a national movement, but it's composed of individual people taking action in their workplaces, an environment that affects them more directly than state or local government. When Hollywood actresses speak out about sexual assault by Harvey Weinstein or radio producers speak out about being bullied and harassed by John Hockenberry, they are advocating for change in an environment that directly affects them, their workplace.

The successes of #MeToo—the arrests and prosecutions of Harvey Weinstein, Bill Cosby, Larry Nassar, and others—suggest that activism focused on locality may have a higher success rate than activism focused at the national or global level. Nassar, after assaulting hundreds of young women on the US gymnastics team, is now incarcerated for the rest of his life, and the organization's board members who enabled him have been forced to resign. Many of the women assaulted by Nassar have left the sport, but they know they've made gymnastics safer for the young women who follow them.

Activists within #MeToo are acutely aware of efficacy as part of their calculus. In 2017 and 2018, I helped organize an annual prize given by the MIT Media Lab for "pro-social disobedience," designed to recognize and reward people who break rules and resist authority in support of broader change. In 2018 we honored leaders of the #MeTooSTEM movement, along with #MeToo founder Tarana Burke, for their work on sexual harassment in the academy, specifically opening a discussion about the relationships between senior faculty and graduate students in the sciences, where faculty have enormous power over their students' future careers. Because most professors are protected by tenure, it often requires extraordinary circumstances for them to lose their jobs. So Dr. Sherry Marts and Dr. BethAnn McLaughlin aim their work at influencing institutions like the National Academy of Sciences, asking these groups that focus on honoring extraordinary achievement to distance themselves from known harassers. Such a public rebuke helps young scientists identify these men as people to avoid at conferences and events. Removing honorary affiliations should be easier to achieve than firing tenured faculty.

The Media Lab's disobedience prize took a dark turn when Joi Ito, who created the prize (with LinkedIn creator Reid Hoffman), admitted to having a set of financial relationships with Jeffrey Epstein, a financier who had previously been convicted for sexual abuse of a fourteen-year-old girl. Drs. Marts and McLaughlin both denounced the Media Lab's involvement with Epstein. Marts posted on her blog, "[Ito] stood on a stage, looked Burke, McLaughlin, and me in the eye and congratulated us for our work to end sexual violence, harassment, and bullying, and did not even blink. He has not apologized to us for his behavior and for the potential harm of bringing our work into question by associating us with an organization that accepted funding from a sexual predator. He owes us that apology."[38] McLaughlin used funds from the award to return to the MIT campus and provide counseling for those affected by the Epstein scandal. For McLaughlin, Ito's decision to work with Epstein cemented the importance of working with those victimized by an academic environment that too often looks the other way at sexual harassment and fails to consider the crushing psychological effects that tolerating harassers can have on the workplace.

Some men have expressed concern about the #MeToo movement, fearing that behavior that was previously ignored is now being deemed unacceptable. A concern that makes more sense to me is that activism—whether around sexual harassment, gender discrimination, racism, or other biased behavior—is coming to the workplace because that's where people feel most empowered to make change. At a moment when many people are alienated from national-level politics but simultaneously are politically engaged (and often enraged), it is logical that they would try to change discriminatory behaviors in their workplaces first. News organizations have begun referring to the "era of #MeToo" to contextualize a work climate in which the previously accepted is no longer tolerated. It's possible that we'll start seeing a broader movement for workplace justice on axes other than sexual discrimination as people try to make change in an environment that they feel more empowered to influence.

Efficacy and Online Spaces

In the last decade, major social movements have been unfolding in online spaces as well as in physical ones. That's no coincidence: a critical element of movements like #MeToo and Black Lives Matter is a theory of change that demands that mainstream media pay attention to the issues they are raising.

This focus on media attention is not new—the civil rights movement relied heavily on television to bring images of the struggle in southern cities into homes across the nation. The local press in many southern cities wouldn't cover protests against racism, so movement leaders targeted national newscasts, allowing Black southerners to learn about actions taken in nearby communities.[39]

In a similar way, television and social media helped launch the Arab Spring. Activists in Sidi Bouzid used Facebook video to document their protests, which were uncovered by Tunisian media outlets. Tunisian activists in Europe then packaged the video and brought it to Al Jazeera, which broadcast it on its Arabic-language service, reaching an audience in Tunis who were otherwise unaware of the protests occurring only two hundred kilometers away. We can credit social media for helping to oust Tunisian president Ben Ali if only because other local protest movements, including one in Gafsa a few years earlier, died because they never received national attention.[40]

In the past twenty years, a shift in the architecture of media has radically changed the relationship between producers of news and their audiences. We're used to talking about the ways digital media has destroyed the economic model of journalism, but we're less used to discussing the ways audiences now produce and disseminate media themselves. The political power that comes from amplifying media has changed the nature of political participation.

In the broadcast age, the relationship between media producers and citizens was straightforward. Companies both produced and distributed media, gaining revenue by selling ad insertions in the distribution stream. Broadcasters told citizens what to pay attention to and invited them, perhaps, to do something with the information they received. In a participatory media ecosystem, by contrast, different people produce and distribute news. *The New York Times* still has its printing press and delivery trucks, obviously, but the ability of a news story to reach a wide audience now depends heavily on digital media distributors, especially Google and Facebook. Because those platforms control the audience, they now also have a dominant position in advertising, capturing 90 percent of all the growth in digital advertising in 2017.[41]

In addition to voting, protesting, etc., citizens can engage by producing media or amplifying existing media

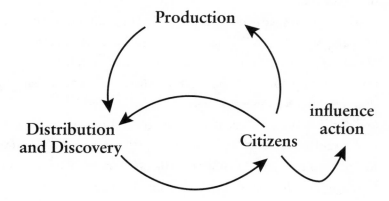

Individual citizens have two powerful roles within this new model. First, they can create their own media, which sometimes competes with professional media producers for attention and is sometimes amplified by those professionals. Second, they can influence the distributors by voting content up and down with their attention, helping amplify some stories and suppressing others. Both of these are possible forms of political activism, and they use a common method: agenda setting and framing.[42]

Agenda setting, an idea advanced by the journalism scholars Maxwell McCombs and Donald Shaw, asserts that media's power comes from influencing what issues appear in public discourse.[43] The power of agenda setting is well summarized by the political scientist Bernard Cohen, who noted, "The press may not be successful much of the time in telling people what to think, but it is stunningly successful in telling its readers what to think about."[44] Media continue to have this power, but individuals and groups now have the possibility of telling the press what to pay attention to through social media.

Kony 2012 was an agenda-setting campaign. In the process of making Joseph Kony famous, it asked news outlets why they weren't paying attention to the Lord's Resistance Army and the suffering of children in northern Uganda. One of the missed opportunities of the campaign is that it didn't demand increased coverage for sub-Saharan Africa in general, a systemic weakness of US media.[45]

#IfTheyGunnedMeDown (discussed in Chapter 4) is a reframing campaign. When US media pay attention to the deaths of people of color at the hands of the police, they often focus on the potential culpability of the victims, choosing images that imply that they were dangerous or breaking the law. Patrisse Cullors, one of the founders of the Black Lives Matter movement, observed that "dead 17-year-old Trayvon was posthumously placed on trial for his own murder."[46] Campaigns like #IfTheyGunnedMeDown leverage the attention paid to these deaths but shift the frame.

My former lab, Center for Civic Media, studied the effects of reframing police violence by the Black Lives Matter movement. We examined 343 cases between 2013 and 2016 where unarmed people of color were killed by police. We found that deaths that occurred after Michael Brown's death, the focus of a great deal of antiracist activism, were eleven times more likely to receive media coverage than deaths that preceded Brown's. We also found a change in the way media outlets covered these deaths. Before Brown's death, 2 percent of stories about unarmed people of color killed by police contained the name of another victim. After Brown, 22 percent did, showing that reporters were far more likely to cover a story not as an isolated incident but as part of a pattern of police violence against people of color.[47] And while attention to the deaths of unarmed people of color waned by 2016, not to return until reactions to George Floyd's death in 2020, our study suggested that the reframing was a lasting one, and that subsequent stories about these deaths were more likely to mention the larger pattern.

Reframing and agenda setting work, and the people who use these tools know they work. Campaigns try to go viral on social media not just to raise money but to gain mainstream media attention. Individuals and groups who've figured out how to hack the media feel a powerful sense of efficacy precisely because their efforts end up having rapid and measurable effects.

One remarkable aspect of the Trump presidency has been Trump's own embrace of "meme magic," the idea that pro-Trump imagery and video can motivate and mobilize voters. In July 2019 the president invited two hundred conservative media makers to the White House, including "Carpe Donktum," who creates fake videos that Trump has shared online. Addressing the assembled crowd, Trump lauded them for producing advocacy materials that were better than what he could get from his own staff. "The crap you think of is incredible," he crowed.

Have memes of Trump as a professional wrestler hitting the

CNN icon with a chair helped cement his steady approval rating among his base? Or does making memes give some Trump supporters a sense of efficacy, a belief that they're able to be part of their leader's reelection campaign? Given the high visibility of Trump's Twitter posts, which have driven numerous news cycles over the past four years, it's probably unwise to dismiss "meme magic" out of hand.

Do Something

In 1993 the actor Andrew Shue and his childhood friend Michael Sanchez formed a nonprofit organization called Do Something. Their idea was simple: "to encourage and inspire young people to get involved in their communities."[48] The breadth and vagueness of that goal is reflected both in the organization's name and in the wide variety of projects it has launched. Popular Do Something campaigns include Free to Pee, which encourages participants to post signs demanding gender-inclusive restrooms; Elephant Tusk Force, in which participants flag ivory items on craigslist to stop elephant poaching; and Update Your Status, which encourages students to get tested for HIV and to post an Instagram pic of their knuckles with TESTED written across them.[49]

The point of Do Something is not that any of these campaigns will accomplish major change around the issues they address, but that taking action on a social issue is a precursor to deeper forms of engagement. Do Something believes it is training a generation of young people, many as young as high school students, to see that it's possible to organize, to lead a group of their peers, and to make change in the world.

Perhaps the most remarkable story to come out of Do Something is the way the organization itself has done something about teens and mental health. Do Something organizers spend a great deal of time communicating via text message, the medium most used by their target audience. In 2011 the Do Something organizer Stephanie Shih received a text message from a young woman that said, "He won't stop raping me. He told me not to tell anyone." Shih traded messages with her, and learned that the "he" she referred to was her father. Shih directed the young woman to the Rape, Abuse and Incest National Network (RAINN), but the experience left her so shaken, she brought it to Do Something's director, Nancy Lublin.

Lublin and Shih realized that many teens are too scared to call rape crisis or suicide hotlines. They are more comfortable texting, but no mental health hotlines were well-equipped to operate primarily by text. The two women formed Crisis Text Line, a national service staffed by volunteers who've completed a thirty-four-hour online course in counseling via text, and who agree to serve a weekly four-hour shift for a year. At least once a day, on average, Crisis Text Line intervenes, leading to the rescue of someone believed to be at imminent danger of suicide.[50]

Crisis Text Line breaks from many of the conventions of mental health care. Conventional wisdom in the psychiatric profession holds that people in distress should seek help from counselors able to address their set of issues—hence RAINN as a network specifically for people suffering rape and sexual assault. But "people don't experience life in an issue-specific way," Lublin explains. And Crisis Text Line is a dedicated user of data analytics, using A/B testing to determine what responses from counselors are most associated with positive outcomes. From their analytics, they know when certain behaviors are most common (four a.m. for self-harm, eleven p.m. for depression) and what mental health issues are most reported in which states.

While many of the projects launched by Do Something have lower stakes, Crisis Text Line has clearly been transformational, not just for those it has counseled but for the thousands of counselors who have participated. As the project raised awareness of suicide as the third-highest cause of death for teenagers, Crisis

Text Line also has served tens of thousands of teens at risk and has given thousands of counselors a meaningful way to help their community. The training counselors receive in how to listen gives them a skill invaluable in their own interactions with friends, family, and their own kids.

The sense of wanting to do something is one of the most powerful forces that social movements can harness. The idea that people can transform the world for the better is one of the most powerful motivators imaginable. The questions of who we, as individuals, might influence, what levers we should seek to pull, and whether we should operate within, around, or against institutions all are less important than the question of whether we do something or do nothing. There is no one right way to participate, just more and less effective ways to participate. The least effective of all is disengagement.

Faced with a world in which so many have lost trust in so many institutions, our challenge is simple. We must harness mistrust so that we don't lose the power, strength, and creativity of those who've lost faith in institutions. Our work is to help people—starting with ourselves—channel energy and passion into doing something that matters.

Afterword

KATRINA AND COVID-19

IN THE SUMMER OF 2005, HURRICANE KATRINA KILLED MORE than a thousand Gulf Coast residents and displaced more than a million, but its deadly impact was not immediately apparent. Katrina made landfall early on Monday, August 29, as a Category 3 hurricane, significantly weaker than it had been the day before, when its winds reached 160 miles per hour as a Category 5 hurricane. Many thought New Orleans had dodged a bullet. Not until the following day did the scale of the destruction become clear. Levees began to break on the morning of the twenty-ninth, and by the thirtieth, 80 percent of the city was under water.

In the days that followed, the natural tragedy of the hurricane was amplified by the tragedies of failing systems and institutions. As refugees overwhelmed the Superdome, New Orleans's "shelter of last resort," law enforcement began sending flood victims to the Ernest N. Morial Convention Center so they could be evacuated from the flooded city. It took until Friday, four days after the storm made landfall, for the National Guard to arrive with food, water, and medicine for those forced out of their homes and into the convention center.[1] On September 2, as journalists around the world shared images of corpses rotting in the sweltering building, FEMA director Michael Brown told CNN that "the federal government did not even know about the convention center people until today."[2]

While some flood walls and levees failed because of the size of Katrina's storm surge, others breached because of poor engineering and shoddy maintenance. The Army Corps of Engineers tasked the American Society of Civil Engineers with understanding what had happened to New Orleans's "Hurricane Protection System." The ASCE review committee began its report, "A large portion of the destruction from Hurricane Katrina was caused not only by the storm itself but also by the storm's exposure of engineering and engineering-related policy failures."[3] Not only did FEMA fail to bring relief supplies in a timely manner, it also prevented the Red Cross from aiding evacuees for fear that it would encourage them to remain in the city.[4] And while some observers blamed residents for not being proactive and following instructions to flee the city—ignoring the fact that many low-income residents had nowhere to flee to and could not afford a hotel room—the neighboring community of Gretna, Louisiana, blocked a bridge with armed police officers to prevent evacuees from "overwhelming" their town.[5]

Writing on the tenth anniversary of the disaster, the former *New Orleans Times-Picayune* reporter John McQuaid reflected, "What Hurricane Katrina, the floodwall and levee collapses, and the aftermath taught me is that America, and its institutions, simply don't work—and that people like it that way."[6]

The name *Katrina* has become shorthand for two different forms of institutional failure. It evokes a crisis in which so many interconnected systems fail that it becomes difficult to know who to blame. And it evokes a crisis that disproportionately affects disadvantaged people, particularly the low-income brown and Black people least able to prepare and who were most harmed by the failure of safety nets.

I remember watching Katrina from the safety of my dry and unthreatened home in western Massachusetts, a sense of horror and dread rising as the destruction of a great American city came into focus. On Friday, September 2—the day the National Guard began evacuating refugees from the convention center—I received an email from David Geilhufe, a member of the loose association of "techies for social change" that I have been privileged to be part of in my career. David observed that thousands of people fleeing New Orleans were posting "lost but safe" messages to a wide range of websites—the comments section on a radio station's articles about the hurricane, for instance—alerting friends and family, or seeking family members they'd been separated from. David wanted to create a central database for this information to help reunite families: Katrina PeopleFinder.

I volunteered to take on one facet of the problem: entering unstructured data into a shared database. While some "lost but safe" messages could be translated into computer-readable formats, most were "natural text," human language that computers find difficult to parse. With help from dozens of friends—most notably my ex-wife, who has a remarkable posse of Internet friends—we recruited 2,100 online volunteers and entered 87,000 messages into the database in forty-eight hours.[7] Years after Katrina, in response to the earthquake in Haiti, Google built a tool called Google Person Finder, using the data format of Katrina PeopleFinder. Google makes the code available open source for use in subsequent disasters.[8]

At the time, our modest volunteer effort was one of the feel-good stories popular after natural disasters.[9] A particularly optimistic tech writer declared it an example of the Recovery 2.0 movement, a way of responding to disasters by sharing information and by cooperating to aid or circumvent overwhelmed institutions.[10]

In retrospect, I understand the effort another way. My friends and I were helpless to do anything in the face of a disaster that had upended the worlds of more than a million people. Desperate to help and morose in the face of the catastrophic failure of systems that should have protected our fellow citizens, we found something small we could do and threw ourselves into doing it.

It's fifteen years later, and now we're sewing masks.

It's mid-May 2020 as I write this afterword, and the United States has just achieved the grim milestone of 100,000 deaths due to COVID-19. It's not clear at this point whether the country has experienced the worst of the virus, or another wave of infection is coming.

What is clear is that the US response to the novel coronavirus has been vastly less successful than that of other nations. South Korea reported its first case of COVID-19 on January 20, a day before the first case was reported in the United States. Four months later South Korea had kept its deaths to under three hundred and was approaching a small new outbreak with the tools it had successfully used to manage the first wave: rapid, low-cost testing; aggressive contact tracing; free treatment; and salary support while people are quarantined.[11] In the United States, by contrast, we do not yet know whether the community spread of the disease has slowed sufficiently to allow for safe reopening of businesses. Desperate to return to normal, Americans are ignoring public health advice to maintain social distancing and wear protective masks. Their actions are cheered by a president who has minimized the dangers of the virus and stubbornly refused to protect himself or those around him during the crisis.

As with Katrina, there's lots of blame to go around in understanding America's institutional failures around COVID-19. Rather than use coronavirus tests developed in Germany and promoted by the WHO, the government relied on a test developed by the Centers for Disease Control (CDC); it was slow to arrive and did not function correctly.[12] The FDA prevented the CDC test from being used in independent health labs—anyone using it had to send it back to CDC headquarters in Atlanta to receive results. Further, the FDA blocked university and private labs from developing their own tests. The net result was that the United States was largely blind to the extent of coronavirus during the month of February as infections spread throughout the nation.[13]

But failures at the CDC and the FDA don't capture the whole picture, much as blaming the destruction of Katrina on FEMA or the Army Corps of Engineers offers only a partial truth. Pandemic response in the United States has been complicated by our massive prison population—inmates are unable to socially distance and often lack access to soap, hand sanitizer, and masks. In one prison in Marion, Ohio, more than eighteen hundred inmates—three-quarters of the prison population—tested positive for the virus.[14] Many employees had no paid sick leave when the pandemic began to spread, and some came to work despite feeling ill. Many of those who lost their jobs in the economic downturn have also lost their health insurance, a result of the country's unique system of employer-subsidized health insurance. Much as Katrina revealed the unforgivable fragility of levee walls that everyone knew were weak and badly maintained, COVID-19 is showing the inadequacy of many American institutions.

Like Katrina, COVID-19 is disproportionately affecting America's most vulnerable. In New York City, the epicenter of the nation's largest outbreak to date, the death rate for Black residents from COVID was twice the rate for white residents.[15] Latinx Americans are also disproportionately affected, and Native Americans have experienced some of the nation's highest community death rates, particularly on reservations that have inadequate health care and often lack basic infrastructure, like running water.

Unlike Katrina, COVID is a global phenomenon, and the United States has been forced to compare its response to those of other nations. The country is fond of thinking of itself as number one, the most powerful and technologically advanced nation on the planet. But the United States is now number one in cases of the disease and number one in deaths. Its shambolic response is evoking disbelief from citizens of other nations. As *Irish Times* columnist Fintan O'Toole put it, "Over more than two centuries, the United States has stirred a very wide range of feelings in the rest of the world: love and hatred, fear and hope, envy and contempt, awe and anger. But there is one emotion that has never been directed towards the US until now: pity."[16]

The United States may not be number one for long. Cases of COVID-19 are growing quickly in Brazil and Russia, countries where governmental response to the pandemic has been less than decisive. Jair Bolsonaro, sometimes termed a "tropical Trump,"[17] has dismissed the dangers of the virus, failed to practice social distancing, and urged businesses to reopen, over the objections of regional governors and health ministers.[18] The situation in Russia has been one of confusion, with Vladimir Putin shutting the border with China in late January and declaring a "national paid vacation" on March 25. But Russia is reopening after only six weeks of shutdown, despite rising infection rates and death tolls, and Russians find themselves choosing between the optimism of Putin and the caution of the Moscow mayor Sergei Sobyanin, who has resisted the reopening and put more stringent distancing measures in place. Caught between the two leaders, many Russians are confused about the threat they face and what measures they should take to protect themselves.[19]

As I write, the United States, Russia, Brazil, and Britain lead the world in coronavirus cases. All four are led by right-wing nationalist governments that have weaponized doubt to gain political power. In Britain, a misinformation-filled campaign against the vast institution that is the European Union brought Boris Johnson to power, while in the United States, Trump's war on the media and the "deep state" has followed Steve Bannon's advice to "flood the zone with shit."[20] All four countries are at a deep disadvantage in combating the coronavirus, because no one knows who to believe.

At moments of crisis like the pandemic, governments have two ways to mobilize their citizens to take steps to defend public health and welfare. Autocracies can demand compliance, as

China did in imposing a region-wide lockdown in Wuhan, mobilizing workers to build hospitals and forcing anyone diagnosed with coronavirus into isolation. By contrast, democracies can only ask citizens to follow medical guidelines and recommendations. Compliance in democracies depends primarily on two factors: the consistency of the message, and public confidence in the messenger.

Leaders like Bolsonaro and Trump, who personally display skepticism about the danger of the virus through their behavior, muddle the message pushed by medical authorities to maintain social distance and wear masks. Their followers echo their behavior, turning rejecting medical advice into a political position. An American wearing a face mask in May 2020 is as much a reflection of her position on Donald Trump as it is an assessment of her risk of catching or spreading the disease.

Adding to the confusion coming from political leaders, public confidence in scientific and medical experts has been systematically undercut by an approach to public discourse that recognizes no truth, just claims to power. When Dr. Anthony Fauci, director of the National Institute of Allergy and Infectious Diseases, speaks, some in his audience hear the voice of an entrenched "deep state" bureaucrat and tune him out, just as President Trump has told them to do. Others, more receptive to his message, wonder how badly hollowed out the National Institutes of Health, the CDC, and other expert agencies have been by decades of underinvestment in public goods. Was the CDC's failure to test adequately for the virus bad luck, or was it the predictable result of a decades-long project to limit and weaken public institutions?

While we can and should sew masks, donate blood, and cheer for essential workers, a pandemic reminds us of the limitations of personal and decentralized responses to a crisis. In early March 2020, as it became increasingly clear that the coronavirus was spreading throughout US communities, individuals were left to make decisions about what steps they should take to prepare themselves. I boarded a plane to Seattle on March 2, worried that I was making a poor decision but feeling unable to synthesize the little I knew into a reasonable risk-reward equation. When my university banned work-related airplane travel three days later, I breathed a sigh of relief—I needed someone to take responsibility for decision making in the face of incomplete information, and if my state and federal governments weren't comfortable taking a position, at least my employer was.

Some problems can be meaningfully shifted by a single person's principled actions—the movement started by a single tweet, the app that changes the landscape on privacy. Pandemics cannot. They require millions of people to cooperate, and that cooperation can be made possible only by trusted institutions. If the United States escapes with "only" a few hundred thousand deaths due to coronavirus, it will be because institutions did their jobs—state governments maintained shutdowns when the disease was spreading and reopened carefully when hospitals were below capacity; employers allowed workers to stay at home and altered workplaces to make them safer; corporations, universities, and government labs worked toward vaccines and other treatments.

My friend the activist Eli Pariser asked me whether the coronavirus pandemic had turned me into an institutionalist or simply confirmed my insurrectionist tendencies. I told him that I was persuaded that we desperately need institutions we believe in, but that the crisis had deepened my suspicions that many of our institutions were no longer fit for the purpose or up to the task.

"Ah," he said, "you've become a resurrectionist."

If an institutionalist believes we should strengthen and celebrate the institutions we have, and an insurrectionist believes our institutions no longer meet our needs and need reform or replacement, a resurrectionist believes both. We need institutions that deserve our passionate support and defense, and if the institutions we rely on now do not clear that bar, we need to demand new ones that take their place. Should the CDC, the FDA, and the WHO prove unable to guide us through this crisis, we need passionate dissenters to show us how and why they've failed, and how new institutions can do better in the future. But we must also be honest with ourselves and ask whether other institutions—Congress, the presidency, the United Nations, news media—share the blame and the need for reform or replacement.

Katrina demanded that America take a close look at its gravest weaknesses and make real, lasting change in how we support the poor, the sick, and the elderly. That national reckoning did not occur, and it's not clear that the Obama or Trump administration would have handled the crisis any better. The magnitude of the coronavirus pandemic—and its associated economic impacts—presents another opportunity to ask what institutions are working and who they are working for.

A prediction for this postmortem: we are likely to find that institutions fail when we no longer recognize ourselves as a single nation, when we no longer feel responsibility for or obligation to our fellow citizens. A nation divided by whether wearing a cloth face mask is an infringement of civil liberties or a way of protecting our most vulnerable is one that will have trouble funding vaccine research or agreeing to take (in the numbers required) a new vaccine.

If there is cause for optimism in the face of pandemic, it is this: many countries have succeeded in stopping the spread of the virus, and those that have are being rewarded with the trust of their citizens. Surveying citizens in eleven countries in May 2020, Edelman's Trust Barometer team found surges of trust in government, especially in China, South Korea, and Germany, where the government seems to have the upper hand in combatting the virus.[21] In New Zealand, Prime Minister Jacinda Ardern enjoys very high popularity as the country's case count nears zero.[22]

If trust in institutions is easy to lose and slow to regain, celebrating the successful performance of institutions in the face of a global crisis may be a shortcut in determining which institutions deserve our trust and which require a rebirth.

Mistrust in institutions demands that we consider efficacy when we decide what actions we wish to take to change the world. We are not obligated to make change through institutions that have closed themselves to our meaningful participation, and we don't need to apologize for making change by wielding the levers we are best positioned to move. But we can't stop with repairing the levees and rebuilding houses in the Lower Ninth Ward; nor can we stamp out the virus and go back to our jobs, our gyms, and our bars. We need to imagine, demand, and build institutions that rebuild levees before they collapse and isolate patients before an outbreak becomes a pandemic. My biggest fear is not that mistrust makes us disengage, but that we fail to imagine change at the scale we truly need.

ACKNOWLEDGMENTS

THIS BOOK REFLECTS ON LESSONS LEARNED DURING THE nine years I spent at MIT, directing the Center for Civic Media and teaching within the Media Lab and the Comparative Media Studies/Writing department. I am grateful to Alberto Ibargüen for recruiting me to MIT, and to both programs for giving me a home at MIT. Thank you to the foundations and other sponsors who made our work possible and to all my colleagues at MIT for their generosity of spirit. I'm especially grateful to Mitch Resnick, Hal Abelson, James Paradis, and Ed Schiappa, who provided guidance and mentoring during my time at MIT.

I benefitted immensely from the community of scholars and activists at Center for Civic Media, and most of the lessons I've learned about social change were from my staff and students. Thanks to everyone who has ever sat around our table, in person or virtually, with special thanks to Lorrie LeJeune, Rahul Bhargava, Sasha Costanza-Chock, Emily Ndulue, Cindy Bishop, Dennis Jen, Emilie Reiser, Aashka Dave, Anushka Shah, Eric Pennington, Anissa Pierre, Don Blair, and Dan Minty for helping build a culture of openness and inclusion that allowed ideas to thrive. Thanks especially to J. Nathan Matias, Erhardt Graeff, Mols Sauter, Neha Narula, Alexis Hope, Joy Buolamwini, Pedro

Reynolds-Cuellar, Catherine D'Ignazio, Anna Chung, Gordon Magnum, Jia Zhang, Laura Perovich, Chelsea Barabas, Sands Fish, Alexandre Gonçalves, Chris Peterson, Rodrigo Davies, Heather Craig, Ali Hashmi, Jude Mwenda, Matt Stempeck, Rubez Chong, Arwa Mboya, and Willow Brugh for conversations that directly or indirectly shaped this book.

I had the privilege of developing many of the ideas for this book in dialogue with the Youth and Participatory Politics Research Network, created by the MacArthur Foundation. Thanks to Joseph Kahne, Cathy Cohen, Danielle Allen, Jennifer Earl, Lissa Soep, Henry Jenkins, Howard Gardner, Elyse Eidman-Aadahl, Carrie James, and Sangita Shresthova for their help working through my ideas about civic engagement. I'm especially grateful to Danielle Allen and Jennifer Light for convening a series of conversations that led to the book *From Voice to Influence*—those meetings were a shaping influence on my work and thought. I am grateful also to two commissions on citizenship that brought me into conversation with amazing scholars, activists, and government leaders: the American Academy of Arts and Sciences' Commission on the Practice of Democratic Citizenship and the Knight Commission on Trust, Media and Democracy.

Every time I sit down to write, I remember lessons from my friends at the Berkman Klein Center's book club: Doc Searls, David Weinberger, Judith Donath, Eszter Hargittai, Colin Maclay, Christian Sandvig, Wendy Seltzer, Rey Junco, Lokman Tsui, and Zeynep Tufekci. Together, we will club our books into submission.

I am grateful to a wide circle of friends who've helped me think through the ideas in this book. Thanks to Sunil Abraham, Emily Bell, danah boyd, Dominique Cardon, Kate Crawford, Steve Coll, Ian Condry, Darius Cuplinskas, Kate Darling, Cory Doctorow, Henry Farrell, Adam Foss, Patrick Gaspard, Masha Gessen, Eric Gordon, Jo Guldi, Janet Haven, Sanjana Hattotuwa, Sherrilyn Ifill, Dragana Kauric, Stephen King, Ivan Krastev, Nathan Kurz,

Ronaldo Lemos, Lawrence Lessig, Rebecca MacKinnon, Colin McCormick, Lori McGlinchey, BethAnn McLaughlin, Martha Minow, Moisés Naim, Martha Nissenbaum, Quinn Norton, Dele Olojede, Mabel von Oranje, John Palfrey, Eli Pariser, Bruno Patino, Justin Reich, Istvan Rev, Deb Roy, Anya Schiffrin, Michael Schudson, Clay Shirky, Micah Sifry, Ivan Sigal, Jonathan Soros, Tom Steinberg, Bryan Stephenson, Chris Stone, TL Taylor, Jenny Toomey, Fred Turner, Zeynep Tufekci, Ttcat, Siva Vaidhyanathan, Darren Walker, Jing Wang, and Jillian York for conversations and insights that shaped my thinking on this topic.

I am deeply grateful to Brendan Curry, my editor at W. W. Norton, for his confidence in my ideas and my writing, and his efforts to sharpen and hone both. Thanks to everyone at W. W. Norton for bringing this book to life even as COVID-19 was shutting down life as usual.

I am grateful beyond measure for the love and support of my family: Amy, Drew, Don, Donna, Liz, Aya, Evan, and everyone on Team Drew, especially Rachel and Sandy.

Most of this book was written in the public libraries of Berkshire County, Massachusetts. Libraries are one of our most precious public goods and a perpetual example of ways we could treat each other better as neighbors and citizens. God bless the librarians.

NOTES

INTRODUCTION

1. Heather Bellow, "Shays' Rebellion Monument in Sheffield Gets Preservationist Cleanup," *Berkshire Eagle*, May 28, 2018, https://www.berkshireeagle.com/stories/shays-rebellion-monument-in-sheffield-gets-preservationist-cleanup,540751.

2. Thomas Jefferson to James Madison, January 30, 1787, in *American History: From Revolution to Reconstruction and Beyond*, http://www.let.rug.nl/usa/presidents/thomas-jefferson/letters-of-thomas-jefferson/jefl53.php.

3. Leonard L. Richards, *Shays's Rebellion: The American Revolution's Final Battle* (Philadelphia: University of Pennsylvania Press, 2002).

4. Sidney M. Milkis and Michael Nelson, *The American Presidency: Origins and Development, 1776–2014* (Washington, DC: CQ Press, 2003).

5. Ibid.

6. Madeleine Albright, *Fascism: A Warning* (New York: HarperCollins, 2018).

7. "David Brooks: Trump Is the Wrong Answer to the Right Question," *Brian Lehrer Show*, WNYC, May 17, 2016, https://www.wnyc.org/story/david-brooks-republican-values/.

8. Rashad Robinson, conversation with author, August 14, 2018.

Chapter 1: IS THIS THING WORKING?

1. "Underwear Protest at India Attack," BBC News, February 10, 2009; and Geetanjali Krishna, "A Kick in the Knickers," *Business Stan-*

dard, January 25, 2013, https://www.business-standard.com/article/opinion/geetanjali-krishna-a-kick-in-the-knickers-109021400041_1.html.

2. Jennifer Preston, "Movement Began with Outrage and a Facebook Page That Gave It an Outlet," *New York Times,* February 6, 2011.

3. Dan Balz, "Don't Be Too Quick to Mistake Tea Party for Perot Movement," *Washington Post,* April 18, 2010.

4. Megan Garber, "How Pop Culture Primed the U.S. for a Trump Win," *Atlantic,* November 16, 2016.

5. Sam Dillon, "Failing Grades on Civics Exam Called a 'Crisis,'" *New York Times,* May 4, 2011.

6. "Survey of Young Americans' Attitudes toward Politics and Public Service: 27th Edition, March 18—April 1, 2015," Institute of Politics, John F. Kennedy School of Government, Harvard, Spring 2015, http://www.iop.harvard.edu/sites/default/files_new/IOPSpring15%20PollTopline.pdf.

7. "Voter Turnout Demographics," United States Elections Project, n.d., http://www.electproject.org/home/voter-turnout/demographics.

8. Danielle Allen, "What Is Education For?" *Boston Review,* May 9, 2016, http://bostonreview.net/forum/danielle-allen-what-education.

9. Joseph Gershtenson and Dennis L. Plane, "Trust in Government," *2006 American National Election Studies Pilot Report* (April 10, 2007), https://www.electionstudies.org/wp-content/uploads/2018/04/nes011890.pdf.

10. "2020 Edelman Trust Barometer," *Edelman,* January 19, 2020, https://www.edelman.com/trustbarometer.

11. "Confidence in Institutions," Gallup, November 11, 2019, https://news.gallup.com/poll/1597/confidence-institutions.aspx.

12. "The Rise of HMOs," Rand Corporation, https://www.rand.org/content/dam/rand/pubs/rgs_dissertations/RGSD172/RGSD172.ch1.pdf.

13. Chris Hayes, *Twilight of the Elites: America After Meritocracy* (New York: Crown, 2012).

14. Massimo Calabresi, "While Trump Is Tweeting, These 3 People Are Undoing American Government As We Know It," *Time,* October 26, 2017.

15. "Don't Vote," *Quinn Said,* November 6, 2012, https://www.quinnnorton.com/said/?p=638.

16. Michael Schudson, *The Good Citizen: A History of American Civic Life* (New York: Simon & Schuster, 1998).

17. Michael M. Phillips, "Civil-Rights Leader Rustin Gets His Due 50

Years Later," *Wall Street Journal,* August 27, 2013; Steve Hendrix, "Bayard Rustin, Organizer of the March on Washington, Was Crucial to the Movement," *Washington Post,* August 21, 2011; and Jesse Rhodes, "Eating on the March: Food at the 1963 March on Washington," Smithsonian Institution, August 23, 2013, https://www.smithsonianmag.com/arts-culture/eating-on-the-march-food-at-the-1963-march-on-washington-1291334/.

18. "Public Statement by Eight Alabama Clergymen: Denouncing Martin Luther King's Efforts," April 12, 1963, MassResistance.org, https://www.massresistance.org/docs/gen/09a/mlk_day/statement.html.

19. David Johnson and Chris Wilson, "Women's Marches: See Just How Big They Were Across America," *Time,* April 19, 2017.

Chapter 2: WHY WE LOST TRUST

1. Damon Beres, "Most Honest Cities: The Reader's Digest 'Lost Wallet' Test," *Reader's Digest,* January 13, 2020, https://www.rd.com/culture/most-honest-cities-lost-wallet-test/.

2. Gallup, "Gallup Database: 2006 Survey Results," Gallup, October 18, 2014, https://news.gallup.com/poll/24487/gallup-database-2006-survey-results.aspx.

3. John F. Helliwell, and Shun Wang, "Trust and Well-Being," NBER Working Paper no. 15911, April 15, 2010, http://www.nber.org/papers/w15911.

4. Francis Fukuyama, *Trust: The Social Virtues and the Creation of Prosperity* (New York: The Free Press, 1995). See also Francis Fukuyama, *The End of History and the Last Man* (New York: Free Press, 1992).

5. Paul J. Zak and Stephen Knack, "Trust and Growth," *Economic Journal* 111, no. 470 (2001): 295–321, https://doi.org/10.1111/1468-0297.00609.

6. Robert D. Putnam, *Bowling Alone: The Collapse and Revival of American Community* (New York: Simon & Schuster, 2000).

7. Frederick A. O. Schwarz, Jr., *Democracy in the Dark: The Seduction of Government Secrecy* (New York: New Press, 2012).

8. "2020 Edelman Trust Barometer," *Edelman,* January 19, 2020, https://www.edelman.com/trustbarometer.

9. R. Inglehart et al., eds., World Values Survey: Round Six—Country-Pooled Datafile 2010–2014 (Madrid: JD Systems Institute, 2014), version http://www.worldvaluessurvey.org/WVSDocumentationWV6.jsp.

10. "Section 1: Trust in Government 1958-2010," Pew Research Cen-

ter, December 31, 2019, http://www.people-press.org/2010/04/18/section-1-trust-in-government-1958-2010/.

11. Kevin Mattson, "Examining Carter's 'Malaise Speech,' 30 Years Later," NPR, July 12, 2009.

12. "Public Opinion," European Commission, n.d., http://ec.europa.eu/commfrontoffice/publicopinion/index.cfm/Chart/getChart/themeKy/18/groupKy/98/chartType/barChart/savFile/521.

13. Amanda Taub, "How Stable Are Democracies? 'Warning Signs Are Flashing Red,'" *New York Times,* November 29, 2016.

14. Ronald Inglehart. "The Danger of Deconsolidation: How Much Should We Worry?" *Journal of Democracy* 27, no. 3 (2016): 18–23.

15. "Confidence in Institutions," Gallup, November 11, 2019, http://news.gallup.com/poll/1597/confidence-institutions.aspx.

16. Cameron Easley, "Public's Confidence in Presidency Erodes During Trump's White House Tenure," *Morning Consult,* January 24, 2018, https://morningconsult.com/2018/01/24/publics-confidence-presidency-erodes-trumps-white-house-tenure/.

17. "2017 Edelman Trust Barometer Reveals Global Implosion of Trust," *Edelman,* January 15, 2017, https://www.edelman.com/news-awards/2017-edelman-trust-barometer-reveals-global-implosion.

18. Karl Marlantes, "Vietnam: The War That Killed Trust," *New York Times,* January 7, 2017.

19. Barry Sussman and Kenneth E. John, "War Bequeaths a Distrust of Government," *Washington Post,* April 15, 1985.

20. "Public Trust in Government: 1958–2019," Pew Research Center, April 11, 2019, http://www.people-press.org/2017/05/03/public-trust-in-government-1958-2017/.

21. Julian Zelizer, "Distrustful Americans Still Live in Age of Watergate," CNN, July 7, 2014.

22. "Demography of the United States," Wikipedia, December 21, 2019. Calculations were done by the author.

23. Richard Rothstein, *The Color of Law: A Forgotten History of How Our Government Segregated America* (New York: Liveright, 2017).

24. Erica Frankenberg and Rebecca Jacobsen, "Trends—School Integration Polls," *Public Opinion Quarterly* 75, no. 4 (2011): 788–811, https://doi.org/10.1093/poq/nfr016.

25. Michelle Alexander, *The New Jim Crow: Mass Incarceration in the Age of Colorblindness* (New York: New Press, 2010).

26. Ta-Nehisi Coates, "The Case for Reparations," *Atlantic,* September 24, 2019.

27. George Monbiot, "The Self-Hating State," Monbiot.com, April 22, 2013, http://www.monbiot.com/2013/04/22/the-self-hating-state/.

28. "Great Depression, Great Recession," Roosevelt Institute, September 15, 2010, http://rooseveltinstitute.org/great-depression-great-recession/.

29. "FDR: From Budget Balancer to Keynesian," FDR Presidential Library and Museum, https://fdrlibrary.org/budget.

30. Edward Nelson and Kalin Nikolov, "Monetary Policy and Stagflation in the UK," SSRN, October 15, 2002, https://papers.ssrn.com/sol3/papers.cfm?abstract_id=315180.

31. Alistair Osborne, "Margaret Thatcher: One Policy That Led to More than 50 Companies Being Sold or Privatised," *Telegraph,* April 8, 2013.

32. Tony Judt, *Ill Fares the Land* (London: Penguin Books, 2010).

33. Andrew Chatzky and James McBride, "China's Massive Belt and Road Initiative," Council on Foreign Relations, January 28, 2020, https://www.cfr.org/backgrounder/chinas-massive-belt-and-road-initiative.

34. Massimo Calabresi, "While Trump Is Tweeting, These 3 People Are Undoing American Government as We Know It," *Time,* October 26, 2017.

35. Thomas Piketty, *Capital in the Twenty-First Century* (Cambridge, Mass.: Harvard University Press, 2013).

36. John Cassidy, "Piketty's Inequality Story in Six Charts," *New Yorker,* March 26, 2014, as well as Piketty, *Capital in Twenty-First Century.* See also Paul Krugman, "Why We're in a New Gilded Age," *New York Review of Books,* May 8, 2014; Allison Schrager, "Is Income Inequality Always a Bad Thing?," *Quartz,* December 16, 2016, https://qz.com/836927/is-income-inequality-always-a-bad-thing/; and T. M. Scanlon, "The 4 Biggest Reasons Why Inequality Is Bad for Society," *TED Talks,* June 3, 2014, https://ideas.ted.com/the-4-biggest-reasons-why-inequality-is-bad-for-society/.

37. Elizabeth Tricomi et al., "Neural Evidence for Inequality-Averse Social Preferences," *Nature* 463 (2010): 1089–91, https://www.nature.com/articles/nature08785.

38. Walter Scheidel, *The Great Leveler: Violence and the History of Inequality from the Stone Age to the Twenty-First Century* (Princeton: Princeton University Press, 2017). See also Paul Mason, "*The Great Leveller* by Walter Scheidel Review—An End to Inequality?," *Guardian,* March 29, 2017; and "Stanford Historian Uncovers a Grim Correlation Between Violence and Inequality over the

Millennia," *Stanford News*, April 30, 2020, https://news.stanford
.edu/2017/01/24/stanford-historian-uncovers-grim-correlation
-violence-inequality-millennia/.

39. Jason Deparle, "The Safety Net Got a Quick Patch. What Happens After the Coronavirus?," *New York Times,* March 31, 2020.

40. Gunhild Gram Giskemo, "Exploring the Relationship Between Socio-Economic Inequality, Political Instability and Economic Growth: Why Do We Know So Little?," CMI Working Paper, 2012, https://www.cmi.no/publications/file/4379-exploring-the-relationship-between-socio-economic.pdf.

41. Jay Ulfelder, "It's Harder Than It Looks to Link Inequality with Global Turmoil," *FiveThirtyEight,* January 7, 2016, https://fivethirtyeight.com/features/its-harder-than-it-looks-to-link-inequality-with-global-turmoil/.

42. Anne Case and Angus Deaton, "Rising Morbidity and Mortality in Midlife Among White Non-Hispanic Americans in the 21st Century," *PNAS* 112, no. 49 (2015): 15078–83, https://www.pnas.org/content/112/49/15078.

43. Michael Bible, "Is the US Facing an Epidemic of 'Deaths of Despair'? These Researchers Say Yes," *Guardian,* March 28, 2017.

44. Andrew Gelman, "Correcting Statistical Biases in 'Rising Morbidity and Mortality in Midlife Among White Non-Hispanic Americans in the 21st Century': We Need to Adjust for the Increase in Average Age of People in the 45–54 Category," *Statistical Modeling, Causal Inference, and Social Science,* November 6, 2015, http://andrewgelman.com/2015/11/06/correcting-rising-morbidity-and-mortality-in-midlife-among-white-non-hispanic-americans-in-the-21st-century-to-account-for-bias-in/.

45. J. D. Vance, *Hillbilly Elegy: A Memoir of a Family and Culture in Crisis* (New York: Harper, 2016).

46. Tracy Jan, "Report: No Progress for African Americans on Homeownership, Unemployment and Incarceration in 50 Years," *Washington Post,* February 26, 2018.

47. Leon Aron, "Everything You Think You Know About the Collapse of the Soviet Union Is Wrong," *Foreign Policy,* June 20, 2011.

48. Timur Kuran, *Private Truths, Public Lies: The Social Consequences of Preference Falsification* (Cambridge, Mass.: Harvard University Press, 1995).

49. Denis Volkov, "Timur Kuran: 'An Atmosphere of Repression Leads to Preference Falsification Among Opinion Leaders,'" Institute of Modern Russia, October 14, 2015, https://imrussia.org/en/opinions/2445

-timur-kuran-%E2%80%9Can-atmosphere-of-repression-leads-to
-preference-falsification-among-opinion-leaders%E2%80%9D.

50. Michael Schudson, "When the Media Had Enough: Watergate, Vietnam and the Birth of the Adversarial Press," *Salon,* October 10, 2015.

51. Nick Bryant, "All the President's Unreported Women: JFK Never Had Problems like Bill Clinton's," *Independent,* October 23, 2011.

52. Michael Schudson, *The Rise of the Right to Know: Politics and the Culture of Transparency, 1945–1975* (Cambridge, Mass.: Harvard University Press, 2018).

53. U.S. Census, "Table A-1. Years of School Completed by People 25 Years and Over, by Age and Sex: Selected Years 1940 to 2019," CPS Historical Time Series Visualizations, March 11, 2020, https://www.census.gov/library/visualizations/time-series/demo/cps-historical-time-series.html.

54. U.S. Census, Table 2, "Educational Attainment of the Population 25 Years and Over, by Selected Characteristics: 2019," Educational Attainment in the United States: 2019, March 30, 2020, https://www.census.gov/data/tables/2019/demo/educational-attainment/cps-detailed-tables.html.

55. Susan Bassnett et al., "Participation Rates: Now We Are 50," *Times Higher Education,* June 10, 2015.

56. "Government Gets Lower Ratings for Handling Health Care, Environment, Disaster Response," Pew Research Center, December 14, 2017, http://www.people-press.org/2017/12/14/government-gets-lower-ratings-for-handling-health-care-environment-disaster-response/?utm_content=buffer27a84.

Chapter 3: WHAT WE LOSE WHEN WE LOSE TRUST

1. "76: Mob," *This American Life,* PRI, December 14, 2017.

2. Leopoldo Franchetti and Sidney Sonnino, *La Sicilia nel 1876* (Florence: G. Barbera, 1877), https://archive.org/details/lasicilianel00sonngoog; and Diego Gambetta, "Mafia: The Price of Distrust," in *Trust: Making and Breaking Cooperative Relations,* ed. Diego Gambetta (London: Blackwell, 1988) 158–75, http://citeseerx.ist.psu.edu/viewdoc/download?doi=10.1.1.25.2167&rep=rep1&type=pdf.

3. Diego Gambetta, *The Sicilian Mafia: The Business of Private Protection* (Cambridge, Mass.: Harvard University Press, 1996).

4. Diego Gambetta, "*The Sicilian Mafia,* 20 Years After Publication," *Sociologica: Italian Journal of Sociology Online* 2 (May–August 2011): 1–11, https://doi.org/10.2383/35869.

5. Adam Asmundo and Maurizio Lisciandra "The Cost of Protection Racket in Sicily," *Global Crime* 9, no. 3 (2011): 221–40, https://doi .org/10.1080/17440570802254338.

6. Francis Fukuyama, *Trust: The Social Virtues and the Creation of Prosperity* (New York: Free Press, 1995), 97–111.

7. "Coronavirus: Brazil's President Rejects COVID-19 as a 'Little Flu' and Ignores Distancing Rules," Sky News, April 11, 2020, https:// news.sky.com/story/coronavirus-brazils-president-rejects-covid-19 -as-a-little-flu-and-ignores-distancing-rules-11971799.

8. "COVID-19 in Brazil: 'So What?,'" *Lancet,* May 9, 2020, https:// www.thelancet.com/journals/lancet/article/PIIS0140-6736(20)31095 -3/fulltext.

9. Rafael Soares, "Coronavírus: Tráfico e Milícia Ordenam Toque de Recolher em Favelas do Rio," *Globo Extra,* March 24, 2020, https:// extra.globo.com/casos-de-policia/coronavirus-trafico-milicia -ordenam-toque-de-recolher-em-favelas-do-rio-24324363.html.

10. Caio Barretto Briso and Tom Phillips, "Brazil Gangs Impose Strict Curfews to Slow Coronavirus Spread," *Guardian,* March 25, 2020.

11. On low landline teledensity, see "African Telecommunications Indicators 2004," International Telecommunication Union, May 2004, https://www.itu.int/net/wsis/tunis/newsroom/stats/AFRICA_2004 .pdf. GSMA 2012 shows teledensities around 60 percent via mobile; see "Sub-Saharan Africa Mobile Observatory 2012," GSM Association, November 13, 2012, https://www.gsma.com/publicpolicy/wp -content/uploads/2012/03/SSA_FullReport_v6.1_clean.pdf.

12. Michael Booth, "Colorado Springs Cuts into Services Considered Basic by Many," *Denver Post,* January 30, 2010.

13. Ibid.

14. Caleb Hannan, "The Short, Unhappy Life of a Libertarian Paradise," *Politico,* June 30, 2017.

15. "History," MySociety, n.d., https://www.mysociety.org/about/history/; and "FixMyTransport," MySociety, n.d., https://www.mysociety.org /category/fixmytransport/.

16. Tom McKay, "Florida State House Declares Porn Is a Health Risk, Assault Weapons Totally Fine Though," *Gizmodo,* February 21, 2018.

17. Nathan Bomey, "MetLife, Rental Car Agencies Dump NRA Discounts," *USA Today,* February 23, 2018.

18. Laura M. Holson, "Dick's Sporting Goods Will Destroy the Assault-Style Weapons It Didn't Sell," *New York Times,* April 18, 2018.

19. Adele Peters, "'Power Is the Ability to Change the Rules': How

Rashad Robinson Holds Companies Accountable," *Fast Company,* October 25, 2017, https://www.fastcompany.com/40474488/power -is-the-ability-to-change-the-rules-how-rashad-robinson-holds -companies-accountable?utm_content=bufferc5274.

20. Andrew Orlowski, "US Congress Finally Emits All 3,000 Russian 'Troll' Facebook Ads. Let's Take a Look at Some," *Register,* May 10, 2018, https://www.theregister.co.uk/2018/05/10/congress_russian_ facebook_troll_ads/; and Nick Penzenstadler, Brad Heath, and Jessica Guynn, "We Read Every One of the 3,517 Facebook Ads Bought by Russians. Here's What We Found," *USA Today,* May 13, 2018.

21. Claire Allbright, "A Russian Facebook Page Organized a Protest in Texas. A Different Russian Page Launched the Counterprotest," *Texas Tribune,* November 1, 2017.

22. Deb Reichmann, "U.S. Intelligence Agencies Expect Russia to Target 2018 Midterms," *NewsHour,* PBS, February 13, 2018.

23. Sheera Frenkel and Matthew Rosenberg, "Top Tech Companies Met with Intelligence Officials to Discuss Midterms," *New York Times,* June 25, 2018.

24. Will Oremus, "Americans Are Losing Trust in Facebook—Here's Why They'll Keep Using It Anyway," *Business Insider,* March 31, 2018.

25. Siva Vaidhyanathan, "The Real Reason Facebook Won't Fact Check Political Ads," *New York Times,* November 2, 2019.

26. "Making Ads and Pages More Transparent," Facebook, November 7, 2019, https://newsroom.fb.com/news/2018/04/transparent-ads -and-pages/.

27. Harlan Yu and David G. Robinson, "The New Ambiguity of 'Open Government,'" *UCLA Law Review* 59, disc. 178 (February 2012): 180–208, https://www.uclalawreview.org/pdf/discourse/59-11.pdf.

28. "How a Team of Ukrainian Journalists Rescued Documents from Yanukovych's House," PRI, February 27, 2014.

29. "'Everything Will Be Exposed,' Ukrainian Reporter Says," *Deutsche Welle,* June 25, 2014, https://www.dw.com/en/everything-will -be-exposed-ukrainian-reporter-says/a-17735243.

30. Alessandra Prentice, "Ukrainians Shocked as Politicians Declare Vast Wealth," Reuters, October 31, 2016.

31. Max Skubenko, "MPs' Salaries in Ukraine: Would Paying Politicians More Lead to Better Performance?," *VoxUkraine,* January 13, 2017, https://voxukraine.org/en/mps-salaries-in-ukraine/.

32. Marc P. Berenson, "Trust, Governance & Citizenship in Post-Euromaidan Ukraine," King's Russia Institute Policy Paper, June

27, 2016, https://www.kcl.ac.uk/sspp/departments/kri/Documents/Trust,-Governance-and-Citizenship-in-Post-Euromaidan-Ukraine.pdf.

33. Eugene Kiely, "A Guide to Clinton's Emails," *FactCheck,* October 28, 2016, https://www.factcheck.org/2016/07/a-guide-to-clintons-emails/.

34. Matthew Yglesias, "Against Transparency," *Vox,* September 6, 2016.

35. Katy Waldman, "It's All Connected: What Links Creativity, Conspiracy Theories, and Delusions? A Phenomenon Called Apophenia." *Slate,* September 16, 2014.

36. Gregor Aisch, Jon Huang, and Cecilia Kang, "Dissecting the #PizzaGate Conspiracy Theories," *New York Times,* December 10, 2016.

37. Abdurashid Solijonov, "Voter Turnout Trends Around the World," International Institute for Democracy and Electoral Assistance, 2016, https://www.idea.int/sites/default/files/publications/voter-turnout-trends-around-the-world.pdf.

38. "The Party's (Largely) Over," *Economist,* October 21 2010.

39. Ingrid van Biezen, "The Decline in Party Membership Across Europe Means That Political Parties Need to Reconsider How They Engage with the Electorate," LSE Europe, May 6, 2013, http://blogs.lse.ac.uk/europpblog/2013/05/06/decline-in-party-membership-europe-ingrid-van-biezen/.

40. Jana Kasperkevic, "Occupy Wall Street: Four Years Later," *Guardian,* September 16, 2015.

41. Carlotta Gall, "Erdogan's Victory in Turkey Election Expands His Powers," *New York Times,* June 24, 2018.

42. Zeynep Tufekci, *Twitter and Tear Gas: The Power and Fragility of Networked Protest* (New Haven, Conn.: Yale University Press, 2017).

43. Ivan Krastev, *In Mistrust We Trust: Can Democracy Survive When We Don't Trust Our Leaders?* (New York: TED Books, 2013).

44. Roberto Stefan Foa and Yascha Mounk, "The Democratic Disconnect," *Journal of Democracy* 27, no. 3 (2016): 5–17, https://www.journalofdemocracy.org/sites/default/files/Foa%26Mounk-27-3.pdf.

45. Alfred Regnery, "Goldwater's 'The Conscience of a Conservative' Transformed American Politics," *Washington Times,* November 17, 2014.

46. Barry Goldwater, *The Conscience of a Conservative* (Shephardsville, Ky.: Victor Publishing, 1960), 7.

47. Matthew Dallek, "The Conservative 1960s," *Atlantic,* December 1995.

48. Ryota Kanai et al., "Political Orientations Are Correlated with Brain Structure in Young Adults," *Current Biology* 21, no. 8 (2011): 677–80, https://doi.org/10.1016/j.cub.2011.03.017.

49. R. Chris Fraley et al., "Developmental Antecedents of Political Ideology: A Longitudinal Investigation from Birth to Age 18 Years," *Psychological Science* 23, no. 11 (2012): 1425–31, https://doi.org/10.1177/0956797612440102.

50. John Bargh, "At Yale, We Conducted an Experiment to Turn Conservatives into Liberals. The Results Say a Lot About Our Political Divisions," *Washington Post,* November 22, 2017.

51. David L. Altheide, "The News Media, the Problem Frame, and the Production of Fear," *Sociological Quarterly 38,* no. 4 (1997): 647–68, https://www.jstor.org/stable/4121084.

52. Michael M. Grynbaum, "Trump Calls the News Media the 'Enemy of the American People,' " *New York Times,* February 17, 2017.

53. Ethan Zuckerman, "Stop Saying 'Fake News.' It's Not Helping," . . . *My Heart's in Accra,* January 30, 2017, http://www.ethanzuckerman.com/blog/2017/01/30/stop-saying-fake-news-its-not-helping/.

54. *American Values: Trust, Media and Democracy: A Gallup/Knight Foundation Survey,* Gallup, 2018, https://kf-site-production.s3.amazonaws.com/publications/pdfs/000/000/242/original/KnightFoundation_AmericansViews_Client_Report_010917_Final_Updated.pdf.

55. Amber Phillips, " 'Disgraceful' and 'Tragic': John McCain's Excoriation of Trump on Russia, Annotated," *Washington Post,* July 16, 2018.

56. George Will, "This Sad, Embarrassing Wreck of a Man," *Washington Post,* July 17, 2018.

57. Igor Bobic, "GOP Senator Offers the Craziest Theory for Why Trump Didn't Stand Up to Putin," *HuffPost,* July 18, 2018.

58. Hannah Arendt, *The Origins of Totalitarianism* (New York: Schocken, 1951), 382.

59. "Deadline Club Awards 2018 Dinner: Conversation with Judy Woodruff and Lesley Stahl," YouTube, May 22, 2018, https://www.youtube.com/watch?v=nq6Tt--uAfs.

60. Hannah Arendt, "Lying in Politics: Reflections on The Pentagon Papers," *New York Review of Books,* November 18, 1971.

61. Arendt, *Origins of Totalitarianism,* 382.

62. "Godwin's Law," *Wikipedia,* May 3, 2020.

63. Arendt, *Origins of Totalitarianism,* 387.

64. Ibid., 388.

65. Peter Pomerantsev, *Nothing Is True and Everything Is Possible:*

The Surreal Heart of the New Russia (New York: PublicAffairs, 2015), 42.

66. Ilya Yablokov, "Conspiracy Theories as a Russian Public Diplomacy Tool: The Case of *Russia Today* (*RT*)," *Politics* 35, no. 3–4 (2015): 301–15, https://doi.org/10.1111/1467-9256.12097.

67. Pomerantsev, *Nothing Is True,* 73.

68. Madeleine Albright, *Fascism: A Warning* (New York: HarperCollins, 2018).

69. Janine Kritschgau, "David Brooks Says Trump Was the Wrong Answer to the Right Question," *Skidmore News,* December 7, 2017, http://skidmorenews.com/new-blog/2017/12/5/david-brooks-says -trump-was-the-wrong-answer-to-the-right-question.

70. Marian Watson Virga, "Lessons on How to Reclaim a City: Addiopizzo," *Times of Sicily,* April 2, 2017, http://www.timesofsicily .com/lessons-reclaim-city-addiopizzo/.

Chapter 4: THE LEVERS OF CHANGE

1. "#MeToo: A Timeline of Events," *Chicago Tribune,* May 26, 2020.

2. "Harvey Weinstein Timeline: How the Scandal Unfolded," BBC News, May 29, 2020; and Jodi Kantor and Megan Twohey, "Harvey Weinstein Paid Off Sexual Harassment Accusers for Decades," *New York Times,* October 5, 2017.

3. #MeToo: Timeline."

4. Zahara Hill, "A Black Woman Created the 'Me Too' Campaign Against Sexual Assault 10 Years Ago," *Ebony,* December 14, 2018.

5. Cassandra Santiago and Doug Criss, "An Activist, a Little Girl and the Heartbreaking Origin of 'Me Too,'" CNN, October 17, 2017.

6. Sheryl Estrada, "*Time* Magazine Excluding Tarana Burke from #MeToo Cover Speaks Volumes," *DiversityInc,* December 11, 2017, http://www.diversityinc.com/news/time-magazine-excluding -tarana-burke-metoo-cover-speaks-volumes.

7. Emma Brockes, "#MeToo Founder Tarana Burke: 'You Have to Use Your Privilege to Serve Other People,'" *Guardian,* January 15, 2018.

8. Ibid.

9. Malcolm Gladwell, "Small Change," *New Yorker,* October 4, 2010.

10. Susan Davis, "'Me Too' Legislation Aims to Combat Sexual Harassment in Congress," NPR, November 15, 2017.

11. Lauren Prince and Valerie Kipnis, "Sexual Assault Hotlines Are Feeling the Impact of #Metoo," *Vice,* January 22, 2018.

12. Liz Brody, "In Their Own Words: The Army of Women Who Took Down Larry Nassar," *Glamour*, October 30, 2018.

13. "Justice Department Files Antitrust Suit Against Microsoft for Unlawfully Monopolizing Computer Software Markets," Department of Justice, May 18, 1998, https://www.justice.gov/archive/atr/public/press_releases/1998/1764.htm.

14. *United States v. Microsoft Corporation,* Civil Action No. 98-1232 (TPJ) (filed February 1, 2000), Brief of Professor Lawrence Lessig as *Amicus Curiae,* https://cyber.harvard.edu/works/lessig/ab.pdf.

15. Lawrence Lessig, "Tyranny in the Infrastructure," *Wired,* July 1, 1997.

16. Lawrence Lessig, *Code: Version 2.0* (Creative Commons, 2006): 120–24.

17. *Loving v. Virginia,* 388 U.S. 1 (1967).

18. Frank Newport, "In U.S., 87% Approve of Black-White Marriage, vs. 4% in 1958," Gallup, July 25, 2013, http://news.gallup.com/poll/163697/approve-marriage-blacks-whites.aspx.

19. Lydia Saad, "Americans Slow to Back Interracial Marriage," Gallup Vault, June 21, 2017, http://news.gallup.com/vault/212717/gallup-vault-americans-slow-back-interracial-marriage.aspx?g_source=link_NEWSV9.

20. Justin McCarthy, "U.S. Support for Gay Marriage Edges to New High," Gallup, May 15, 2017, http://news.gallup.com/poll/210566/support-gay-marriage-edges-new-high.aspx.

21. Lindsay Dunsmuir, "Many Americans Have No Friends of Another Race: Poll," Reuters, August 8, 2013.

22. Gordon Allport, *The Nature of Prejudice* (Boston: Addison-Wesley, 1954).

23. Edward Schiappa, Peter B. Gregg, and Dean E. Hewes, "The Parasocial Contact Hypothesis," *Communication Monographs* 72, no. 1 (2005): 92–115, https://doi.org/10.1080/0363775052000342544.

24. "The 21 Best Memes Celebrating the Supreme Court's Same-Sex Marriage Ruling," *Orlando Weekly*, June 26, 2015, http://photos.orlandoweekly.com/the-21-best-memes-celebrating-the-supreme-courts-same-sex-marriage-ruling/?slide=1.

25. John Hoffman, "Sharing Our Way Toward Equality: Social Media and Gay Rights," *Nonprofit Quarterly*, May 14, 2012, https://nonprofitquarterly.org/2012/05/14/sharing-our-way-toward-equality-social-media-and-gay-rights/.

26. Hatewatch Staff, "Breitbart Exposé Confirms: Far-Right News

Site a Platform for the White Nationalist 'Alt-Right,'" Southern Poverty Law Center, October 6, 2017, https://www.splcenter.org/hatewatch/2017/10/06/breitbart-expos%C3%A9-confirms-far-right-news-site-platform-white-nationalist-alt-right.

27. Robert M. Faris et al., "Partisanship, Propaganda, and Disinformation: Online Media and the 2016 U.S. Presidential Election," Berkman Klein Center for Internet & Society Research Paper (2017), https://dash.harvard.edu/handle/1/33759251.

28. Sleeping Giants (@slpng_giants), "@Sofi Are you aware that you're advertising on Breitbart, the alt-right's biggest champion, today? Are you supporting them publicly?," Twitter, November 17, 2016, https://twitter.com/slpng_giants/status/799048412289077248.

29. Paul Farhi, "The Mysterious Group That's Picking Breitbart Apart, One Tweet at a Time," *Washington Post,* September 22, 2017.

30. Patrick Coffee, "*The Daily Caller* Names Founder of Sleeping Giants, Which Organized Breitbart Advertiser Boycotts," *Adweek,* July 17, 2018.

31. Lucia Moses, "Breitbart Ads Plummet Nearly 90 Percent in Three Months as Trump's Troubles Mount," *Digiday,* June 6, 2017, https://digiday.com/media/breitbart-ads-plummet-nearly-90-percent-three-months-trumps-troubles-mount/.

32. Daniel Victor, "Advertisers Drop Laura Ingraham After She Taunts Parkland Survivor David Hogg," *New York Times,* March 29, 2018.

33. David Hogg (@davidhogg111), "Soooo @IngrahamAngle what are your biggest advertisers . . . Asking for a friend. #BoycottIngramAdverts," Twitter, March 29, 2018, https://twitter.com/davidhogg111/status/979161878990598144.

34. David Hogg (@davidhogg111), "Pick a number 1-12 contact the company next to that # Top Laura Ingraham Advertisers 1. @sleepnumber 2. @ATT 3. Nutrish 4. @Allstate & @esurance 5. @Bayer 6. @RocketMortgage Mortgage 7. @LibertyMutual 8. @Arbys 9. @TripAdvisor 10. @Nestle 11. @hulu 12. @Wayfair," Twitter, March 29, 2018, https://twitter.com/davidhogg111/status/979168957180579840.

35. Victor, "Advertisers Drop Ingraham."

36. Jeremy Barr, "Laura Ingraham's Advertisers Haven't Fully Returned," *Hollywood Reporter,* May 16, 2018.

37. John Voelcker, "Electric Cars: Some Are Real, Most Are Only 'Compliance Cars'—We Name Names," *Green Car Reports,* May 3, 2012, https://www.greencarreports.com/news/1068832_electric-cars-some-are-real-most-are-only-compliance-cars--we-name-names; and "What Is ZEV?," Union of Concerned Scientists, August 7,

2012, https://www.ucsusa.org/clean-vehicles/california-and-western -states/what-is-zev.

38. Chris Woodyard, "Automakers Hawk Electric 'Compliance Cars' to Meet Rules," *USA Today,* May 9, 2013.

39. Bob Sorokanich, "The Tesla Roadster Is Not the 'Fastest Car in the World,'" *Road & Track*, November 17, 2017, https://www .roadandtrack.com/new-cars/news/a30536/tesla-model-s-p100d -quickest-not-fastest/.

40. Michael J. Coren, "Tesla's Model 3 Dominates US Electric Cars Sales. The Nissan Leaf Is Winning Around the World," *Quartz*, March 16, 2020, https://qz.com/1703260/teslas-model-3-may-never -catch-up-to-the-nissan-leaf/.

41. Peter Maass, "How Laura Poitras Helped Snowden Spill His Secrets," *New York Times Magazine,* August 13, 2013.

42. Orin Kerr, "Edward Snowden's Impact," *Washington Post,* April 9, 2015.

43. Donald J. Trump (@realDonaldTrump), "Snowden is a spy who has caused great damage to the U.S. A spy in the old days, when our country was respected and strong, would be executed," Twitter, April 18, 2014, https://twitter.com/realdonaldtrump/status/4573149 34473633792?lang=en.

44. Brooke Auxier, "How Americans See Digital Privacy Issues amid the COVID-19 Outbreak," Pew Research Center, May 4, 2020, https://www.pewresearch.org/fact-tank/2020/05/04/how-americans -see-digital-privacy-issues-amid-the-covid-19-outbreak/.

45. Andy Greenberg, "Signal, the Snowden-Approved Crypto App, Comes to Android," *Wired*, November 2, 2015.

46. Nick Statt, "WhatsApp Co-Founder Jan Koum Is Leaving Facebook After Clashing over Data Privacy," *Verge*, April 30, 2018.

47. Lawrence Lessig, *Code: Version 2.0* (Creative Commons, 2006), 3.

48. R. L. Nave, "C. J. Lawrence," *Jackson Free Press*, August 14, 2014, http://www.jacksonfreepress.com/news/2014/aug/14/cj-lawrence/; and C. J. Lawrence, "Yes let's do that: Which photo does the media use if the police shot me down? #IfTheyGunnedMeDown," Twitter, August 10, 2014, https://twitter.com/CJLawrenceEsq/ status/498537843170353152.

49. Tanzina Vega, "Shooting Spurs Hashtag Effort on Stereotypes," *New York Times,* August 12, 2014.

50. German Lopez, "There Are Huge Racial Disparities in How US Police Use Force," *Vox*, November 14, 2018.

51. Joshua Correll et al., "Across the Thin Blue Line: Police Officers

and Racial Bias in the Decision to Shoot," *Journal of Personality and Social Psychology* 92, no. 6 (2007): 1006–23, https://doi.org/10.1037/0022-3514.92.6.1006.

52. Phillip Atifa Goff et al. "The Essence of Innocence: Consequences of Dehumanizing Black Children," *Journal of Personality and Social Psychology* 106, no. 4 (2014): 526–45, https://doi.org/10.1037/a0035663.

53. Kevin Zeese, "Black Lives Matter Gets Laws Passed in 24 States," PopularResistance.org, August 4, 2015, https://popularresistance.org/in-one-year-blacklivesmatter-gets-laws-passed-in-24-states/.

54. Ivan Penn, "California Will Require Solar Power for New Homes," *New York Times,* May 9, 2018.

55. Tom DiChristopher, "Solar Power: Here's Where Your State Now Ranks," CNBC, March 15, 2018.

56. Candice Elliott, "Are Economic Boycotts a More Effective Way to Create Change?," *Listen Money Matters,* n.d., https://www.listenmoneymatters.com/economic-boycotting/.

57. Bob Graham, *America, the Owner's Manual: Making Government Work for You* (Washington, DC: CQ Press, 2009): This good-hearted book is a great example of this paradigm at work.

58. William A. Gamson, *Power and Discontent* (Homewood, IL: Dorsey Press, 1968).

59. "The Choir," episode 82, *Criminal,* January 12, 2018, https://thisiscriminal.com/episode-82-the-choir-01-12-2018/.

Chapter 5: INSTITUTIONALISTS TO THE RESCUE

1. Jennifer Palkha, interview by author, July 25, 2018.

2. Jennifer Pahlka, "Delivery-Driven Government," *Medium,* May 30, 2018.

3. Drew DeSilver, "What Does the Federal Government Spend Your Tax Dollars On? Social Insurance Programs, Mostly," Pew Research Center, April 4, 2017, http://www.pewresearch.org/fact-tank/2017/04/04/what-does-the-federal-government-spend-your-tax-dollars-on-social-insurance-programs-mostly/.

4. "Total Charitable Donations Rise to New High of $390.05 Billion," Giving USA, June 12, 2017, https://givingusa.org/giving-usa-2017-total-charitable-donations-rise-to-new-high-of-390-05-billion/.

5. Palkha interview.

6. Jennifer Pahlka, "Why I'm Going to the White House Today," *Medium,* June 19, 2017.

7. Lisa Rein, "Interior Department Reactivates Twitter Accounts After Shutdown Following Inauguration," *Washington Post,* January 21, 2017.

8. Ibid.

9. Sean Rossman, "Parody Parks Service Twitter Takes Aim at Trump," *USA Today,* January 25, 2017.

10. Wynne Davis, "It's Not Just the Park Service: 'Rogue' Federal Twitter Accounts Multiply," *All Tech Considered,* NPR, January 27, 2017.

11. TNN, "4 Dalits Stripped, Beaten up for Skinning Dead Cow," *Times of India,* July 13, 2016, https://timesofindia.indiatimes.com/city/rajkot/4-Dalits-stripped-beaten-up-for-skinning-dead-cow/articleshow/53184266.cms.

12. "10 Things to Know about Jignesh Mevani, the Man Leading Gujarat's Dalit Agitation," *India Today,* August 5, 2016, https://www.indiatoday.in/fyi/story/jignesh-mevani-the-man-leading-gujarat-dalit-agitation-333488-2016-08-05; Trilochan Sastry, "A Journey for Liberty," *Hindu,* September 20, 2016, https://www.thehindu.com/opinion/op-ed/A-journey-for-liberty/article14571413.ece.

13. Merry Mou, "Justice in the Judiciary: Adam Foss at MIT Media Lab Defiance Conference," *Medium,* July 21, 2017.

14. Adam Foss, "A Prosecutor's Vision for a Better Justice System," TED, February 2016, https://www.ted.com/talks/adam_foss_a_prosecutor_s_vision_for_a_better_justice_system.

15. Jamiles Lartey, "John Legend and This Former Prosecutor Have One Goal: Keep Teens Out of Prison," *Guardian,* July 5, 2016.

16. Shaun King, "Philadelphia DA Larry Krasner Promised a Criminal Justice Revolution. He's Exceeding Expectations," *Intercept,* March 20, 2018.

17. Chris Palmer, "6 Months in, Philly DA Larry Krasner Cementing National Stature Among Reform Advocates," *Philadelphia Inquirer,* June 12, 2018.

18. Danielle Kurtzleben, "How to Win the Presidency with 23 Percent of the Popular Vote," NPR, November 2, 2016.

19. Meg Anderson, "Critics Move to Scrap the Electoral College, But It's Not Likely to Work," NPR, November 17, 2016.

20. Jonathon Keats, "John Koza Has Built an Invention Machine," *Popular Science,* March 18, 2019; and Pagan Kennedy, "Who Made That Scratch-Off Lottery Ticket?," *New York Times,* July 5, 2013.

21. Jedediah Purdy et al., "Is the Electoral College Doomed?," *Politico,* September–October, 2017.

22. James Madison, "Debates in the Federal Convention of 1787," Teaching American History, http://teachingamericanhistory.org/convention/debates/0917-2/.

23. Bruce Bartlett, "Enlarging the House of Representatives," *New York Times,* January 7, 2014; and Daniel Weiss, "Reapportionment Then and Now," *Campaigns & Elections*, February 28, 2011, https://www.campaignsandelections.com/campaign-insider/reapportionment-then-and-now.

24. Bartlett, "Enlarging the House."

25. Michael G. Neubauer and Joel Zeitlin, "Outcomes of Presidential Elections and the House Size," *PS: Political Science and Politics* 36, no 4 (2003): 721–25, https://doi.org/10.1017/S1049096503003019.

26. Fabrice Barthélémy, Mathieu Martin, and Ashley Piggins, "The Size of the House of Representatives, Not the American People, Can Determine the Outcome of Presidential Elections," London School of Economics US Centre, April 27, 2014, http://blogs.lse.ac.uk/usappblog/2014/04/24/the-size-of-the-house-of-representatives-not-the-american-people-can-determine-the-outcome-of-presidential-elections/.

27. Bartlett, "Enlarging the House"; George F. Will, "Congress Just Isn't Big Enough," *Washington Post,* January 14, 2001; and Bruce Bartlett, "The Ultimate Congressional Reforms," *Forbes,* July 11, 2012. See also Drew DeSilver, "US Population Is Growing, but House of Representatives Is Same Size as in Taft Era," Pew Research Center, May 31, 2018, http://www.pewresearch.org/fact-tank/2018/05/31/u-s-population-keeps-growing-but-house-of-representatives-is-same-size-as-in-taft-era/.

28. Noah Kunin, "Why I'm Staying at 18F," *Medium,* November 8, 2016.

29. Noah Kunin, "Why I'm Leaving 18F," *Medium,* July 5, 2017.

Chapter 6: COUNTER-DEMOCRACY
AND CITIZEN MONITORING

1. Bobby Seale, interview by Blackside, Inc., November 4, 1988, at Washington University Digital Gateway, http://digital.wustl.edu/e/eii/eiiweb/sea5427.0172.147bobbyseale.html.

2. " 'Policing the Police': How the Black Panthers Got Their Start," *Fresh Air,* NPR, September 23, 2015.

3. Thad Morgan, "The NRA Supported Gun Control When the Black Panthers Had the Weapons," History.com, March 22, 2018, https://

www.history.com/news/black-panthers-gun-control-nra-support
-mulford-act.

4. Black Panther Party, "The Ten-Point Program," October 15, 1966, Marxists.org, https://www.marxists.org/history/usa/workers/black -panthers/1966/10/15.htm.

5. Charles E. Jones, ed., *The Black Panther Party (Reconsidered)* (Baltimore: Black Classic Press, 2005).

6. Tom Cleary, "Feidin Santana: 5 Fast Facts You Need to Know," Heavy.com, April 9, 2015, https://heavy.com/news/2015/04/feidin -santana-video-recorded-walter-scott-michael-slager-shooting -murder-cell-phone-interview-video-photo-south-carolina -bystander-witness-name/.

7. Jason Ryan, "Man Who Filmed Walter Scott's Killing: 'It Wasn't a Fight . . . It Was an Injustice,'" *Daily Beast*, November 4, 2016.

8. Stephen Rex Brown, "Ramsey Orta Says He's Been Beaten by Prison Guards, Thrown in Solitary as Retaliation for Filming Eric Garner Death," *New York Daily News*, October 29, 2017.

9. WeCopWatch and WITNESS, "Video as Evidence: Documenting #NoDAPL," February 16, 2017, https://s3-us-west-2.amazonaws .com/librarywebfiles/Training+Materials/Training+PDFs/ Video+as+Evidence+Guides/English/VaE_NoDAPL_16Feb2017_v1_1 .pdf.

10. Avi Asher-Schapiro and Tess Owen, "Walking the Beat with Copwatch, the People Who Police the Police," *Vice*, September 8, 2015.

11. Pierre Rosanvallon, *Counter-Democracy: Politics in an Age of Distrust,* trans. Arthur Goldhammer (Cambridge, UK: Cambridge University Press, 2008), 274.

12. Mark Warren, "Democracy and Distrust: A Discussion of *Counter-Democracy: Politics in an Age of Distrust,*" *Perspectives on Politics* 8, no. 3 (2010): 892–95, https://doi.org/10.1017/S1537592710001349; and Philippe C. Schmitter, "Democracy and Distrust: A Discussion of *Counter-Democracy: Politics in an Age of Distrust,*" *Perspectives on Politics* 8, no. 3 (2010): 887–89, https://doi.org/10.1017/ S1537592710001325.

13. "About OIG," Office of the Inspector General, n.d., Social Security Administration, https://oig.ssa.gov/about-oig.

14. Antonella Napolitano, "Monithon, a Government 'Monitoring Marathon' in Italy," TechPresident.com, May 14, 2014, http:// techpresident.com/news/wegov/25011/monithon-monitoring -marathon-citizens; Ethan Zuckerman, "Monithon and Monitorial Citizenship in Italy," . . . *My Heart's in Accra,* May 19, 2014,

http://www.ethanzuckerman.com/blog/2014/05/19/monithon-and
-monitorial-citizenship-in-italy/.

15. "Interview with Steve Mann on the Rise of Sousveillance," *Narrative*, May 6, 2013, http://blog.getnarrative.com/2013/05/steve-mann/ and Ethan Zuckerman, "Why We Must Continue to Turn the Camera on Police," *MIT Technology Review,* July 11, 2016, https://www.technologyreview.com/s/601878/why-we-must-continue-to-turn-the-camera-on-police/.

16. Colleen Kimmett, "Five Things We Can Learn from Brazil's School Meal Program," *Tyee,* May 11, 2016, https://thetyee.ca/News/2016/05/11/Brazil-School-Meal-Program.

17. Michael Schudson, *The Good Citizen: A History of American Civic Life* (Cambridge, Mass.: Harvard University Press, 1999).

18. "About," Safecast, April 6, 2020, https://blog.safecast.org/history/.

19. "One Lawyer's Fight for Young Blacks and 'Just Mercy,'" *Fresh Air,* NPR, October 20, 2014.

20. Regina Moorer, "Equal Justice Initiative," *Encyclopedia of Alabama,* November 28, 2018, http://www.encyclopediaofalabama.org/article/h-3465.

21. Rosanvallon, *Counter-Democracy,* 71.

22. Maegan Vazquez, "Top Immigration Official: Family Detention Centers Are 'Like Summer Camp,'" CNN, August 1, 2018.

23. Laura Jarrett, "Federal Judge Orders Reunification of Parents and Children, End to Most Family Separations at Border," CNN, June 27, 2018.

24. Joe Concha, "Poll: Majority of Republicans Agree Media Is 'Enemy of the People,'" *Hill,* August 14, 2018.

25. Knight Foundation, "10 Reasons Why Americans Don't Trust the Media," *Medium,* January 16, 2018.

Chapter 7: PRODUCTIVE DISRUPTION

1. Max Ehrenfreund, "Charted: The 20 Deadliest Jobs in America," *Washington Post,* January 28, 2015.

2. Susan Crawford, "Getting over Uber," *Wired,* October 16, 2015.

3. Luke Villapaz, "Uber CEO Travis Kalanick Declares War on Taxi Industry in Interview," video, *International Business Times,* May 30, 2014, https://www.ibtimes.com/uber-ceo-travis-kalanick-declares-war-taxi-industry-interview-video-1592433.

4. "Uber for X," Product Hunt, https://www.producthunt.com/e/uber-for-x.

5. "The Global Unicorn Club: Current Private Companies Valued at $1B+," CB Insights, https://www.cbinsights.com/research-unicorn-companies.

6. S. Lock, "Hotel Industry—Statistics & Facts," Statista.com, June 18, 2019, https://www.statista.com/topics/1102/hotels/.

7. Jack Hungelmann, "Uber and Lyft: Insuring the Drivers," IRMI.com, January 2017, https://www.irmi.com/articles/expert-commentary/uber-lyft-insurance.

8. Dan Mangan, "Medical Bills Are the Biggest Cause of US Bankruptcies: Study," CNBC, July 24, 2013.

9. Cyrus Farivar, "What's Uber and Lyft Drivers' Median Hourly Wage? $10 or Lower, Report Finds," *Ars Technica,* March 6, 2018, https://arstechnica.com/tech-policy/2018/03/whats-uber-and-lyft-drivers-median-hourly-wage-under-4-report-finds/.

10. Yanbo Ge et al., "Racial and Gender Discrimination in Transportation Network Companies," NBER Working Paper no. 22776 (October 2016), http://www.nber.org/papers/w22776; and Natalie Shoemaker, "Your Name May Influence How Long You Wait for an Uber or Lyft, MIT Study Finds," BigThink.com, November 7, 2016, https://bigthink.com/natalie-shoemaker/your-name-may-influence-how-long-you-wait-for-an-uber-lyft-ride.

11. Sam Levin, "Airbnb Gives In to Regulator's Demand to Test for Racial Discrimination by Hosts," *Guardian,* April 27, 2017.

12. Hannah Jane Parkinson, "#AirBnBWhileBlack Hashtag Highlights Potential Racial Bias on Rental App," *Guardian,* May 5, 2016.

13. Kristen Houser, "Uber and Lyft Still Allow Racist Behavior, but Not as Much as Taxi Services," *Futurism,* July 16, 2018, https://futurism.com/racial-discrimination-ridehaiing-apps.

14. Nikita Stewart and Luis Ferré-Sadurní, "Another Taxi Driver in Debt Takes His Life. That's 5 in 5 Months," *New York Times,* May 27, 2018; and Ginia Bellafante, "A Driver's Suicide Reveals the Dark Side of the Gig Economy," *New York Times,* February 6, 2018.

15. India has hundreds of minimum wages, which differ by state and skill level. This figure is for skilled workers in Rajasthan, where MKSS is based. "Rajasthan Minimum Wage w.e.f. January 1, 2018 to June 30, 2018," Paycheck.in, https://paycheck.in/salary/minimumwages/rajasthan/rajasthan-minimum-wage-w-e-f-january-1-2018-to-june-30-2018; and "List of Minimum Wages by Country," *Wikipedia,* May 6, 2020.

16. Noe Jacomet, "How the G0v Movement Is Forking the Taiwanese Government," *Medium*, May 23, 2018.

ﬡ

17. Stephen A. Higginson, "A Short History of the Right to Petition Governments for the Redress of Grievances," *Yale Law Journal* 96, no. 1 (1986): 142–66, https://www.jstor.org/stable/796438?seq=1#page_scan_tab_contents.

18. Eric Jaffe, "How Open Data and Civic Participation Helped Taiwan Slow Covid," *Medium: Sidewalk Talk*, March 27, 2020.

19. Louise Matsakis, "YouTube Will Link Directly to Wikipedia to Fight Conspiracy Theories," *Wired*, March 13, 2018.

20. John Naughton, "In a Hysterical World, Wikipedia Is a Ray of Light—and That's the Truth," *Guardian*, September 2, 2018.

21. Ibid.

22. Joseph Reagle and Lauren Rhue, "Gender Bias in Wikipedia and Britannica," *International Journal of Communication* 5 (2011): 1138–58, http://ijoc.org/index.php/ijoc/article/view/777.

23. Matt Shipman, "Study Finds Gender Bias in Open-Source Programming," Phys.org, May 1, 2017, https://phys.org/news/2017-05-gender-bias-open-source.html.

24. Daniel Oberhaus, "Nearly All of Wikipedia Is Written by Just 1 Percent of Its Editors," *Vice*, November 7, 2017.

25. Ibid.

26. "Welcome to Turkopticon 2 Beta!," *Turkopticon,* https://turkopticon.info/.

27. J. Nathan Matias, "Supporting Change from Outside Systems with Design and Data: Stuart Geiger on Successor Systems," MIT Center for Civic Media, December 9, 2014, https://civic.mit.edu/2014/12/09/supporting-change-from-outside-systems-with-design-and-data-stuart-geiger-on/.

28. Slatin Group, "Accessible NYC Transportation," *NYC: The Official Guide*, July 5, 2017, https://www.nycgo.com/articles/accessible-nyc-transportationl and "Taxicabs of New York City," Wikipedia.

29. Winnie Hu, "Uber Discriminates Against Riders with Disabilities, Suit Says," *New York Times,* July 18, 2017.

Chapter 8: DECENTRALIZATION

1. Susanne Tarkowski Tempelhof, "Lessons of the Libyan Endgame," *New York Times,* August 23, 2011.

2. Peter Rothman, "Interview: Bitcoin Pioneer Susanne Tarkowski Tempelhof on Bitnation and M+," *h+ Media*, February 18, 2015, http://hplusmagazine.com/2015/02/18/interview-bitcoin-pioneer-susanne-tarkowski-tempelhof-on-bitnation-and-m/.

3. Matthew Frankel, "How Many Cryptocurrencies Are There?," *Mot-

ley Fool, March 16, 2018, https://www.fool.com/investing/2018/03/16/how-many-cryptocurrencies-are-there.aspx.

4. Stayawhile, "Faces of Crypto: Susanne Tarkowski Tempelhof," *Medium*, October 19, 2017.

5. Boluwatife Arebisola, "Bitnation—World's First Decentralized Borderless Voluntary Nation," *Medium*, April 9, 2018.

6. "Enter Pangea: The Internet of Sovereignty," Bitnation, November 12, 2018, https://tse.bitnation.co/.

7. Ibid.

8. Antonio Madeira, "The DAO, the Hack, the Soft Fork and the Hard Fork," *CryptoCompare*, March 12, 2019, https://www.cryptocompare.com/coins/guides/the-dao-the-hack-the-soft-fork-and-the-hard-fork/; and Samuel Falkon, "The Story of the DAO—Its History and Consequences," *Medium*, August 12, 2018.

9. "Report of Investigation Pursuant to Section 21(a) of the Securities Exchange Act of 1934: The DAO," Securities and Exchange Commission, release no. 82107, July 25, 2017, https://www.sec.gov/litigation/investreport/34-81207.pdf.

10. James Bridle, "The Rise of Virtual Citizenship," *Atlantic*, February 21, 2018.

11. "Passport Dealers of Europe: Navigating the Golden Visa Market," Transparency International, March 6, 2018, https://www.transparency.org/news/feature/navigating_european_golden_visas.

12. "X-Road®," e-estonia, November 7, 2019, https://e-estonia.com/solutions/interoperability-services/x-road/; "Estonia Takes the Plunge," *Economist*, June 28, 2014; and Nathan Heller, "Estonia, the Digital Republic," *New Yorker*, December 11, 2017.

13. "Enter Pangea: The Internet of Sovereignty," Bitnation, November 12, 2018, https://tse.bitnation.co/.

14. "Refugee Emergency Response," Bitnation, n.d., https://web.archive.org/web/20180517124009/https://refugees.bitnation.co/; and Erin Lace, "Bitnation Registers First Refugees on the Blockchain," *Cointelegraph*, September 18, 2015, https://cointelegraph.com/news/bitnation-registers-first-refugees-on-the-blockchain.

15. Turner Wright, "Ethereum Now Rivals Bitcoin for Daily Value Transfers," *Cointelegraph*. April 16, 2020, https://cointelegraph.com/news/ethereum-now-rivals-bitcoin-for-daily-value-transfers.

16. Peter Fairley, "The Ridiculous Amount of Energy It Takes to Run Bitcoin," *IEEE Spectrum: Technology, Engineering, and Science News*, September 28, 2017, https://spectrum.ieee.org/energy/policy/the-ridiculous-amount-of-energy-it-takes-to-run-bitcoin.

17. Ben Kaiser, Mireya Jurado, and Alex Ledger, "The Looming Threat

of China: An Analysis of Chinese Influence on Bitcoin," arXiv.org, October 5, 2018, https://arxiv.org/pdf/1810.02466.pdf.

18. Jonathan Miles, "The Billionaire King of Techtopia," *Details,* August 23, 2011, available at https://longreads.com/picks/the-billionaire-king -of-techtopia/.

19. Ibid.

20. Peter Thiel, "The Education of a Libertarian," *Cato Unbound,* April 13, 2009, https://www.cato-unbound.org/2009/04/13/peter -thiel/education-libertarian.

21. Mary L. G. Theroux, "The Quest for a New Tech Land of the Free," *Wired,* February 2014.

22. Mike Ives, "As Climate Change Accelerates, Floating Cities Look Like Less of a Pipe Dream," *New York Times,* January 27, 2017.

23. "MS The World," CruiseMapper, n.d., https://www.cruisemapper .com/ships/ms-The-World-1119.

24. Seasteading, "The One Universal Human Right," *Diary of a Seasteader,* September 26, 2007, http://seasteading.livejournal .com/27761.html.

25. Thiel, "Education of a Libertarian."

26. Albert O. Hirschman, *The Rhetoric of Reaction: Perversity, Futility, Jeopardy* (Cambridge, Mass.: Harvard University Press, 1991).

27. Albert O. Hirschman, *Exit, Voice, and Loyalty: Responses to Decline in Firms, Organizations, and States* (Cambridge, Mass.: Harvard University Press, 1970): 99–102.

28. Ibid., 113.

29. Yochai Benkler, *The Wealth of Networks: How Social Production Transforms Markets and Freedom* (New Haven, Conn.: Yale University Press, 2006).

30. Jürgen Habermas, *The Structural Transformation of the Public Sphere* (1962), trans. Thomas Burger and Frederick Lawrence (Cambridge, Mass.: Polity Press, 1989), 176.

31. Elisa Shearer and Katerina Eva Matsa, "News Use Across Social Media Platforms 2018," Pew Research Center, September 10, 2018, http://www.journalism.org/2018/09/10/news-use-across-social -media-platforms-2018/.

32. Zeynep Tufekci, *Twitter and Tear Gas: The Power and Fragility of Networked Protest* (New Haven, Conn.: Yale University Press, 2017).

33. Ethan Zuckerman, "The First Twitter Revolution?," *Foreign Policy,* January 15, 2011.

34. Mike Isaac and Daisuke Wakabayashi, "Russian Influence Reached

126 Million Through Facebook Alone," *New York Times,* October 30, 2017; and Sarah Frier and Steven T. Dennis, "Instagram Was Bigger Russian Election Tool Than Facebook, Senate Report Says," Bloomberg.com, December 17, 2018.

35. Arab American Institute (AAI) et al. to Facebook, Inc., October 30, 2017, reprinted in *Politico,* https://www.politico.com/f/?id=0000015f-72d6-d783-a15f-f7d65c8d0000.

36. Sasha Lekach, "The Coder Who Built Mastodon Is 24, Fiercely Independent, and Doesn't Care About Money," *Mashable,* April 6, 2017, https://mashable.com/2017/04/06/eugen-rochko-mastodon-interview/.

37. Ethan Zuckerman, "Mastodon Is Big in Japan. The Reason Why Is . . . Uncomfortable," *Medium,* August 18, 2017.

38. Alex Ciarniello, "What is Mastodon and Why Should You Care?" *Intel,* February 4, 2020, https://www.echosec.net/blog/what-is-mastodon-and-why-should-you-care.

39. Eleanor, "Statement on Gab's Fork of Mastodon," *Join Mastodon,* July 4, 2019, https://blog.joinmastodon.org/2019/07/statement-on-gabs-fork-of-mastodon/; and Ben Makuch, "The Nazi-Free Alternative to Twitter Is Now Home to the Biggest Far Right Social Network," *Vice: Motherboard,* July 11, 2019.

40. Mastodon Monitoring Project, April 5, 2019, https://mnm.social, accessed via Archive.org snapshot April 5, 2019.

41. Josh Constine, "2.5 Billion People Use at Least One of Facebook's Apps," *TechCrunch,* July 25, 2018, https://techcrunch.com/2018/07/25/facebook-2-5-billion-people/.

42. John Dougherty and Michael Edison Hayden, "'No Way' Gab Has 800,000 Users, Web Host Says," *SPLC Hatewatch,* February 14, 2019, https://www.splcenter.org/hatewatch/2019/02/14/no-way-gab-has-800000-users-web-host-says; and David Gilbert, "Here's How Big Far Right Social Network Gab Has Actually Gotten," *Vice,* August 16, 2019.

43. Ethan Zuckerman, "Who Filters Your News? Why We Built Gobo .social," . . . *My Heart's in Accra,* November 16, 2017, http://www.ethanzuckerman.com/blog/2017/11/16/who-filters-your-news-why-we-built-gobo-social/.

44. "U.S. Supreme Court Rejects CFAA Appeal by Power Ventures Against Facebook," *Lexology,* October 16, 2017, https://www.lexology.com/library/detail.aspx?g=f11a87fc-e9ab-4760-a75b-472c70f598ec; and Corynne McSherry et al., "Facebook v. Power Ventures," Electronic Frontier Foundation, March 10, 2014, https://www.eff.org/cases/facebook-v-power-ventures.

45. John Keefe, "How to Buy into Journalism's Blockchain Future (in Only 44 Steps)," Nieman Lab, September 19, 2018, http://www.niemanlab.org/2018/09/how-to-buy-into-journalisms-blockchain-future-in-only-44-steps/.

46. Matthew Iles, "What's Next for Civil," *Medium,* October 16, 2018, https://blog.joincivil.com/whats-next-for-civil-66f2737f5c31.

47. Matthew De Silva, "The Crypto Token that Wants to Save Journalism Is Offering Refunds," *Quartz,* October 16, 2018, https://qz.com/1426382/consensys-bought-most-of-the-cvl-tokens-in-civil-medias-disappointing-ico/.

48. Rick Edmonds, "R.I.P. Civil—Lessons from a Failed Startup," *Poynter,* June 2, 2020.

Chapter 9: DO SOMETHING

1. Scott R. Caseley, "Children at War" (interview with Jason Russell), NewEnglandFilm.com, February 1, 2007, https://newenglandfilm.com/magazine/2007/02/children-at-war.

2. danah boyd, "The Power of Youth: How Invisible Children Orchestrated Kony 2012," Social Media Collective, March 14, 2012, https://socialmediacollective.org/2012/03/14/the-power-of-youth-how-invisible-children-orchestrated-kony-2012.

3. Ethan Zuckerman, "Unpacking Kony 2012," . . . *My Heart's in Accra,* March 8, 2012, http://www.ethanzuckerman.com/blog/2012/03/08/unpacking-kony-2012/.

4. Dale Archer, "Jason Russell's Psychosis," *Psychology Today,* March 24, 2012.

5. Nick Allen, "Joseph Kony 2012: Filmmaker Jason Russell Arrested on Suspicion of Masturbating in Public," *Telegraph,* March 17, 2012.

6. Kristof Titeca and Matthew Sebastian, "Why Did Invisible Children Dissolve?," *Washington Post,* December 30, 2014.

7. Ibid.

8. "Condorcet's Essay on the Application of Analysis to the Probability of Majority Decisions," in Condorcet, *Foundations of Social Choice and Political Theory,* ed. and trans. Iain McLean and Fiona Hewitt (Northampton, MA: Edward Elgar, 1994): 245–46.

9. Anthony Downs, *An Economic Theory of Democracy* (New York: Harper, 1957).

10. Ibid.

11. Angus Campbell, Gerald Gurin, and Warren E. Miller, *The Voter Decides* (Evanston, IL: Row, Peterson & Co., 1954), 187.
12. Ibid.
13. George I. Balch, "Multiple Indicators in Survey Research: The Concept "Sense of Political Efficacy,'" *Political Methodology* 1, no. 2 (1974): 1–43, http://www.jstor.org/stable/25791375.
14. Ibid.
15. Ibid.
16. Christine Bennett Button, "Political Education for Minority Groups," in Richard G. Niemi and Associates, *The Politics of Future Citizens* (San Francisco: Jossey-Bass, 1974), pp. 167–98.
17. "Modi Traces Back Mahatma Gandhi's Historic South African Train Ride," *Hindu BusinessLine*, January 17, 2018, https://www .thehindubusinessline.com/news/modi-traces-back-mahatma -gandhis-historic-south-african-train-ride/article8828839.ece.
18. Ramachandra Guha, *Gandhi: The Years That Changed the World, 1914–1948* (New York: Knopf, 2018).
19. Saurabh Bhattacharya, "Martin Luther King Jr.," MKGandhi.org, n.d., https://www.mkgandhi.org/associates/martinluther.htm.
20. Malcolm Gladwell, "Small Change," *New Yorker,* October 4, 2010.
21. "Red Equal Sign," *Know Your Meme*, March 18, 2020, https:// knowyourmeme.com/memes/events/red-equal-sign.
22. "Showing Support for Marriage Equality on Facebook," Facebook, March 29, 2013, https://www.facebook.com/notes/facebook -data-science/showing-support-for-marriage-equality-on-facebook/ 10151430548593859.
23. J. Nathan Matias, Matt Stempeck, and Molly Sauter, "Green vs. Pink: Change Your Profile, Change the World!," MIT Center for Civic Media, March 28, 2013, available at https://natematias.com/ media/Green-Vs-Pink-03.28.2013.pdf.
24. Julia Preston, "How the Dreamers Learned to Play Politics," *Politico*, September 9, 2017.
25. Albert Sabaté, "The Rise of Being 'Undocumented and Unafraid,'" ABC News, December 4, 2012.
26. Elizabeth Flock, "Susan G. Komen Stops Planned Parenthood Funding: Who Does the Decision Hurt More?," *Washington Post*, February 1, 2012.
27. Deanna Zandt, "Planned Parenthood Saved Me," DeannaZandt.com, https://www.deannazandt.com/portfolio_page/planned-parenthood -saved-me.

28. Evgeny Morozov, "From Slacktivism to Activism," *Foreign Policy,* September 5, 2009.

29. Walter Stephen, ed., *Think Global, Act Local: The Life and Legacy of Patrick Geddes,* 2nd ed. (Edinburgh: Luath Press, 2016).

30. Reid Wilson, "Governors in All 50 States Get Better Marks Than Trump for COVID Response," *Hill,* April 30, 2020.

31. Bruce Katz and Jeremy Nowak, *The New Localism* (Washington, DC: Brookings Institution Press, 2017).

32. Charles Garrett, *The La Guardia Years: Machine and Reform Politics in New York City* (New Brunswick, NJ: Rutgers University Press, 1961), 274.

33. "Partisan vs. Nonpartisan Elections," National League of Cities, n.d., https://www.nlc.org/partisan-vs-nonpartisan-elections. Ironically, New York is one of the three cities with party elections.

34. "Trust in Government," Gallup, n.d., https://news.gallup.com/poll/5392/trust-government.aspx.

35. Justin McCarthy, "Americans Still More Trusting of Local Than State Government," Gallup, October 8, 2018, https://news.gallup.com/poll/243563/americans-trusting-local-state-government.aspx.

36. Richard F. Fenno, *Home Style: House Members in their Districts* (Boston: Little, Brown, 1978).

37. Morgan McDaniel, "Why Do You Loathe Congress but Love Your Congressman?," *Mic,* May 9, 2013, https://mic.com/articles/40765/why-do-you-loathe-congress-but-love-your-congressman.

38. "Privilege Blindness, #MeToo, and the MIT Media Lab," Smarts Consulting, August 30, 2019, smartsconsulting.com/askdrsmarts/2019/8/30/want-to-invent-the-future-start-by-checking-your-privilege.

39. William G. Thomas III, "Television News and the Civil Rights Struggle: The Views in Virginia and Mississippi," *Southern Spaces,* November 3, 2004, https://southernspaces.org/2004/television-news-and-civil-rights-struggle-views-virginia-and-mississippi/.

40. Ethan Zuckerman, "The First Twitter Revolution?," *Foreign Policy,* January 15, 2011.

41. Sarah Sluis, "Digital Ad Market Soars to $88 Billion, Facebook and Google Contribute 90% of Growth," *AdExchanger,* May 10, 2018, https://adexchanger.com/online-advertising/digital-ad-market-soars-to-88-billion-facebook-and-google-contribute-90-of-growth/.

42. Ethan Zuckerman, "Four Problems for News and Democracy," *Medium,* April 1, 2018.

43. Maxwell E. McCombs and Donald L. Shaw, "The Agenda Setting Function of Mass Media," *Public Opinion Quarterly* 36, no. 2 (1972): 176–87.

44. Bernard C. Cohen, *The Press and Foreign Policy* (Princeton, NJ: Princeton University Press, 1963).

45. Ethan Zuckerman, *Rewire: Digital Cosmopolitans in the Age of Connection* (New York: W. W. Norton, 2013).

46. Patrisse Cullors, "Opinion: #BlackLivesMatter Will Continue to Disrupt the Political Process," *Washington Post,* August 18, 2015.

47. Ethan Zuckerman et al., "Whose Death Matters? A Quantitative Analysis of Media Attention to Deaths of Black Americans in Police Confrontations, 2013–2016," *International Journal of Communication* 13 (2019): 27.

48. Patricia Brennan, "Keeping His Goal in Sight," *Washington Post,* June 9, 1996.

49. Campaigns featured on the homepage of DoSomething.org, December 28, 2018.

50. Alice Gregory, "R U There?," *New Yorker,* February 9, 2015.

Afterword: KATRINA AND COVID-19

1. David Zucchino, "'They Just Left Us Here to Die,'" *Los Angeles Times,* September 4, 2005; and John Burnett, "At a Shelter of Last Resort, Decency Prevailed over Depravity," *Morning Edition*, NPR, August 25, 2005.

2. Faiz Shakir, "FEMA Director: We Did Not Know New Orleans Convention Center Was a Hurricane Shelter," *ThinkProgress,* September 2, 2005, https://archive.thinkprogress.org/fema-director-we -did-not-know-new-orleans-convention-center-was-a-hurricane -shelter-1f43b6f2ce2e/.

3. American Society of Civil Engineers, "The ERP report: What Went Wrong and Why," ASCE Library, June 2007, https://ascelibrary.org/ doi/pdf/10.1061/ciegag.0000126.

4. "Red Cross: State Rebuffed Relief Efforts," CNN.com, September 9, 2005; and Chris Edwards, "Hurricane Katrina: Remembering Federal Failures," *Cato at Liberty,* August 27, 2015, https://www .cato.org/blog/hurricane-katrina-remembering-federal-failures.

5. John Burrett, "Evacuees Were Turned Away at Gretna, La.," *Morning Edition*, NPR, September 20, 2005.

6. John McQuaid, "The Lessons American Never Learned from Hurricane Katrina," *Atlantic,* September 3, 2015.

7. Ethan Zuckerman, "Recovery 2.0—Thoughts on What Worked and Failed on PeopleFinder So Far," . . . *My Heart's in Accra,* September 6, 2005, http://www.ethanzuckerman.com/blog/2005/09/06/

recovery-20-thoughts-on-what-worked-and-failed-on-peoplefinder -so-far/.

8. "Person Finder Help," Google.com, https://support.google.com/ personfinder/?hl=en.

9. Pamela Licalzi O'Connell, "Internet Matchmaking: Those Offering Help and Those Needing It," *New York Times,* November 14, 2005.

10. Jeff Jarvis, "Recovery 2.0, a Call to Convene," *Buzzmachine*, September 5, 2005, https://buzzmachine.com/2005/09/05/recovery-20-a -call-to-convene/.

11. Soo Rin Kim, Dr. Tiffany Kung, and Dr. Mark Abdelmalek, "Trust, Testing and Tracing: How South Korea Succeeded Where the US Stumbled in Coronavirus Response," ABC News, May 1, 2020.

12. "Contamination at C.D.C. Labs Resulted in Delayed Coronavirus Tests," *New York Times,* April 18, 2020.

13. Shawn Boburg et al., "Inside the Coronavirus Testing Failure: Alarm and Dismay Among the Scientists Who Sought to Help," *Washington Post,* April 3, 2020.

14. Rick Rojas and Michael Cooper, "Georgia, Tennessee and South Carolina Say Businesses Can Reopen Soon," *New York Times,* April 20, 2020.

15. "COVID-19 in Racial and Ethnic Minority Groups," Centers for Disease Control and Prevention, April 22, 2020, https://www.cdc .gov/coronavirus/2019-ncov/need-extra-precautions/racial-ethnic -minorities.html.

16. Fintan O'Toole, "Donald Trump Has Destroyed the Country He Promised to Make Great Again," *Irish Times*, April 25, 2020.

17. "Jair Bolsonaro: Brazil's Firebrand Leader Dubbed the Trump of the Tropics," BBC News, December 31, 2018.

18. Nick Paton Walsh et al., "Bolsonaro Calls Coronavirus a 'Little Flu.' Inside Brazil's Hospitals, Doctors Know the Horrifying Reality," CNN, May 25, 2020.

19. Michele A. Berdy, "How Russia's Coronavirus Crisis Got So Bad," *Politico,* May 24, 2020.

20. Sean Illing, "'Flood the Zone with Shit': How Misinformation Overwhelmed Our Democracy," *Vox,* February 6, 2020.

21. "2020 Edelman Trust Barometer Update: Trust and the COVID-19 Pandemic," *Edelman,* May 5, 2020, https://www.edelman.com/ research/trust-2020-spring-update.

22. Charles Anderson, "Jacinda Ardern and Her Government Soar in Popularity During Coronavirus Crisis," *Guardian,* April 30, 2020.

INDEX

Page numbers in *italics* indicate figures.

A/B testing, 205
accountability, 53–54, 129
Accra, Ghana, 1–2
action
　acting locally, 195–200
　taking, 204–6
　voting as, 185–86
activism. *See also specific move-*
　　ments
　code-based, 105
　different ways to work for,
　　189–95
　digital, 79–83, 189, 193–94
　efficacy and, 194–95, 196
　media and, 136
　norms-based, 100–101
　smart, 54–55
　undocumented immigrants and,
　　192–93
　voice-based, 192–94
activists, 16–17, 19. *See also spe-*
　　cific leaders and movements
Acton, Brian, 96

Addiopizzo, 78
advertising, 201
affirmative action, 87
Africa, 52, 180–84, 195, 202. *See*
　　also specific countries
African-Americans, 20, 124–25, 138
　civic education and, 187
　COVID-19 and, 211
　discrimination against, 33–35
　inequality and, 42–43
　justice system and, 114, 134–36
　lynching and, 135–36
　police brutality and misconduct
　　against, 101, 124–26, 135–36,
　　202
　ride-sharing services and,
　　145–46
agenda setting, 202
Airbnb, 143, 146
Alabama, racial discrimination
　　laws in, 104
Alabama Court of Criminal
　　Appeals, 134

Alaska, 119
Albright, Madeleine, 76
Alexander, Michelle, 34
Alexandria, Egypt, 3–4
"algorithmic reputation token" (XPAT), 161, 165
Ali, Ben, 200
Alinsky, Saul, 186
Al Jazeera, 200
Allen, Danielle, 5
Alternative for Germany (AfD), 63
Amazon, 56, 143
Ambedkar, Babasaheb, 112
American Boychoir School, 106
American National Election Study, 5
American Revolution, 67, 68
American Society of Civil Engineers, 208
American Society of Newspaper Editors, 57
Americans with Disabilities Act, 86
American Technology Council, 109
"amoral familism," 49
anime-manga community, 176
anti-abortion activists, 193–94
anti-austerity protests, 63–64
antigovernment rhetoric, conservatism and, 69
anti-immigrant sentiments, 35
antipolitics, 2–5, 20
antivaccination activists, 45–46
antiwar movement, 82
Appelbaum, Binyamin, 110
Apple, 56, 95, 158
Arab Spring, 9, 43–44, 63, 64, 159, 174, 200
Ardern, Jacinda, 215
Arendt, Hannah, 72, 73–74, 165–66
Arizona, 68
Army Corps of Engineers, 208

arrests, documentation of, 126
Assange, Julian, 75
asymmetric power, 139–40
AT&T, 146
attorneys, activist, 114–16
Australia
   institutional mistrust in, 30
   mandatory voting in, 14
authoritarianism, 70, 76, 212–13
   in Europe, 76
   nationalist, 69
   tolerance for, 61
awareness, 43–46

baby boomers, 66
Bach, Steve, 52–53
Backpage.com, 176
Badlands National Park, 110
Bailey, Bobby, 180–82
Bakshy, Eytan, 191
Balch, George, 186
ballot initiatives and questions, 15
banks, mistrust of, 6, 29–30
Bannon, Steve, 90, 212
Bargh, John, 69–70
Bartlett, Bruce, 121
Belo Horizonte, Brazil, 130–31
Belt and Road Initiative, 37
Ben Ali, Zine al-Abidine, 63, 174
Benghazi, Libya, 160
Benkler, Yochai, 90, 174
Bennett, Ralph Kinsey, 21
bGeigie, 133
Biden, Joe, 12
big business, mistrust of, 6
Bitcoin, 160–68, 179
Bitnation, 161–66, 168, 169, 179
Black Americans, *see* African-Americans
Black Lives Matter, 83, 100–101, 102, 126, 200, 202, 203

Black Panthers, 20, 124–25, 140, 186

Black Twitter, 100

Black With No Chaser, 101–2

Blasey Ford, Christine, 18

Bloody Sunday, 87

Bolsonaro, Jair, 50–51, 212, 213

borders, closure of, 173–74

Boston, Massachusetts, 114

Boston Globe, 29

Bourbons, 48

Boxer, Barbara, 117

boycott campaigns, 54, 91–92

brain structure, political ideology and, 69

brands, smart activism and, 54–55

Brazil, 50–52, 129–31, 212

Breitbart, 90–91

Brexit, 10, 27, 38, 62, 66–67, 71

Britain, 35, 67, 76
    Brexit and, 10, 27, 38, 62, 66–67, 71
    COVID-19 and, 212
    disengagement from politics in, 62–63
    educated readership in, 45
    Great Depression and, 35
    India and, 188–89
    mistrust of institutions in, 7
    National Health Service in, 158

Brooks, David, 77

Browder v. Gayle, 104

Brown, Michael (FEMA director), 207–8

Brown, Michael (police shooting victim), 98–99, 100, 101–2, 203

Brown v. Board of Education of Topeka, 33, 87

Brugger, Peter, 60

bureaucracy, 38

"deep state" and, 110–13 (*see also* "deep state")
    demonization of, 37–39
    institutions and, 156–57
    mistrust of, 7
    technology and, 107–9

Burke, Tarana, 80–81, 198

Bush, George W., 27, 120
    administration of, 46

Bush, Jeb, *11*, 12, 67

Cairo, Egypt, Tahrir Square protests in, 3

California, 116, 120, 124–25, 137, 146, 177
    Air Resources Board, 93, 94
    Proposition 8, 191
    solar energy and, 102–3

Cambodia, 22, 32

Cambridge Analytica scandal, 56

Cameron, David, 67

Campbell, Angus, 185–86

Canada, 22

capitalism, "golden age of," 36

"Carpe Donktum," 203

Carter, Jimmy, 5, 27, 102–3

Case, Anne, 42

"catch and Kill," 81

Catholic Church, 29, 140, 147

censorship, 85

census, 119

Center for Civic Media, MIT, 115, 177, 203

Centers for Disease Control (CDC), 210–11, 213, 215

Central Africa, 180–84, 195

change, 78, 206
    through code, 94–98, 102–6, 177, 192
    code-based theories of, 98

change (*continued*)
 different ways to work for,
  189–95
 through law, 13, 85–90, 192
 levers of, 79–106, 192
 through markets, 13, 90–94,
  102–6, 192
 media and, 200
 through norms, 88–89, 98–106,
  136, 192
 scale needed, 216
 social networks and, 175–78
 through voting, 185–86
checks and balances, 38
Chernobyl, 132
Chevrolet, 94
children, detained by ICE, 137
China, 37, 50, 152
 Belt and Road Initiative and, 37
 Bitcoin in, 167–68
 COVID-19 and, 213
 interpersonal trust in, 23
 trust of institutions in, 7, 25,
  215
chokeholds, 126
Chrysler, 93
Cidade de Deus favela, Rio de
  Janeiro, Brazil, 51–52
cigarettes, 85–86
cities, 196–97
Citizenfour, 95
citizens. *See also* citizenship
 citizen monitoring, 124–40
 citizen power, 150–51
 good, 13–20
 media and, 201, 202
 voices of, 151–52
citizenship
 engaged, 20
 "informed," 131–34
 "monitorial," 131–34, 140

refugees and, 165–66
 as "right to have rights,"
  165–66
 voluntary, 164–66, 168
"citizenship as a service," 164–65
Citizens United, 121
City of God, 51
civic duty, 15–16
civic dynamics, 46
civic education, 4–5, 13, 187
civic engagement, 13–20, 70. *See
  also* voting
 efficacy and, 16–17, 18–19, 187
 thick vs. thin, 188–95
 voice-based activism, 192–93
civic functions, 53–54
civic institutions, 49
civic life
 consequences of mistrust on, 76
 exclusion from, 20
civic piety, guarding against, 19
civics, 78
 insurrectionism and, 18–19
 new, 78
Civil.co, 177–79
Civilian Conservation Corps, 35
civil participation. *See* civic
  engagement
Civil Rights Act, 7–8, 33, 87, 89
civil rights movement, 20, 82,
  87–88, 89, 91, 104, 105, 135,
  186
 Gandhi and, 188–89
 institutional mistrust and, 31,
  32–35
 media and, 200
 press and, 200
 in the United States, 16–17
Clinton, Bill, 34, 44, 44*n*
Clinton, Hillary, 11–12, *11*, 55,
  59–60, 61, 99, 117

closed societies, trust and, 25–26
CNN, 139, 207–8
Coates, Ta-Nehisi, 34–35
code, 85–90, 102
    change through, 94–98, 102–6,
        177, 192
    definition of, 97–98
    law and, 85–90
coded racism, 34
Code for America, 107–9
Cohen, Bernard, 202
Colding-Jørgensen, Anders, 194
collectivism, fear of, 37
Colorado Springs, Colorado,
        52–53
Color of Change, 54–55
Comet Ping Pong Pizza, 60
communications, 46
Communications Decency Act, 85
Communism, 37, 68
community ties, trust and, 46
Complexo de Maré, 52
compliance, democracy and, 213
Condorcet, Nicolas de, 184
ConsenSys, 179
conservatism
    antigovernment rhetoric and, 69
    institutionalism and, 68
    insurrectionism and, 67–68, 69,
        70
Consortium of Pub-Going, Loose,
        and Forward Women, 3
conspiracy theorists, 60–61
contact tracing, 95–96
contributions, 189, 190
cooperation, institutions and, 214
Copenhagen, Denmark, 194
Coppola, Francis Ford, 46
Copwatch, 126, 127, 133, 136, 140
coronavirus. See COVID-19
corruption, 65

Cosby, Bill, 198
counter-democracy, 124–40
    legitimacy of counter-
        democratic institutions, 138–40
    technology and, 129
counternarratives, 45–46
COVID-19, 41, 50–52, 95–96, 111,
        143, 145, 153, 210–15
    borders and, 173–74
    disruption and, 146–47
    government and, 215
    immigration and, 173–74
    institutionalism and, 214–15
    institutions and, 158
    insurrectionism and, 214–15
    mobilization and, 212–13
    trust in government and, 215
Crawford, Susan, 142
Crimea, 59, 75
criminal organizations, 48–49, 50,
        78
crisis response, decentralization
        and, 213–14
Crisis Text Line, 205–6
Cruz, Ted, 12
cryptocurrency, 160–63, 165–70
    environmental costs of, 166–67,
        167n
    journalism and, 177–78
cryptonations, 165
Cullors, Patrisse, 100, 202
cultural conservatives, 68
CVL, 178
Cyprus, 163–64

Daily Caller, 90
Dakota Access oil pipelines, 126
Dalits, 111–13, 122
Darfur, Sudan, atrocities in,
        180–82
Dave, 4

Davis, Kim, 88

"deaths of despair," whites and, 42

Deaton, Angus, 42

decentralization, 159–79
   crisis response and, 213–14
   institutions and, 159–79
   social networks and, 175–79

"decentralized borderless voluntary nation" (DBVN), 161

"deep state," 11, 34, 73, 110–13, 212, 213

Dela, Efo, 1–2, 20

Delta, 54

democracy, 184. *See also* democratic institutions; representative democracy
   compliance and, 213
   crisis of confidence in, 28–29
   trust and, 25–26
   voting and, 184–85

democratic institutions
   accountability of, 129
   bolstering, 77
   crisis of confidence in, 28–29
   legitimacy and, 138–39
   mistrust of, 128
   transformation of, 77–78, 128

democratic oversight, media and, 136

Democratic Party, 27, 60, 67, 69–70, 118, 120, 121
   insurrectionists vs. institutionalists, 11–12, *11*
   media and, 71

Democratic Republic of Congo, 180–81

Denhollander, Rachael, 83

deregulation, 13, 36–37

desegregation, 87–88

Designated Survivor, 4

destabilization, 73

Development, Relief, and Education for Alien Minors (DREAM) immigration reform act, 192

Dey, Nikhil, 147–50

Dick's Sporting Goods, 54

digital activism, 79–83, 189, 193–94

digital advertising, 90–91, 201

digital identity cards, 165–66

digital jurisdiction, 163–65

digital media, 201

digital nations, 163–65, 167–68, 170–71, 174

disability advocates, 156–57

discrimination, against African-Americans, 33–35

disengagement, 20, 70, 76
   among youth, 104
   mistrust and, 61–70

disinformation campaigns, 2016 US presidential election and, 174–75

disrupters, become institutions, 154–56, 158

disruption
   COVID-19 and, 146–47
   dark side of, 144
   market forces and, 141–51
   productive, 141–58

Distributed Autonomous Organization (DAO), 162–63

distributed currencies, 168. *See also* distributed systems

distributed systems, 166, 179

district attorneys, 114–16

District of Columbia, 118

documentation
   of arrests, 126
   of public works projects, 128–31

donations, 189, 190
Do Something, 204–6
Down, Anthony, 184–85
Downs's paradox, 184–85
Dream Walk, 192
Duda, Andrzej, 67
Dumsor protests, 1–2
dysfunctional systems, insurrec-
    tionism in, 17–19

eBay, escrow system and, 23–24
e-citizenship, 164–65
economic crisis of 2007–8, 28,
    29–30
Economic Policy Institute, 42–43
economic stagnation, 36
Edelman, 7, 25–26, 30, 215
education, 4–5, 13, 36, 45, 46. *See
    also* civic education
"e-Estonia," 164–65
efficacy, 16, 104
    activism and, 194–95, 196
    civil participation and, 16–19
    high vs. low, 186–87
    institutionalism and, 186–87
    insurrectionism and, 186–87
    internal vs. external, 186–87
    local government and, 197–98
    motivation and, 196
    online spaces and, 200–206
    participation and, 187
    perception and, 194–95
    social change and, 104–5,
        180–206
    voting and, 185–86
Egypt, 3–4, 64, 159
    overthrow of government in,
        63–64
    protests in, 3, 9
8chan, 61
8kun, 61

18F, 122–23
Eisenhower, Dwight D., 68
elections
    2000 US presidential election,
        120
    2016 US presidential election,
        2, 8, 10, 11–12, *11*, 59, 67, 90,
        117, 122, 174–75
    local, 196
    partisanship and, 196
    voting and, 184
Electoral College, 116–23
electric cars, 92–94, 102
Elephant Tusk Force, 204
elites, 40–41
emission laws, 94
encryption, 96
Encyclopaedia Britannica, 155
encyclopedias, 155
engagement, 128–29. *See also* civic
    engagement
    with media, 201–2
    thick and thin, 188–95
environmental monitoring,
    132–33
environmental movement, 196
Epstein, Jeffrey, 199
equality, 41, 87–88. *See also*
    inequality
Equal Justice Initiative (EJI),
    135–37, 138
equal marriage, 33, 88, 190–92
Erdoğan, Recep Tayyip, 64, 65
Erin, 183–84
Ernest N. Morial Convention
    Center, 207
Estonia, 164–65
Ethereum, 162–63
ethnonationalism, 33–35, 76, 173
"ethos of democratic oversight,"
    128

Euromaidan revolution, 58

Europe. *See also* European Union; *specific countries*
  authoritarianism in, 76
  disengagement from politics in, 62–63
  trust in government and, 28

European Union, 10, 38, 62, 63, 66–67, 128–29, 164, 173. *See also specific countries*

exclusion, insurrectionism and, 20

exit, right to, 170–74

Facebook, 55, 57, 59, 65, 89, 96, 98, 160, 174, 177, 179
  2016 US presidential election and, 174–75
  digital media and, 201
  equal marriage campaign and, 191–92
  Khaled Said Facebook page, 3–4
  "pivot to privacy" and, 98
  trust in, 56

factuality, 74

Fafsa, Tunisia, 200

failure, institutional, 207–16

fairness, 40–41

"fake news," 11, 71–72

false narratives, 46

family separation, 137–38

family ties, 49

far right, 63, 90–91

far-right media, 90–91

fascism, 76

Fauci, Anthony, 213

FBI (Federal Bureau of Investigation), 38

fear, 70
  media and, 70
  political ideology and, 69–70

Federal Trade Commission, 84

federated decentralization, 175–76

FEMA (Federal Emergency Management Agency), 207–8, 211

Fenno, Richard, 196–97

Ferguson, Missouri, 98–99

Fiat, 93

fiction, 72–74

Fight Online Sex Trafficking Act (FOSTA), 176

Filippi, Primavera di, 164

firearms, open carry of, 124–25

First Amendment, 25

FixMyStreet, 53–54

FixMyTransport, 53–54

Floating Island Project, 169

Florida, 103

Floyd, George, 203

Foa, Roberto Stefan, 28–29, 61

Ford, Gerald, 27

Foss, Adam, 114–16

Fox News, 91, 139

Fraley, R. Chris, 69

framing, 202

France, 35, 49
  disengagement from politics in, 63
  institutional mistrust in, 30

Franchetti, Leopoldo, 47

Franken, Al, 80

Freedom Rides, 33

Freedom Summer, 87

free markets, 36–37

Free to Pee, 204

French Polynesia, 169

French Revolution, 67, 127, 138, 139

Friedman, Milton, 36

Friedman, Patri, 169–71

Fukushima Daiichi nuclear power plant, 132–33

Fukuyama, Francis, 23, 46, 49

g0v movement, 151, 153–54, 157
Gab.ai, 176
Gaddafi, Muammar, 159
Gallup/Knight study, 2018, 71
Gallup polls, 27, 29, 30, 87, 88,
    196–97
Gallup World poll 2006, 22
Gambetta, Diego, 48–49
Gamson, William, 105
Gandhi, Mahatma (Mohandas),
    112, 188–89, 193
Gandhi, Sonia, 150
Garner, Eric, 125–26
Garza, Alicia, 100
gay marriage. *See* equal marriage
gay rights advocates, 88–89
Geddes, Patrick, 196
Geiger, Stuart, 156
Geilhufe, David, 209
General Motors, 158
General Services Administration,
    108, 122
Germany, 49
    COVID-19 test developed in,
        210
    interpersonal trust in, 23
    mistrust of institutions in, 7, 30
    Nazi Germany, 73, 76
    trust in government and, 215
Gezi Park, Istanbul, Turkey, 64–65
Ghana, 1–2
GI Bill, 36
gig economy, 141–45
Gladwell, Malcolm, 82, 189
globalization, 77
Gobo, 177
The Godfather, 46
Godwin's Law, 73
"going viral," 181
"golden visa," 164
Goldwater, Barry, 68

Gomez, Reagan, 100
good citizen, being a, 18–19
Google, 3, 55, 56, 95, 154, 158,
    201
Google Person Finder, 209
Gore, Al, 120
government. *See also* local govern-
    ment; US federal government;
    specific government
    COVID-19 and, 215
    mistrust of, 5–8, 6, 34, 196
    monitoring and documenting,
        128–31
    no longer in charge, 50–52
    portrayed as incompetent,
        37–39
    technology and, 107–9
    trust in, 25–27, 43, 215
government data, 58
government institutions. *See also*
    specific institutions
    self-fulfilling attacks on, 38–39
government spending, 36
GPS readings, 130
Graeff, Erhardt, 152–53
"great compression," 41
Great Depression, 35
Greece, 65
Greenwald, Glenn, 95
Gretna, Louisiana, 208
Gujarat, India, 111–13, 122
Gulf of Tonkin incident, 32–33
Gulu, Sudan, 180–81
gun control, national movements
    for, 45–46

Habermas, Jürgen, 174
Haiti, earthquake in, 209
Han dynasty, 152
Hapsburgs, 48
Hardwiche, John, 106

Hariri, Saad, 64

hashtags, 100, 101, 102

Hawaii, 119

Hayes, Chris, 8

health insurance, 7

Heart of Texas, 55

Helliwell, John, 22

Hencken, Randolph, 170

high-trust societies, 22–25
transparency in, 58–59

highways, 37

Hindu nationalists, 112

Hindus, 112, 122

Hirschman, Albert, 171–73

HIV testing, 204

HMOs, 7

Hockenberry, John, 198

Hoffman, Reid, 199

Hogg, David, 91–92, 104–5

Hong Kong, 64, 94–95

House Size Effect, 120

housing discrimination, prohibition of, 87

human rights, 170

Human Rights Campaign (HRC),
89, 190–92

Hungary, 58, 67, 70, 173

Hurricane Katrina, 46, 207–10,
211, 215

hyperpartisanship, in United
States, 29

identity cards, digital, 165–66

#IfTheyGunnedMe Down, 99,
101–2, 202

Iles, Matthew, 179

immigrant rights movement,
192–93

immigration, 67, 90, 173–74
COVID-19 and, 173–74
executive power and, 111

"zero-tolerance" immigration
policy, 137

income, redistribution of, 39, 43

India, 3, 111–13, 122
Britain and, 188–89
independence of, 188–89
media, 148–49
minimum wage in, 147–50
press in, 148–49
right to information in, 148–49
right to work in, 150
trust in government and, 25
trust of institutions in, 7

inequality, 39–43. *See also* racial
inequities
African-Americans and, 42–43
mistrust and, 42
political instability and, 41–42
race and, 42–43
resentment and, 40–41
as state of nature, 41–42
in United States, 42
whites and, 42–43

inflation, 36

Informed Citizen model, 15–16,
131–34

infrastructure, 36, 37, 55

Inglehart, Ron, 29

Ingraham, Laura, 92

Initial Coin Offering, 165

inspector general corps, 128

institutional failure, in United
States, 207–16

institutionalism, 109. *See also*
institutionalists
conservatism and, 68
COVID-19 and, 214–15
efficacy and, 186–87
vs. insurrectionism, 166
law and, 114–23
radical, 113–23

social change and, 121–22
institutionalist revolutionaries, 113
institutionalists, 107–23
    effective, 109
    vs. insurrectionists, 8–13, *11*, 20,
        67, 186, 187–88, 214–15
    radical, 19, 113, 114–16, 158
institutional mistrust
    civil rights movement and, 31,
        32–35
    in Italy, 30
    Nixon and, 31–32
    racism and, 31, 32–35
    Trump and, 30
    in the United States, 30, 50
institutions, 76
    bureaucracy and, 156–57
    cooperation and, 214
    COVID-19 and, 158
    decentralization and, 159–79
    disruptive, 154–56
    frustration with, 13, 17–18
    inflexibility of, 154
    local, 196–98
    maturation of, 7
    mistrust of, 6, 7, 46, 66, 104,
        187, 206, 216
    questioning of, 45
    razing, 12
    reforming, 12, 46
    replacing, 12–13
    resurrection of, 214–16
    self-fulfilling attacks on, 38–39
    technology's role in overthrow-
        ing, 149–50
    trust in, 7
    underperformance of, 46
insurrectionism, *11*, 168–69. *See
    also* insurrectionists
    civics and, 18–19
    conservatism and, 67–68, 69, 70

COVID-19 and, 214–15
    in dysfunctional systems, 17–19
    efficacy and, 186–87
    exclusion and, 20
    vs. institutionalism, 166
    from the left, 11–12, *11*
    liberalism and, 67, 68
    radical, 174
    from the right, 11–12, *11*, 77
    taking seriously, 10–13
insurrectionists, vs. institution-
    alists, 8–13, *11*, 20, 67, 186,
        187–88, 214–15
integration, 33
intelligence agencies, 55, 96. *See
    also specific agencies*
intermarriage, 87, 88
internal efficacy, 104
international women's march, 8,
    64
Internet, 46, 96, 160
Internet Explorer, 84–90
Internet Research Agency, 55
interstate highway system, 68
Invisible Children, 180–82, 187,
    195
iPhone apps, 96
Irish Times, 211–12
ISIS, 159
Islamic Da'wah Center of Hous-
    ton, 55
Israel, 97
Italy, 49
    disengagement from politics in,
        63
    institutional mistrust in, 30
    mistrust of institutions in, 7
Ito, Joi, 199

Jackson, Mississippi, 99
Jackson, Thomas Penfield, 84

James I, 25
Japan, 49, 176
    2011 tsunami in, 132–33
    mistrust of institutions in, 7, 30
Jim Crow laws, 87
Johnson, Boris, 10–11, 67, 77
Johnson, Lyndon B., 32, 42, 66
    Civil Rights Act and, 8
    election of, 5
Jones, Paula, 44n
journalism. See news media
Judd, Ashley, 79, 80, 81, 82
Judt, Tony, 37
Just Be, Inc., 80

Kalanick, Travis, 142, 157
Kanai, Ryota, 69
Katrina PeopleFinder, 209
Katz, Bruce, 196–97
Kavanaugh, Brett, 18
Keillor, Garrison, 80
Kennedy, John F., 7–8, 66
    assassination of, 5
    marital infidelities of, 44
Kerner Commission, 42
Key, Robert E. Lee, Jr., 134, 138
Keynes, John Maynard, 35, 36
King, Larry, 75
King, Martin Luther, Jr., 17, 20,
        87–88
    Gandhi and, 189
    "I Have a Dream" speech, 7–8
KMT, 151
Knack, Stephen, 24
Kony, Joseph, 180–84, 202
Kony 2012, 181–82
Kony 2012 campaign, 181–84, 202
Koum, Jan, 96
Koza, John, 117–18
Krasner, Larry, 115–16
Krastev, Ivan, 65–66

Krebs, Christopher, 55–56
Kremlin, 75
Kunin, Noel, 122–23
Kuran, Timur, 44, 45

labor, organized, 6, 37, 42
La Cosa Nostra, 46
La Guardia, Fiorello, 196
Lam, Carrie, 64
Lancet, 51
Laos, 32
Latinx Americans, 124, 211
Lauer, Matt, 80
law, 82–83, 85–90
    change through, 13, 85–90, 192
    code and, 85–90
    institutionalism and, 114–23
    as lever for change, 13
    mistrust of, 48–49
Lawrence, C. J., 99, 100, 101–2
Lebanon, 64
Lee, Harper, To Kill a Mocking-
        bird, 134–35
the left, disengagement of, 66–70
Le Pen, Marine, 63
Lessig, Lawrence, 84–90, 98, 146
    Code, 85, 86–87
    Criminal podcast, 105–6
Lewinsky, Monica, 44
"Lex Informatica," 85
LGBTQIA people, 20
liberalism, insurrectionism and,
        67, 68
libertarianism, 168–69, 171
libertarians, 68
Libya, 63–64, 159–60, 168
Limassol, Cyprus, 163–64
local elections, partisanship and, 196
local government
    confidence in, 196–98
    efficacy and, 197–98

local institutions, 196–98
local politics, voter enthusiasm
   for, 196–98
Loehmann, Timothy, 101
"lolicon," 176
London, England, 53–54
Lord's Resistance Army (LRA),
   180–82, 202
Louis C.K., 80
Loving, Mildred, 87
Loving, Richard, 87
Loving v. Virginia, 87, 88
low-trust societies, 22–25, 76
   transparency in, 58–59
Lublin, Nancy, 205
Lugg, 143
Lyft, 145, 158
lynching, African-Americans and,
   135–36

Madhya Pradesh, India, 147
mafias, 48–49, 50, 78
Mahatma Gandhi National Rural
   Employment Guarantee Act,
   149
managed health care, mistrust of, 7
Mangalore, India, 3
Mann, Steve, 129–31
Marchionne, Sergio, 93
March on Washington, 7–8, 16,
   33, 66
Marion, Ohio, COVID-19 outbreak in, 211
Marjory Stoneman Douglas High
   School, school shooting at,
   83, 91–92
market forces, disruption and,
   141–51
markets, 85–90
   change through, 13, 90–94,
      102–6, 192

power of global financial, 65
Marlantes, Karl, 32
Marlinspike, Moxie, 96, 97, 104–5
marriage equality. *See* equal mar-
   riage
Martin, Trayvon, 100, 202
Marts, Sherry, 198–99
Massachusetts, 103, 117
Mastodon, 175–77
Matias, Nathan, 191
May, Theresa, 67
Mazdoor Kisan Shakti Sangathan
   (MKSS) (the Association for
   the Empowerment of Workers
   and Peasants), 147–50, 154
McCain, John, 71, 192
McCombs, Maxwell, 202
McLaughlin, BethAnn, 198–99
McMillian, Walter, 134–35, 138
McQuaid, John, 208
media, 38, 71, 138–40, 197. *See
   also* news media; social
   media; *specific outlets*
activism and, 136
antipolitics in, 4
Arab Spring and, 200
bias in, 101–2
change and, 200
citizens and, 201, 202
civil rights movement and, 200
coverage of Africa, 202
democratic oversight and, 136
digital, 201 (*see also* social
   media)
engagement with, 201–2, *201*
far-right, 90–91
fear and, 70
India, 148–49
mistrust of, 6
participatory, 45, 201
police shootings and, 98–99

media (*continued*)
  political participation and, 201
  Republicans and, 138–39
  right-wing, 69
  in Russia, 75
  shift in architecture of, 201
  Trump's attacks on, 11
MediaRadar, 91
medical misinformation, 45–46
medical system, mistrust of, 6, 7,
    29, 45–46, 213
Medicare, 108
"meme magic," mobilization and,
    203–4
mental health, teens and, 204–6
messaging services, 96–97
#MeToo movement, 18, 19, 79–83,
    86, 105, 198–200
#MeTooSTEM movement,
    198–99
Mevani, Jignesh, 112–13, 122
micronations, 174
Microsoft, 84–90
Milano, Alyssa, 79, 80, 81, 102, 105
Miles, Jonathan, 169
military, trust in, 6
millennials, 66
Minibar, 143
"miscegenation," 87
misinformation, 98
Mississippi Freedom Summer,
    189
mistrust
  consequences of, 76–78
  cost of, 49–50
  disengagement and, 61–70
  harnessing, 206
  inequality and, 42
  of institutions, 104
  mobilization and, 66–70
  protesters and, 7–8

reversing, 46
  what follows, 76–78
MIT (Massachusetts Institute of
    Technology), 115, 157
  Center for Civic Media, 115,
      177, 203
  Center for Energy and Environ-
      mental Policy Research, 145
  Media Lab, 130–31, 198–99
mobile phones, 129, 147
mobilization
  COVID-19 and, 212–13
  "meme magic" and, 203–4
  mistrust and, 66–70
  online, 183–84
  social networks and, 174
Model S, 93
monarchies, trust and, 25
Monbiot, George, 35
Monithons, 128–29
"monitorial citizenship," 131–34,
    140
Monroeville, Alabama, 134
Montgomery Bus Boycott, 16, 33,
    91, 104
Moore, Roy, 80
Morozov, Evgeny, 194
Morrison, Ronda, 134
Moscow, Russia, 212
motivation, efficacy and, 196
Mounk, Yascha, 28–29, 61
Movement for Black Lives,
    100–101
Mr. Smith Goes to Washington, 4
MS *The World*, 170
Mubarak, Hosni, 174
Mulford, Don, 125
Musk, Elon, 92–94, 105, 169
Mussolini, Benito, 76
Muthalik, Pramod, 3
mySociety, 53–54

NAACP (National Association for the Advancement of Colored People), 104

NASA (National Aeronautics and Space Administration), 110

Nassar, Larry, 80, 198

National Academy of Sciences, 198–99

National Archives and Records Administration, 59

National Front (France), 63

National Guard, 207, 209

National Health Service (UK), 158

National Institutes of Health, 213

nationalism, 63, 69
  ethnonationalism, 33–35, 76, 173 (*see also* Nazi Germany)
  white nationalism, 33–35

nationalist authoritarianism, 69

National Memorial for Peace and Justice, 135–36

National Parks Service, 110

National Popular Vote Interstate Compact, 117–18

National Rifle Association, 54

nation-states, vs. digital nations, 163–65, 167–68, 170–71

Native Americans, COVID-19 and, 211

NATO (North Atlantic Treaty Organization), 159

natural disasters, 207–10

Navalny, Alexei, 76

Nazi Germany, 73, 76

Nelson, Stanley, 124

neoliberalism, 37–39, 50, 52

Netscape, 84

Neubauer, Michael G., 120

Neutral Point of View, 154

Never Again, 83

Never-Trumper institutionalists, 67

New Deal, 35–36, 39

New Orleans, Louisiana, 207–10
  "Hurricane Protection System," 208

New Orleans Times-Picayune, 208

news media, 25, 30, 46, 138–40, 177–79, 202, 215. *See also specific outlets*
  civil rights movement and, 200
  as counterinstitution, 45
  cryptocurrency and, 177–78
  vs. digital media, 201
  as "fourth estate," 137
  in India, 148–49
  investigative, 45
  legitimacy of, 138–39
  mistrust of, 6, 29
  transparency and, 57–58
  Trump's attacks on, 70–71, 138–39
  trust in, 138–39
  trust of, 70–71
  in the United States, 44–45

Newton, Huey, 124–25

New York, New York
  COVID-19 and, 211
  taxi system in, 156

New York Times, 79–80, 90, 100, 110, 139, 146, 201

New Zealand
  interpersonal trust in, 22
  trust in government and, 215

Nigeria, 26–27

Nissan, 94

Nixon, Richard, 6, 27, 68
  criminality of, 50
  Gulf of Tonkin incident and, 32–33
  impeachment of, 27, 32–33, 70
  institutional mistrust and, 31–32

Nordic countries, trust in government and, 43
norms
  change through, 85–90, 98–106, 136, 192
  norms-based activism, 100–101
Norris, Pippa, 46
North Charleston, South Carolina, 126
Northern Ireland, 50
Northern League (Italy), 63
North Korea, 76
Norton, Quinn, 13–14, 16, 18
Nowak, Jeremy, 196–97

Oakland, California, 124–25
Oakland City Council, 124
Oakland police, 124–25
Obama, Barack, 27–28, 34, 61, 181
  administration of, 57–58, 152, 215
  inauguration of, 110
Obergefell v. Hodges, 88, 89
Ocasio-Cortez, Alexandria, 68–69, 113
Occupy movement, 11, 14, 64, 150
  Occupy Nigeria, 26–27
  Occupy Wall Street movement, 64
O'Connor, Sandra Day, 4–5, 187
Okonjo-Iweala, Ngozi, 26
"open government," 57–58
Open Government Partnership, 58
Open Society Foundation, 58, 58*n*
Open Whisper Systems, 96
Orbán, Viktor, 58, 67, 70
ordinamento giuridico, 48–49
Orta, Ramsey, 125–26
O'Toole, Fintan, 211–12
Ozzie, Ray, 133

Pahlka, Jen, 107–9, 122–23
Palermo, Sicily, 47, 48, 49, 78

pandemics. *See* COVID-19
Pantaleo, Daniel, 126
"parasocial conact," 89
Pariser, Eli, 214
Parkland, Florida, 54
Parliament (UK), 25, 66
participation. *See* civic engagement; political participation; voting
partisanship
  local elections and, 196
  in the United States, 29
PayPal, 105, 168
Pelosi, Nancy, 153
perception, efficacy and, 194–95
Perot, Ross, 4
Perry, Rick, 12
petitions, 152–53, 189
Pew Research Center, 6
philanthropy, 108
the Philippines, 70
phone companies, 146
Piketty, Thomas, 40, 41–42
Pink Chaddi Campaign, 3
"Pizzagate" conspiracy theory, 60–61
pizzo, 49, 78
plague, 41
Planned Parenthood, 193–94
Planned Parenthood Saved My Life campaign, 193–94
Podemos movement, 11
Podesta, John, 60
Poitras, Laura, 94–95
Poland, 67, 173
police, 124–25
  communities of color and, 101
  mistrust of, 6
  police brutality and misconduct, 83, 98–99, 101, 124–26, 136, 202

policing, 124–26, 133
  racial bias and, 102
political advertising, 98
political ideology
  brain structure and, 69
  fear and, 69–70
political instability, inequality and, 41–42
political participation, 201
political parties, 14–15. *See also specific parties*
  disengagement from, 62–63
  mobilization of the right and, 63
politicians, professional, 14–15
politics
  disengagement from, 61–66
  distancing from label, 2
  mistrust of, 5–8
  professionalization of, 105–6
Polynesia, 169, 172
Pomerantsev, Peter, 74–76
Poole, Laren, 180–82
popular opinion, social justice and, 33
popular vote, 117–18
populism/populist movements, 41, 52, 63
Poseidon Award, 169
power, deference to, 44
powerlessness, 65–66
Power Ventures, 177
preference falsification, 44, 45
"presence," shift in, 45
press. *See* news media
prison population, 115
privacy, 95–96
privatization, 36–37
Producthunt, 143
Prohibition, 119
Promise Tracker, 130–31

prosecutorial reform, 114–16
Prosecutor Impact, 115
prosecutors, 114–16
"pro-social disobedience," 198–99
prostitution, 176
protest movements, 43–44, 63–65, 98–99. *See also specific movements*
  disappointing outcomes of, 64
  mistrust and, 7–8
  participation in, 66
  social media and, 65
public functions, ceded to private actors, 50, 70
public goods, 36, 37–38
public opinion, 44
  equal marriage and, 192
  expression of, 45
  social media and, 70–71
public relations, 70–76
public schools, mistrust of, 6, 29
public works projects, monitoring and documenting, 128–31
Punto Pizzofree, 78
Puro, Marsha Bell, 186
Putin, Vladimir, 71, 74, 76, 212
Putnam, Robert, 25–26, 46

QAnon conspiracy, 61

race, inequality and, 42–43
racial equality, 87–88. *See also* civil rights movement
racial inequities
  challenging, 100–101
  wealth gap, 33–34
racial justice reform, 100–101
racial wealth gap, 33–34

racism/racial bias/racial discrimination, 104
  Airbnb and, 146
  coded, 34
  institutional mistrust and, 31, 32–35
  in policing, 102
  ride-sharing services, 145–46
  structural, 140
  technology companies, 145–46
  US justice system, 140
radical institutionalists, 113–23, 158
radical insurrectionism, 174
Rajasthan, India, 147–48
Rape, Abuse and Incest National Network (RAINN), 83, 205, 206
Reader's Digest, 21–22
readership, educated, 45
Reagan, Ronald, 27, 34, 35, 36–38, 40, 50, 125
Reagle, Joseph, 155
reality television, 74–75
rebellion, 77. *See also* insurrectionism
Recovery 2.0 movement, 209
recycling, 196
Red Command street gang, 51–52
Red Cross, 208
refugees, 165–66, 173–74
Reggi, Luigi, 128–29
regulatory forces, 85–90
Reidenberg, Joel, 85
Reiser, Emilie, 130
religion, organized, mistrust of, 6, 29
representative democracy, 151–52
  trust and, 25–26
  US, 15–16
Republican Party, 27, 33, 34, 67, 68, 69–70, 121
  Electoral College and, 117, 118
  insurrectionists vs. institutionalists, *11*, 12
  media and, 71, 138–39
  Southern Strategy and, 33
  Trump and, 71–72
  Trumpist, 66
resentment, inequality and, 40–41
resurrectionists, 214–16
Reuters/Ipsos poll, 56
revolutions, 43
Rice, Tamir, 101
ride-sharing services, 141–43
  disability advocates and, 156–57
  racial bias and, 145–46
the right
  insurrectionism and, 77
  mobilization of, 66–70
  right-wing media, 69
Rio de Janeiro, Brazil, 51–52
riots, 42
risk, trust and, 22–23
Rivitz, Mark, 90
Roberts, John, 89, 191
Robinson, David, 58
Robinson, Rashad, 54–55
Rochester, New York, 187
Roosevelt, Franklin D., 35–36, 39
Rosanvallon, Pierre, 127–28, 136, 137–38, 140
Rounds, Mike, 71–72
Roy, Aruna, 147–50
RT, 75
RT America, 75
Russell, Jason, 180–82
Russia, 70, 74–76, 212
  interference in 2016 US presidential election, 55–56, 71, 174–75
  news media in, 75
  opposition parties in, 75, 76
  reality television in, 74–75

Russian, 2–5
Russian Revolution, 67

Safecast, 133, 140
Said, Khaled, 3–4
Salt Act of 1882, 188
Salvini, Matteo, 63
Sanchez, Michael, 204–6
Sanders, Bernie, *11*, 12, 68
Santa Lúcia, favela of, Belo Horizonte, Brazil, 130–31
Santana, Feidin, 126
Sauter, Molly, 191
Scheidel, Walter, 41–42
school shootings, 45–46, 54, 83, 91–92
Schudson, Michael, 14–16, 44–45, 131–32
science, mistrust of, 213
Scientific Games, 117
Scott, Walter, 126
Seale, Bobby, 124–25
seasteading, 169–70
Seasteading Institute, 169–70
secret ballot, 15
segregation, 17, 33–34, 87, 104
"self-hating state," 35
Selma, Alabama, 87
sentencing reform, 135–37
September 11, 2001, terror attacks of, 5, 33
sexual abuse/assault/harassment, 79–83, 106, 198, 199. *See also* #MeToo movement
Shaw, Donald, 202
Shih, Stephanie, 205
Shiv Sena, 112
shocks, equality and, 41
Shri Rama Sene, 3
Shue, Andrew, 204–6
Sicily, 46–47, 50, 78
Sidi Bouzid, Tunisia, 200

Signal, 96, 97
Silicon Valley, 109, 142–43
Simmons, Russell, 80
Sinclair, Upton, 154
Singapore, trust of institutions in, 7
Singh, Nikhil Pal, 125
Singh, Shankar, 147–50
60 Minutes, 135
skepticism, 46
Skype, 146, 147, 164
"slacktivism," 194
Slager, Michael, 126
Sleeping Giants, 90–92
smart activism, 54–55
"smart contracts," 162–63, 170
smartphones, 129
SMS messages, encryption of, 96
Snowden, Edward, 94–95, 96, 97
Sobyanin, Sergei, 212
"social attentiveness," 128–29
social change, 12, 13, 17–18, 102–6. *See also* change
    antipolitics and, 4–5
    different ways to work for, 189–95
    efficacy and, 104–5, 180–206
    institutionalist approaches to, 121–22
    online, 180–84
Social Finance, 90
social justice, 33, 100
social media, 18, 55–56, 99, 174–75, 202, 203. *See also* *specific companies*
    Arab Spring and, 200
    "meme magic," 203–4
    protests and, 65
    public opinion and, 70–71
social mobility, 40
social movements, 82, 206. *See also* *specific movements*

social networks. *See also* social
   media; *specific platforms*
   change and, 175–78
   decentralization and, 175–79
   federated decentralization and,
      175–76
   interference in 2016 US presi-
      dential election and, 174–75
   mobilization and, 174
Social Security, 68, 108
solar energy, 94, 102–4
Soros, George, 153
sousveillance, 129, 130–31
South Africa, 188
southern Europe, trust in government and, 43
Southern Italy, 49
Southern Poverty Law Center, 90
Southern Strategy, 33, 68
South Korea, 49
   COVID-19 and, 210
   institutional mistrust in, 30
   trust in government and, 215
Soviet Union, 37, 62, 164. *See also*
   Russia
SpaceX, 92–93, 169
Spacey, Kevin, 80
Spain, 65
   anti-austerity protests in, 64
   interpersonal trust in, 23
   mistrust of institutions in, 7
   Podemos movement in, 11
   trust in government and, 26–27
Spanish Bourbons, 48
Spanish Hapsburgs, 48
split tickets, 15
spyware, 97
stagflation, 36
Stahl, Lesley, 71–73
start-up companies, 143
start-up countries, 169

state collapse, 41
state government, confidence in,
   196–98
Stempeck, Matt, 191
Stevenson, Bryan, 134–37
stock market crash of 1929, 39
Stop Enabling Sex Traffickers Act
   (SESTA), 176
Stork Fountain, 194
street gangs, 51–52
structural racism, 140
Students for a Democratic Society,
   186
"successor systems," 156
Sudan, 180–82
Suffolk Law School, 114
suicide, 205–6
Sunflower Student Movement,
   151, 154
Superdome, 207
surveillance, 95–96
Susan, Nisha, 3
Susan G. Komen Foundation,
   193–94
Sweden, mistrust of institutions
   in, 7
Switter.at, 176, 177
Syria, 64

Tahrir Square protests, 3
Taipei, Taiwan, 151
Taiwan, 151, 153–54, 157
Takei, George, 191
tax cuts, 13, 39, 40
taxes, 39, 103
taxi services, 141–42, 146
   disability advocates and,
      156–57
   in New York City, 156
Tea Party movement, 66–67, 68
"techlash," 56

technology. *See also* technology
    companies
  bureaucracy and, 107–9
  counter-democracy and, 129
  government and, 107–9
  role in overthrowing institu-
    tions, 149–50
technology companies, 55–56,
    142–43, 145–46
teens, mental health and, 204–6
television
  Arab Spring and, 200
  gay and lesbian characters on,
    89
  reality television, 74–75
  television news, 6 (*see also* news
    media)
television news, mistrust of, 6
Tempelhof, Susanne Tarkowski,
    160, 161–63, 165, 168, 170,
    175, 177
Tennessee Valley Authority, 35
1099 economy, 145
the Terror, 139
terror attacks of September 11,
    2001, 5, 33
Tesla, 92–94, 102
Texas, 103
Thatcher, Margaret, 35, 36–38, 50
Thiel, Peter, 168–70, 171, 172, 173
Time magazine, 81
Tocqueville, Alexis de, 43–44
Today show, 81
Tometi, Opal, 100
Toronto, Canada, interpersonal
    trust in, 22
totalitarianism, 72, 73–74
transparency, 70, 98
  global movement toward, 58
  in high-trust societies, 58–59
  in low-trust societies, 58–59

newspapers and, 57–58
  trouble with, 57–61
  unintended consequences of,
    59–60
Transvaal, South Africa, 188
Trump, Donald, *11*, 70, 76. *See
    also* Trump administration
  Access Hollywood scandal and,
    18
  attacks on institutions, 27
  attacks on the press, 70–71,
    138–39, 212
  COVID-19 and, 51, 111, 213
  "deep state" and, 212
  election of, 2, 8, 10, 35, 90, 117,
    122
  emission laws and, 94
  inauguration of, 64, 110
  institutional mistrust and, 30
  as insurrectionist, 10–11, 12
  "meme magic" and, 203–4
  presidency of, 153
  Putin and, 71–72
  QAnon conspiracy and, 61
  rise of, 76
  trust in government and,
    27–28
  2016 US presidential election
    and, 55, 117
  Twitter and, 203–4
  white supremacy and, 35
Trump administration, 8, 12–13,
    38, 55, 94, 215
  American Technology Council
    and, 109
  COVID-19 and, 111
  "deep state" and, 110–11
  deregulation and, 13
  family separation and caging of
    children by, 137–38
  immigration and, 173–74

Trump administration (*continued*)
  refugees and, 173–74
  tax cuts and, 13
  "zero-tolerance" immigration
    policy, 137
trust
  closed societies and, 25–26
  community ties and, 46
  culture of, 49
  democracy and, 25–26
  economic implications of, 49
  effects of, 25
  in government, 26–28 (*see also*
    specific countries)
  key dimensions of, 22–23
  monarchies and, 25
  risk and, 22–23
  as situational, 22–23
  what is lost with loss of, 47–78
  why we lost, 21–46
Trust Barometer, 25–26, 30, 215
"trust trap," 25
trustworthiness, 21–22
truth, 45
Ttcat, 151
Tufekci, Zeynep, 64–66
Tumblr, 99, 193
Tunis, Tunisia, 200
Tunisia, 3, 63, 159, 174, 200
  overthrow of government in,
    63–64
  protests in, 3, 9, 43–44
Turkey, 64–65
Turkopticon, 156
Twitter, 65, 90, 91, 92, 99, 101,
    102, 105, 174, 177, 181, 191
  #MeToo movement and, 79–81
  lolicon and, 176
  "rogue" accounts on, 110
  Trump, Donald and, 203–4
2000 US presidential election, 120

2016 US presidential election, 2, 8,
    10, 11–12, *11*, 59, 90, 122
  disinformation campaigns and,
    174–75
  Electoral College and, 117
  Facebook and, 174–75
  Republican primaries, 67
  Russian interference in, 55–56,
    71, 174–75

Uber, 142–43, 145, 146, 156–57,
    158
Uganda, 180–84, 202
Ukraine, 58–59, 75
Ulfelder, Jay, 42
"Undocumented and Unafraid"
    videos, 192–93
undocumented immigrants, activ-
    ism and, 192–93
United Airlines, 54
United Arab Emirates
  trust in goverment and, 25
  trust of institutions in, 7
United Kingdom Independence
    Party (UKIP), 67
United Muslims of America, 55
United Nations, 159, 165, 215
United States, 49, 76. *See also* US
    federal government; *specific*
    states
  antipolitics in, 4–5
  civil rights movement in, 16–17
  COVID-19 and, 210–15
  crisis of confidence in demo-
    cratic institutions in, 28–29
  disengagement from politics in,
    61–63
  educated readership in, 45
  election reforms in, 15
  Hurricane Katrina and, 207–10,
    211, 215

hyperpartisanship in, 29
inequality in, 42
institutional failure in, 207–16
institutional mistrust in, 30, 50
interpersonal trust in, 21–22
no longer country of last resort, 173–74
press in, 44–45
public works programs in, 35–36
representative democracy in, 15–16
trust in government and, 26–27, 43
United States v. Microsoft Corporation, 83, 84–90
Universal Declaration of Human Rights, Article 13, 170
University of Illinois, 69
Univision, 137
Update Your Status, 204
US Congress, 25, 33, 66, 89–90, 215
   Civil Rights Act and, 7–8
   Fight Online Sex Trafficking Act (FOSTA), 176
   Freedom of Information Act, 57
   ME TOO Congress Act, 83
   mistrust of, 8, 29, 196–97
   possible expansion of, 119–21
   reapportionment of, 119–20
   Senate Armed Services Committee, 32
   Stop Enabling Sex Traffickers Act (SESTA), 176
US Constitution
   amendments to, 9, 117
   Eighteenth Amendment, 119
   Electoral College and, 116–23
   First Amendment, 152
   framers of, 116
US Department of Defense, 182

US Department of Homeland Security, 55–56
US Department of Justice, 38, 84, 95, 111, 147
US Digital Service, 108
US Environmental Protection Agency, 110–11
US federal government. *See also specific branches and agencies*
   attack on, 50
   mistrust of, 5–8, 6
US Food and Drug Administration (FDA), 210–11, 215
US Government Accountability Office, 128
US House of Representatives, 119–20
   Fight Online Sex Trafficking Act (FOSTA), 176
   ME TOO Congress Act, 83
   possible expansion of, 119–22
US Immigration and Customs Enforcement (ICE), 137, 193
US justice system, 114–16
   mistrust of, 6
   racial bias and, 140
   sentencing reform and, 135
US National Security Agency, 94–95, 96, 97
US presidency, 215
   deference to presidential power, 44
   mistrust of, 30, 66, 196
US Securities and Exchange Commission, 163
US Senate, Stop Enabling Sex Traffickers Act (SESTA), 176
US Supreme Court, 6, 33, 88, 89–90, 118, 121, 135
   Brown v. Board of Education of Topeka, 33, 87

US Supreme Court (*continued*)
   equal marriage and, 191
   Jackson v. Hobbs, 135
   Miller v. Alabama, 135
   Obergefell v. Hodges, 88, 89

Vaidhyanathan, Siva, 56
Vance, J. D., 42
venture capitalists, 143–44
Vietnam War, 44
   damage caused by, 32, 33
   resistance to, 27
violence against women, move-
      ment against, 18
Visa, 166–67
voice, 172
voice-based activism, 192–94
voluntary citizenship, 164–66, 168
voter enthusiasm, for local poli-
      tics, 196–98
voter registration, 87
voter turnout, 62
Voter Turnout Database, 62
voting, 194. *See also* elections
   as action, 185–86
   change through, 185–86
   democracy and, 184–85
   efficacy and, 185–86
   "perceived benefit" of, 184–86
   why we vote, 184–88
Voting Rights Act, 33
Vowell, Sarah, 46

Wag! 143
Wales, Jimmy, 155
"wallet test," 21–22
Walmart, 54
war on drugs, 34
Warren, Elizabeth, 68
wars, 41

Washington, George, 118–19, 121
Washio, 143
Watergate, 32, 33, 44, 70, 128
Water Protectors, 126
"weak ties," 25–26
wealth gap, 39–43
Weiner, Anthony, 60
Weinstein, Harvey, 18, 79–80, 81,
      82, 198
Welch, Edgar, 60–61
welfare state, 39
We the People, 152
WeWork, 143
Whats App, 96–97, 146
whistleblowing, 95–96
white nationalism, 33–35
whites
   "deaths of despair" and, 42
   inequality and, 42–43
   rising death rates among, 42
   white resentment, 33–35
   working-class, 42
white supremacy, 33, 35, 176
Whonim, Wael, 3
WikiLeaks, 60, 75
Wikimedia, 155
Wikipedia, 154–56
Will, George, 71, 121
Wilson, Darren, 98–99
Winfrey, Oprah, 181
Witness, 126
women's march, 8
workplace justice, 200
Works Progress Administration,
      35
World Health Organization
      (WHO), 210, 215
World Values Survey 2011–2014,
      26–27, 29, 61
World War II, 39

Wright, Jeffrey, 100
Wyoming, 116, 120

X Prize, 169

Yanukovych, Viktor, 58
"Yanukovychleaks," 58
Yglesias, Matt, 59–60
youth disengagement, 104

YouTube, 154, 174, 193
Yu, Harlan, 58

Zak, Paul, 24
Zandt, Deanna, 193–94
Zeitlin, Joel, 120
Zelizer, Julian, 33
Zimmerman, George, 100
Zittrain, Jonathan, 84